MASTER THE

Sizzling Recipes for Flavorful
Delights and Grilling Techniques.
Enhance Your BBQ Skills with
Top-rated Dishes and Expert Tips

COOKBOOK ACADEMY
by CHEF CIRO RUSSO

Pictures credits: Unsplash.com
The pictures used in this book are just an example on how the recipes could look like.

Book writing: Cookbook Academy Staff

Interior and Cover Designer: Laura Antonioli
Production Manager: LP Business & Management LTD
COOKBOOK ACADEMY 2023 - by Ciro Russo

TABLE OF CONTENTS

Sandwiches and Sides • 185

Dessert • 201

Specials • 223

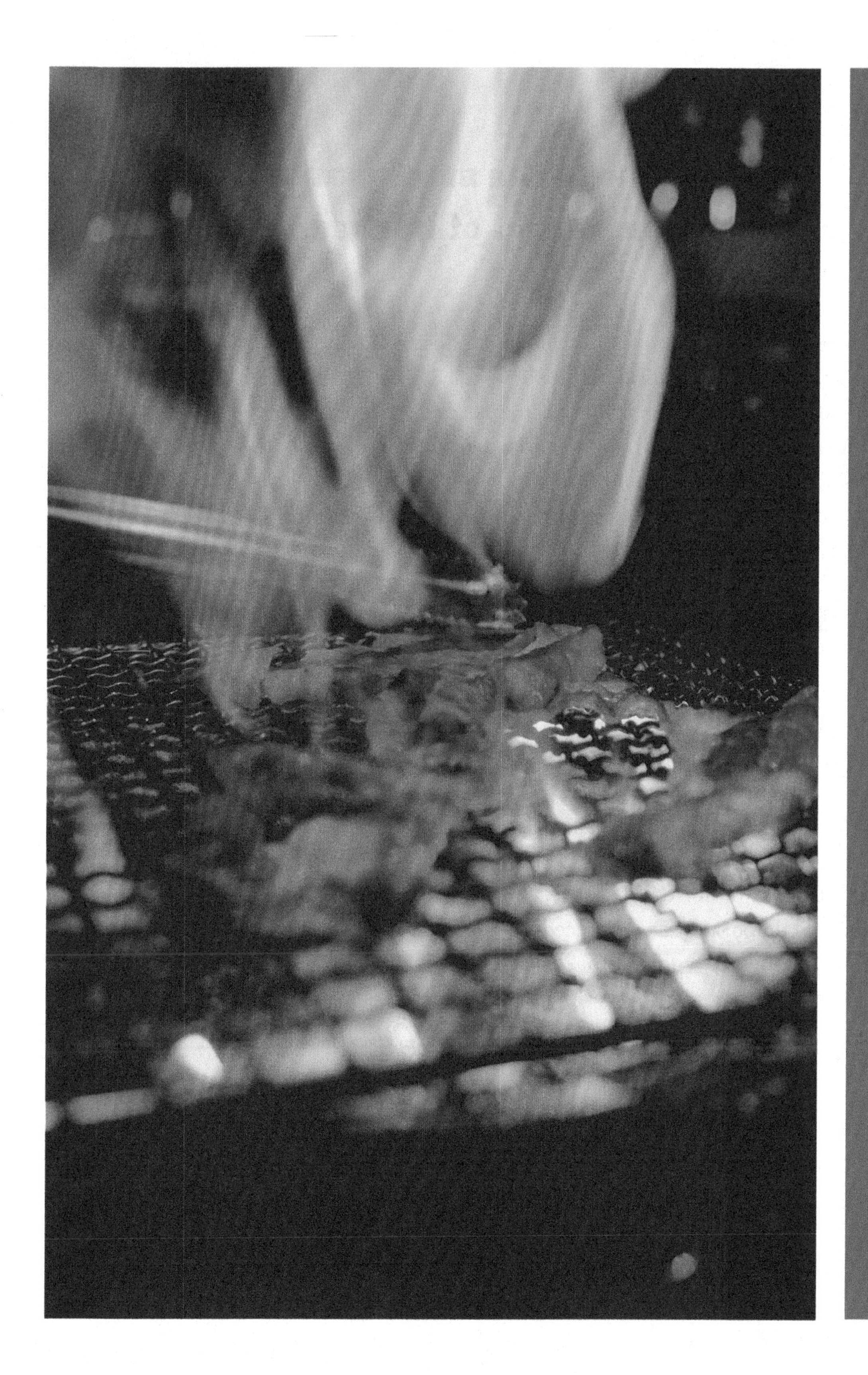

INTRODUCTION

Welcome to the smoky and succulent world of barbecue!

This book is born out of a passion for grilling and a desire to share with you the best recipes and techniques for creating extraordinary dishes. We have dedicated hours of research and experimentation to ensure an unforgettable culinary experience. Whether you're a seasoned grill master or a curious beginner, you'll find within these pages a comprehensive guide to enhance your grilling skills and impress friends and family. Get ready to explore a universe of flavors and let your barbecue become the hero of your summer gatherings and dinners.

Enjoy the journey and bon appétit!

The passion for barbecue is an ancient art rooted in tradition and conviviality. That's why we are thrilled to share our best recipes that encompass everything you need to know to become a grill master. From classic smoked ribs to juicy grilled steaks, you'll discover a variety of recipes that will make your mouth water. But that's not all: we'll also unveil the secrets of perfect marinades, irresistible sauces, and ideal cooking techniques for every type of meat. Each recipe has been tested and perfected to ensure astounding results. Are you ready to lift the lid of your barbecue and embark on an unprecedented culinary journey? Get ready to experience the pleasure of creating authentic culinary masterpieces on your grill. May this book become your faithful guide in the wonderful world of barbecue.

Happy reading and enjoy the kitchen adventures!

9 Essential Tips & Tricks to Master your Barbecue

Beginners should follow the advice and procedures listed below to get the most out of their Barbecue grill and smoker:

1. Do not leave hot cooked food out for more than 45 minutes after preparing the desired recipes. Put it in the refrigerator if you don't plan on eating it right away.
2. Do not allow frozen meat to thaw at room temperature or on a kitchen counter. Meats should always be defrosted in the refrigerator.
3. When switching from high-temperature to medium- or low-temperature cooking, speed up the process by lifting the lid until the thermometer reads the desired temperature. This will not jeopardize the outcome.
4. Cooking a piece of meat at low temperatures for a longer period of time allows your Barbecue to tenderize it.
5. When grilling or smoking foods, always have a meat thermometer on hand. It will allow you to prepare your favorite cuts to your liking while avoiding overdone, tough cuts.
6. When the lid is down, always allow some open space between each piece so that air can move freely. This will cut the cooking time in half and result in a superior finished product.
7. Allow a cut of red meat to rest for 5 to 10 minutes after grilling it, preferably on a hot platter. By doing so, you're letting all of the liquids that have been forced to the outside due to the heat to return to the center and flavor the entire piece.
8. Searing is the way to go for a tasty and crispy surface. Always start with the Barbecue as hot as possible when looking for the crispiest surface on your cuts, then place the piece on it for 50-60 seconds on each side. After that, lower the temperature (the lid is lifted) and continue with the 'traditional' cooking method.
9. Always take the time to thoroughly clean your Barbecue at the end of each grilling session. Spending 5 minutes after each use will extend the life of your Barbecue by hundreds, if not thousands, of hours.

Ratings

In all of our cookbooks you'll find a grade of evaluation on each individual recipe called "Ratings". The "Ratings" goes from 1 to 5 stars and it is determined by the complexity of the dish and the time you'll need to prepare it.

1 star will indicate a very quick and easy meal, while 5 stars will be a more complex recipe with higher preparation time needed. We wanted to offer you this method of evaluating on every dish in order to make it even easier for you to choose the most suitable recipes according to your time availability.

Cookbook Academy Team

CHICKEN AND TURKEY

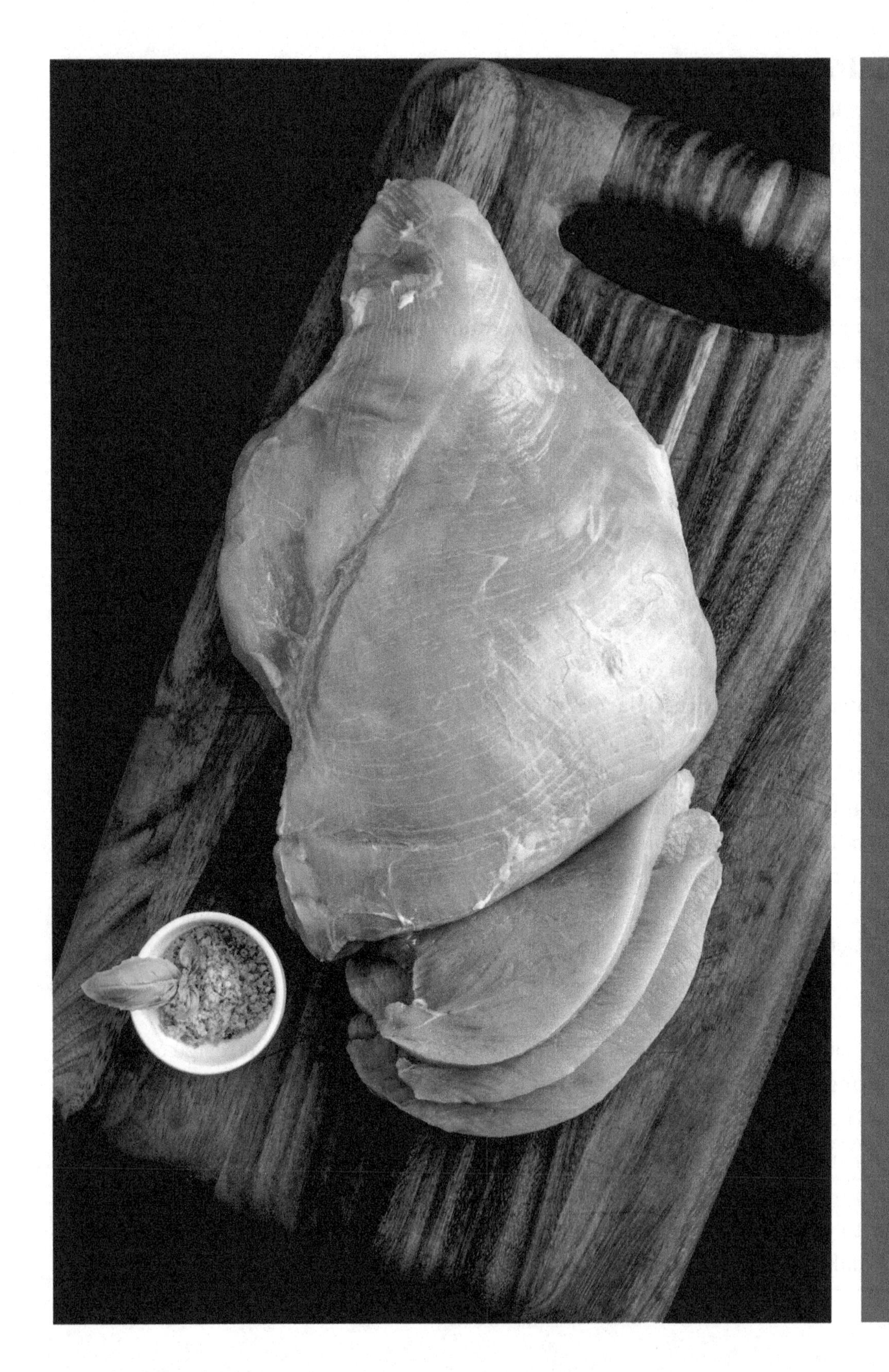

Recommended Sauces for Chicken and Turkey

Sage Butter Sauce:

A creamy and aromatic sauce that pairs perfectly with chicken and turkey. In a skillet, melt butter over medium heat and add finely chopped sage leaves. Cook for a few minutes until the butter starts to lightly brown. Drizzle the sauce over the chicken or turkey before serving.

Curry Sauce:

A rich and spicy sauce that complements chicken and turkey well. In a saucepan, mix coconut milk, red curry paste, minced garlic, grated ginger, lemon juice, brown sugar, and a pinch of salt. Heat the sauce over medium-low heat until it becomes creamy and well blended. Pour it over the chicken or turkey before serving.

Rosemary Honey Sauce:

A sweet and fragrant sauce that pairs well with chicken and turkey. In a bowl, mix olive oil, lemon juice, finely chopped rosemary, honey, minced garlic, salt, and pepper. Brush the sauce onto the chicken or turkey during cooking or use it as a sauce to drizzle over sliced meat before serving.

Sweet Chili Sauce:

A spicy and sweet sauce that adds a touch of liveliness to chicken and turkey. In a small pot, heat sweet chili sauce, apple cider vinegar, brown sugar, minced garlic, and a pinch of salt. Simmer over medium-low heat until the sauce slightly thickens. Brush the sauce onto the chicken or turkey during cooking or serve it as a dipping sauce on the side.

Lime and Cilantro Sauce:

A fresh and citrusy sauce that adds vibrant flavors to chicken and turkey. In a bowl, combine lime juice, finely chopped cilantro, minced garlic, olive oil, salt, and pepper. Pour the sauce over the chicken or turkey before serving or use it as a sauce for dipping slices of meat.

Salt-and-Pepper Boneless Chicken

 **Preparation time** 10 MINUTES |  **Cooking time** 10-14 MINUTES |  **Servings** 4 | ★★★★★ **Ratings**

Ingredients

1½ lbs. boneless, skinless, chicken breasts
2 tbsp. good-quality olive oil
Salt and pepper

Directions

1. Pat-dry the chicken with paper towels and, if needed, pound it to an even thickness. Brush the chicken with oil and sprinkle salt and pepper on both sides.
2. Preheat your barbecue grill to high heat. If using a pellet grill, turn the control knob to the high position. Allow the grill to heat up.
3. Place the chicken breasts on the hot grill and cook for 10 to 14 minutes, flipping halfway through, until the chicken is cooked through and reaches an internal temperature of 165°F (74°C).
4. Transfer the cooked chicken to a platter and let it rest for 5 minutes. This allows the juices to redistribute and ensures a moist and flavorful result.
5. Optional: If desired, slice the chicken across the grain before serving to enhance tenderness.
6. Serve the salt-and-pepper boneless chicken as a main course or use it as a versatile ingredient in other dishes.

Tips: Before grilling the chicken, let it sit at room temperature for about 15-20 minutes. This allows the chicken to cook more evenly and helps it retain its juiciness.

Maple-Glazed Turkey Breast

 **Preparation time** 4 H 30 MINUTES |  **Cooking time** 2 HOURS |  **Servings** 4 | ★★★ **Ratings**

Ingredients

1 turkey breast (about 4-6 lbs)
½ cup maple syrup
2 tbsp. Dijon mustard
2 tbsp. soy sauce
2 tbsp. lemon juice
2 tbsp. vegetable oil
2 cloves garlic, finely minced
1 tsp. salt
½ tsp. black pepper

Directions

1. Preheat the grill to medium-high heat (around 350-400°F).
2. In a bowl, combine the maple syrup, Dijon mustard, soy sauce, lemon juice, vegetable oil, minced garlic, salt, and black pepper to create a marinade.
3. Place the turkey breast in a sealable container and pour the marinade over it. Ensure that the turkey breast is fully coated with the marinade. Marinate in the refrigerator for at least 4 hours, or preferably overnight, turning the turkey breast occasionally to ensure even marination.
4. Preheat the grill and prepare it for indirect grilling.
5. Remove the turkey breast from the marinade and discard the remaining marinade.
6. Place the turkey breast on the grill, away from direct heat. Close the grill lid and grill the turkey breast for approximately 20-25 minutes per pound, or until the internal temperature reaches 165°F.
7. During the last 10-15 minutes of grilling, brush the turkey breast with the remaining marinade to create a sweet and glossy glaze.
8. Once cooked, remove the turkey breast from the grill and let it rest for at least 10-15 minutes before slicing. This will allow the juices to redistribute within the meat, making the turkey breast even more juicy.
9. Slice the turkey breast and serve as the main dish for your barbecue.

Tips: For an extra touch of sweetness and crispiness, you can lightly sprinkle maple syrup on the turkey breast just before placing it on the grill. This will create a delicate caramelized glaze on the surface of the breast during cooking.

Turkey with Apricot Barbecue Glaze

 **Preparation time** 30 MINUTES |  **Cooking time** 30 MINUTES |  **Servings** 4 | ★★★★★ **Ratings**

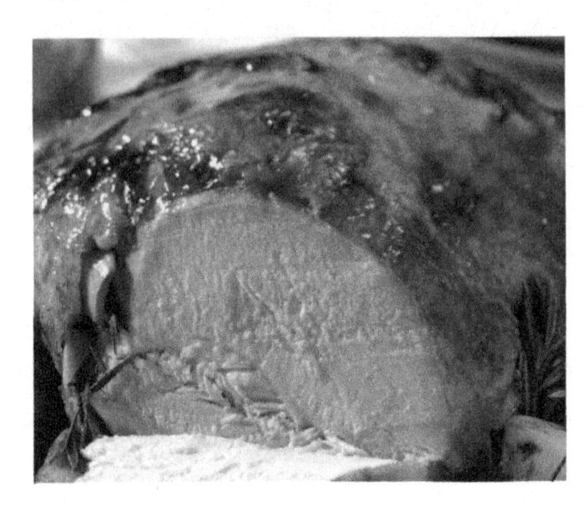

Ingredients

4 turkey breast fillets
4 tbsp. chicken rub
1 cup apricot barbecue sauce

Directions

1. Preheat the grill to medium heat (around 350-400°F).
2. Sprinkle the chicken rub evenly over both sides of the turkey breast fillets, pressing gently to adhere.
3. Place the turkey breast fillets on the grill and cook for about 6-8 minutes per side, or until the internal temperature reaches 165°F.
4. During the last few minutes of grilling, brush the apricot barbecue sauce onto the turkey breast fillets, turning them once or twice to ensure even coating. Allow the glaze to caramelize slightly.
5. Once cooked, remove the turkey breast fillets from the grill and let them rest for a few minutes before serving.
6. Serve the turkey breast fillets with any remaining apricot barbecue sauce on the side for dipping or drizzling.

Tips: For added tenderness and juiciness, you can brine the turkey breast fillets in a solution of water, salt, and sugar for a few hours before grilling. Rinse them well and pat dry before applying the chicken rub.

Perfect Smoked Chicken Patties

 **Preparation time** 20 MINUTES |  **Cooking time** 50 MINUTES |  **Servings** 6 | ★★★★ **Ratings**

Ingredients

2 lb. ground chicken breast
2/3 cup minced onion
1 tbsp. chopped cilantro
2 tbsp. finely chopped fresh parsley
2 tbsp. olive oil
1/8 tsp. crushed red pepper flakes
½ tsp. ground cumin
2 tbsp. fresh lemon juice
¾ tsp. kosher salt
2 tsp. paprika
Hamburger buns for serving

Directions

1. Preheat your smoker to a temperature of 225°F.
2. In a mixing bowl, combine the ground chicken breast, minced onion, chopped cilantro, finely chopped fresh parsley, olive oil, crushed red pepper flakes, ground cumin, fresh lemon juice, kosher salt, and paprika. Mix well to evenly distribute the ingredients.
3. Shape the mixture into patties of your desired size, ensuring they are evenly shaped and compact.
4. Place the chicken patties on the smoker grates and close the lid. Smoke the patties for about 1 to 1 ½ hours, or until they reach an internal temperature of 165°F.
5. Once cooked, remove the smoked chicken patties from the smoker and let them rest for a few minutes.
6. Serve the smoked chicken patties on hamburger buns, and garnish them with your favorite toppings and condiments.

Tips: If you prefer a stronger smoky flavor, you can add some wood chips or chunks to your smoker during the smoking process. Experiment with different types of wood, such as hickory, apple, or mesquite, to find your preferred flavor profile.

Whole Orange Chicken

 **Preparation time** 15 MIN + MARINATE |  **Cooking time** 45 MINUTES |  **Servings** 4 | ★★★★★ **Ratings**

Ingredients

1 whole chicken, 3-4 lbs, backbone removed

2 oranges

¼ cup oil

2 tsp. Dijon mustard

Zest of 1 orange

2 tbsp. chopped rosemary leaves

2 tsp. salt

Directions

1. Preheat your grill to medium-high heat.
2. Rinse the whole chicken inside and out, then pat it dry with paper towels.
3. Cut one of the oranges into slices and stuff them into the cavity of the chicken.
4. In a small bowl, whisk together the juice from the other orange, oil, Dijon mustard, orange zest, chopped rosemary leaves, and salt to create the marinade.
5. Place the chicken in a large resealable bag or a shallow dish and pour the marinade over it, making sure to coat it evenly. Let it marinate in the refrigerator for at least 2 hours or overnight for best results.
6. Remove the chicken from the marinade and discard any excess marinade.
7. Grill the chicken over indirect heat for about 1 to 1 ½ hours, or until the internal temperature reaches 165°F, flipping it occasionally for even cooking.
8. Remove the chicken from the grill and let it rest for about 10 minutes before carving.
9. Serve the Whole Orange Chicken with your favorite side dishes and enjoy!

Tips: Ensure that the chicken is cooked thoroughly by checking the internal temperature with a meat thermometer. Insert it into the thickest part of the thigh without touching the bone; it should read 165°F when done.

Caesar Marinated Pellet Grill Chicken Skewers

 **Preparation time** 10 MINUTES |  **Cooking time** 24 MINUTES |  **Servings** 3 | ★★★★ **Ratings**

Ingredients

¼ cup croutons
1 tsp. lemon zest
½ cup grated Parmesan cheese
¼ cup breadcrumbs
1 lb. ground chicken
2 tbsp. Caesar dressing (plus more for drizzling)
2-4 leaves of romaine lettuce

Directions

1. Preheat your pellet grill to medium heat.
2. In a food processor, pulse the croutons until finely crushed. Transfer to a mixing bowl.
3. Add the lemon zest, grated Parmesan cheese, breadcrumbs, ground chicken, and 2 tablespoons of Caesar dressing to the bowl. Mix well until all ingredients are evenly combined.
4. Take a small portion of the chicken mixture and form it into an oval shape. Repeat until all the mixture is used.
5. Skewer the chicken ovals onto metal or soaked wooden skewers, leaving some space between each piece.
6. Place the skewers on the preheated pellet grill and cook for about 12-15 minutes, or until the chicken is cooked through, flipping them halfway through the cooking time.
7. Remove the skewers from the grill and let them rest for a few minutes.
8. Meanwhile, tear the romaine lettuce leaves into smaller pieces and place them on a serving platter.
9. Once rested, slide the cooked chicken ovals off the skewers onto the bed of romaine lettuce.
10. Drizzle some additional Caesar dressing over the chicken skewers and serve.

Tips: If you prefer a smokier flavor, you can use wood pellets that complement the chicken, such as hickory or applewood.

Balsamic-Rosemary Chicken Breasts

 **Preparation time** 5 MINUTES |  **Cooking time** 6 MINUTES |  **Servings** 4 | ★★★★ **Ratings**

Ingredients

½ cup balsamic vinegar

2 tbsp. olive oil

2 sprigs of rosemary, coarsely chopped

2 lbs. boneless chicken breasts, pounded to a ½-inch thickness

Directions

1. In a small bowl, whisk together the balsamic vinegar, olive oil, and chopped rosemary.
2. Place the pounded chicken breasts in a shallow dish or a resealable bag, and pour the balsamic-rosemary marinade over them. Ensure the chicken breasts are well-coated with the marinade. Let them marinate in the refrigerator for at least 30 minutes or up to 4 hours for maximum flavor.
3. Preheat your grill to medium-high heat.
4. Remove the chicken breasts from the marinade, allowing any excess marinade to drip off.
5. Grill the chicken breasts for about 6-8 minutes per side, or until they are cooked through and reach an internal temperature of 165°F.
6. Remove the chicken breasts from the grill and let them rest for a few minutes before serving.
7. Slice the chicken breasts across the grain into thin strips.
8. Serve the Balsamic-Rosemary Chicken Breasts as a main dish, and they pair well with a variety of sides such as roasted vegetables, rice, or a fresh salad.

Tips: To infuse even more flavor into the chicken, you can reserve a small portion of the marinade before adding it to the chicken breasts. Brush the reserved marinade onto the chicken during the last few minutes of grilling.

Chicken Roast with Pineapple Salsa

 **Preparation time** 10 MINUTES |  **Cooking time** 45 MINUTES |  **Servings** 2 | ★★★★★ **Ratings**

Ingredients

¼ cup extra virgin olive oil
¼ cup freshly chopped cilantro
1 avocado, diced
1 lb. boneless chicken breasts
2 cups canned pineapples
2 tsp. honey
Juice from 1 lime
Salt and pepper to taste

Directions

1. Preheat your grill to medium heat.
2. In a small bowl, combine the olive oil, chopped cilantro, diced avocado, and a pinch of salt. Set aside to use as the pineapple salsa.
3. Season the boneless chicken breasts with salt and pepper to taste.
4. Place the chicken breasts on the preheated grill and cook for about 6-8 minutes per side, or until they reach an internal temperature of 165°F.
5. While the chicken is grilling, drain the canned pineapples and chop them into small pieces. In a separate bowl, mix the chopped pineapples, honey, and lime juice to create the pineapple salsa.
6. Once the chicken is cooked, remove it from the grill and let it rest for a few minutes.
7. Slice the chicken breasts into thin strips or leave them whole, based on your preference.
8. Serve the Chicken Roast with Pineapple Salsa by topping the grilled chicken with the prepared pineapple salsa. Drizzle any remaining salsa over the chicken for added flavor.
9. Garnish with additional cilantro leaves, if desired.

Tips: If you prefer a smoky flavor, you can grill the canned pineapples for a few minutes on each side before chopping them for the salsa.

Duck Poppers

 **Preparation time** 30 MINUTES |  **Cooking time** 4 HOURS |  **Servings** 1 | ★★ **Ratings**

Ingredients

8-10 slices of bacon, cut into evenly sized pieces measuring 4 inches each

3 boneless duck breasts, skin removed and sliced into strips measuring ½ inch

Sriracha sauce

6 jalapenos, deseeded, with the tops cut off and sliced into strips

Directions

1. Preheat your grill to medium-high heat.
2. Wrap each strip of duck breast with a slice of bacon, securing it with a toothpick if needed.
3. Place the bacon-wrapped duck poppers on the preheated grill and cook for about 5-6 minutes per side, or until the bacon is crispy and the duck is cooked through.
4. While the poppers are grilling, brush them with a thin layer of Sriracha sauce for added heat and flavor. Adjust the amount of Sriracha according to your preference.
5. In the last few minutes of grilling, place the sliced jalapeno strips on the grill and cook them until slightly softened and charred.
6. Remove the duck poppers and jalapenos from the grill and let them cool slightly.
7. Carefully remove the toothpicks from the duck poppers.
8. Take a slice of grilled jalapeno and place it on top of each bacon-wrapped duck popper, securing it with a toothpick if desired.
9. Serve the Duck Poppers as an appetizer or main dish, alongside a dipping sauce of your choice or additional Sriracha sauce for those who prefer extra spiciness.

Tips: Make sure to monitor the grilling process closely as duck breasts can cook quickly and may become dry if overcooked.

Smoked Cornish Chicken in Wood Pellets

 **Preparation time** 10 MINUTES |  **Cooking time** 50 MINUTES |  **Servings** 1 | ★★★★ **Ratings**

Ingredients

6 Cornish hens
2-3 tbsp. canola or avocado oil
6 tbsp. spice mix (of your choice)

Directions

1. Preheat your pellet grill to a temperature of 225°F to 250°F (107°C to 121°C) using wood pellets of your choice for smoking.
2. Rinse the Cornish hens under cold water and pat them dry with paper towels.
3. Rub the hens with canola or avocado oil, ensuring they are coated evenly.
4. Sprinkle the spice mix over the hens, making sure to cover them thoroughly on all sides. You can use a store-bought spice mix or create your own blend using your preferred herbs, spices, and seasonings.
5. Once the grill has reached the desired temperature, place the seasoned Cornish hens on the grill grates.
6. Close the grill lid and let the hens smoke for approximately 2 to 2.5 hours, or until they reach an internal temperature of 165°F (74°C) in the thickest part of the meat.
7. During the smoking process, periodically check the temperature of the grill and adjust as needed to maintain a consistent temperature.
8. Once the hens are cooked through, remove them from the grill and let them rest for a few minutes before serving.
9. Serve the Smoked Cornish Chicken as a main dish, garnishing with fresh herbs if desired.

Tips: Consider brining the Cornish hens prior to smoking to infuse them with extra moisture and flavor. Brining involves soaking the hens in a solution of water, salt, sugar, and additional herbs or spices for a few hours before cooking.

Grilled FiletMignon

 **Preparation time** 10 MINUTES |  **Cooking time** 20 MINUTES |  **Servings** 1 |  **Ratings**

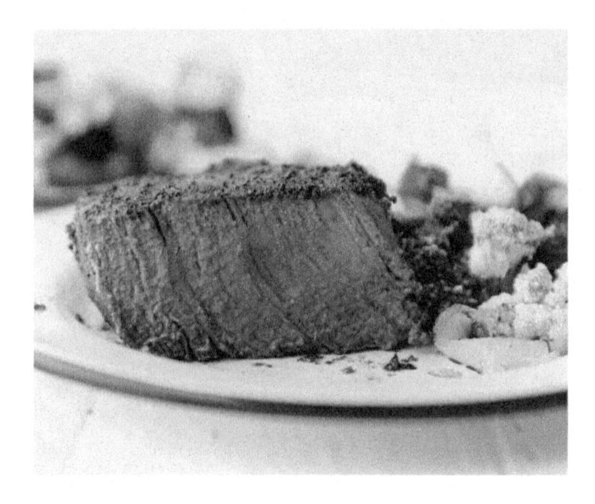

Ingredients

Salt
Pepper
3 filet mignon steaks

Directions

1. Preheat your grill to high heat.
2. Season the filet mignon steaks generously with salt and pepper on all sides, ensuring they are coated evenly.
3. Once the grill is hot, place the steaks on the grates and close the lid.
4. Grill the filet mignon for approximately 4-6 minutes per side, depending on your desired level of doneness. For a medium-rare steak, aim for an internal temperature of 130°F to 135°F (54°C to 57°C).
5. During the grilling process, avoid pressing down on the steaks as this can cause them to lose juices and become less tender.
6. Once the steaks are cooked to your liking, remove them from the grill and let them rest for a few minutes before serving.
7. Serve the Grilled Filet Mignon as a main dish, accompanied by your favorite sides such as roasted vegetables, mashed potatoes, or a fresh salad.

Tips: Letting the steaks rest after grilling allows the juices to redistribute, resulting in a more flavorful and tender bite.

Buffalo Chicken Wings

 **Preparation time** 15 MINUTES |  **Cooking time** 25 MINUTES |  **Servings** 6 | ★★★★ **Ratings**

Ingredients

2 lb. chicken wings
½ cup sweet-spicy dry rub
2/3 cup buffalo sauce
Celery, chopped (for serving)

Directions

1. Preheat your grill to medium-high heat.
2. Rinse the chicken wings under cold water and pat them dry with paper towels.
3. Sprinkle the sweet-spicy dry rub evenly over the wings, making sure to coat them thoroughly on all sides.
4. Place the seasoned chicken wings on the preheated grill and cook for approximately 12-15 minutes per side, or until they are cooked through and the skin is crispy.
5. While the wings are grilling, heat the buffalo sauce in a small saucepan over low heat until warmed through.
6. Once the wings are done, transfer them to a large bowl and pour the warm buffalo sauce over them. Toss the wings in the sauce until they are evenly coated.
7. Serve the Buffalo Chicken Wings hot, garnished with chopped celery on the side for a refreshing crunch.

Tips: For an extra kick of heat, you can add a drizzle of hot sauce or a sprinkle of cayenne pepper to the buffalo sauce.

Chicken Lollipops

 **Preparation time** 30 MINUTES |  **Cooking time** 2 HOURS |  **Servings** 6 |  **Ratings**

Ingredients

12 chicken lollipops
Chicken seasoning
10 tbsp. butter, sliced into 12 cubes
1 cup barbecue sauce
1 cup hot sauce

Directions

1. Preheat your grill to medium-high heat.
2. Season the chicken lollipops generously with chicken seasoning, ensuring they are coated evenly.
3. Insert a cube of butter into the meaty part of each chicken lollipop, pushing it in gently.
4. Place the chicken lollipops on the preheated grill and cook for approximately 15-20 minutes, turning occasionally, until they are cooked through and the internal temperature reaches 165°F (74°C).
5. While the chicken lollipops are grilling, mix the barbecue sauce and hot sauce together in a bowl.
6. Brush the sauce mixture onto the chicken lollipops during the last few minutes of grilling, allowing it to caramelize and create a flavorful glaze.
7. Transfer the grilled chicken lollipops to a serving platter and serve hot.

Tips: Serve the Chicken Lollipops as a delightful appetizer or as part of a main course. Provide extra barbecue sauce and hot sauce on the side for dipping or drizzling, according to personal preference.

Lemon Chicken in Foil Packet

 **Preparation time** 5 MINUTES |  **Cooking time** 25 MINUTES |  **Servings** 4 |  **Ratings**

Ingredients

4 chicken fillets
3 tbsp. melted butter
1 garlic clove, minced
1-½ tsp. dried Italian seasoning
Salt and pepper to taste
1 lemon, sliced

Directions

1. Preheat your grill to medium heat.
2. Cut four pieces of aluminum foil into large squares, enough to wrap each chicken fillet individually.
3. Place each chicken fillet on a separate foil square.
4. In a small bowl, combine melted butter, minced garlic, dried Italian seasoning, salt, and pepper. Mix well.
5. Drizzle the butter mixture evenly over each chicken fillet, ensuring they are coated on both sides.
6. Place a couple of lemon slices on top of each chicken fillet.
7. Fold the foil squares over the chicken to create a sealed packet, making sure there is enough space inside for steam circulation.
8. Place the foil packets on the preheated grill and cook for approximately 15-20 minutes or until the chicken is cooked through and reaches an internal temperature of 165°F (74°C).
9. Carefully open the foil packets, being cautious of the hot steam.
10. Serve the Lemon Chicken in Foil Packets directly on plates or transfer to a platter, allowing each person to enjoy their individual packet.

Tips: You can marinate the chicken fillets in the butter mixture for extra flavor. Simply place the chicken in a shallow dish, pour the marinade over it, and refrigerate for at least 30 minutes before grilling.

Sweet & Spicy Chicken

 **Preparation time** 30 MINUTES |  **Cooking time** 1 H 30 MINUTES |  **Servings** 4 | 

Ingredients

16 chicken wings
3 tbsp. lime juice
Sweet and spicy rub (store-bought or homemade)

Directions

1. Preheat your grill to medium-high heat.
2. Rinse the chicken wings under cold water and pat them dry with paper towels.
3. Place the chicken wings in a large bowl and drizzle them with lime juice. Toss the wings to coat them evenly with the juice.
4. Sprinkle the sweet and spicy rub over the chicken wings, ensuring they are coated on all sides. Use as much or as little as desired, depending on your preferred level of spiciness.
5. Place the seasoned chicken wings on the preheated grill and cook for approximately 15-20 minutes, turning occasionally, until they are cooked through and the skin is crispy and caramelized.
6. Transfer the grilled chicken wings to a serving platter and serve hot.

Tips: Serve the Sweet and Spicy Chicken wings as a delicious appetizer or as part of a main course. Pair them with a cooling dipping sauce like ranch or blue cheese, and serve with celery sticks or carrot sticks for added crunch and freshness.

Turkey Sandwich

 **Preparation time** 5 MINUTES |  **Cooking time** 25 MINUTES |  **Servings** 4 | ★★★★★ **Ratings**

Ingredients

8 bread slices
1 cup gravy
2 cups turkey, cooked and shredded

Directions

1. Toast the bread slices to your desired level of crispness.
2. Warm the gravy in a saucepan over medium heat until heated through.
3. Add the cooked and shredded turkey to the warm gravy and stir to coat the turkey evenly. Allow it to heat for a few minutes until the turkey is warmed.
4. Take two slices of bread and spoon the turkey mixture onto one slice.
5. Place another slice of bread on top to create a sandwich.
6. Repeat the process to make additional sandwiches with the remaining bread slices and turkey mixture.
7. Serve the turkey sandwiches warm.

Tips: If you want a warm sandwich, you can assemble the sandwich and then grill it in a panini press or on a skillet until the bread is toasted and the filling is heated through.

Smoked Turkey

 **Preparation time** 30 MINUTES |  **Cooking time** 6 H 30MINUTES |  **Servings** 8 |  **Ratings**

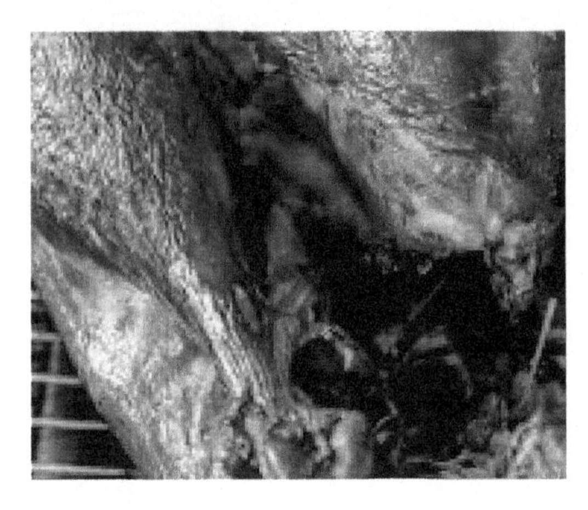

Ingredients

1 cup butter
½ cup maple syrup
2 tbsp. chicken seasoning
1 whole turkey

Directions

1. Preheat your smoker to a temperature of 225°F (107°C).
2. In a small saucepan, melt the butter over low heat. Stir in the maple syrup and chicken seasoning until well combined.
3. Place the whole turkey on a sturdy roasting rack or directly on the smoker grates.
4. Brush the butter-maple syrup mixture all over the turkey, making sure to coat it evenly.
5. Insert a meat thermometer into the thickest part of the turkey, without touching the bone.
6. Place the turkey in the smoker and close the lid. Allow it to smoke for approximately 30 minutes per pound, or until the internal temperature of the thickest part of the turkey reaches 165°F (74°C).
7. While the turkey is smoking, periodically baste it with the remaining butter-maple syrup mixture to keep it moist and add flavor.
8. Once the turkey reaches the desired temperature, carefully remove it from the smoker and transfer it to a carving board. Let it rest for about 20 minutes before carving.
9. Carve the smoked turkey into slices and serve.

Tips: It's essential to maintain a consistent temperature in the smoker throughout the cooking process for optimal results.

Texas Turkey

 **Preparation time** 30 MINUTES |  **Cooking time** 4 H 30MINUTES |  **Servings** 8 | ★★ **Ratings**

Ingredients

1 pre-brined turkey
Salt and pepper to taste
1 lb. butter

Directions

1. Preheat your grill or smoker to a temperature of 325°F (163°C).
2. Remove the pre-brined turkey from its packaging and pat it dry with paper towels.
3. Season the turkey generously with salt and pepper, both inside and outside the bird, to taste.
4. Melt the butter in a saucepan or microwave until it becomes a liquid.
5. Brush the melted butter all over the turkey, making sure to coat it thoroughly.
6. Place the turkey on the grill or in the smoker, breast-side up, and close the lid.
7. Cook the turkey for approximately 12-15 minutes per pound, or until the internal temperature reaches 165°F (74°C) in the thickest part of the thigh.
8. Monitor the temperature throughout the cooking process and adjust the heat as needed to maintain a consistent temperature.
9. Once the turkey reaches the desired temperature, remove it from the grill or smoker and let it rest for about 20-30 minutes before carving.
10. Carve the Texas Turkey into slices and serve.

Tips: Pre-brined turkeys are readily available in stores and already infused with flavor, eliminating the need for additional brining.

Wood Pellet Chicken Breast

 **Preparation time** 10 MINUTES |  **Cooking time** 15 MINUTES |  **Servings** 6 |  **Ratings**

Ingredients

3 chicken breasts
1 tbsp avocado oil
¼ tbsp garlic powder
¼ tbsp onion powder
¾ tbsp salt
¼ tbsp pepper

Directions

1. Preheat your wood pellet grill to a temperature of 375°F (190°C).
2. Rub the chicken breasts with avocado oil, ensuring they are evenly coated.
3. In a small bowl, combine the garlic powder, onion powder, salt, and pepper. Mix well.
4. Sprinkle the seasoning mixture over both sides of the chicken breasts, gently pressing it into the meat.
5. Place the seasoned chicken breasts on the preheated wood pellet grill.
6. Cook the chicken for approximately 20-25 minutes, or until the internal temperature reaches 165°F (74°C).
7. Flip the chicken breasts halfway through the cooking process to ensure even browning and cooking.
8. Once the chicken reaches the desired temperature, remove it from the grill and let it rest for a few minutes.
9. Slice the Wood Pellet Chicken Breast and serve.

Tips: Wood pellet grills provide a unique smoky flavor to your dishes. Use your preferred wood pellets, such as hickory or applewood, to add a delightful smokiness to the chicken.

Succulent Duck Breast

 **Preparation time** 10 MINUTES |  **Cooking time** 10 MINUTES |  **Servings** 4 | ★★★★★ **Ratings**

Ingredients

4 (6-oz.) boneless duck breasts
2 tbsp. chicken rub

Directions

1. Preheat your grill to medium-high heat.
2. Pat dry the duck breasts with paper towels to remove any excess moisture.
3. Sprinkle the chicken rub evenly over both sides of the duck breasts, pressing it gently into the meat.
4. Place the seasoned duck breasts on the preheated grill, skin-side down.
5. Cook the duck breasts for about 4-5 minutes per side, or until the skin is crispy and the internal temperature reaches 130°F (54°C) for medium-rare or 140°F (60°C) for medium.
6. Flip the duck breasts only once during cooking to ensure a crispy exterior and juicy interior.
7. Once cooked to your desired doneness, remove the duck breasts from the grill and let them rest for a few minutes.
8. Slice the Succulent Duck Breast diagonally into thin slices and serve.

Tips: Duck breasts have a thick layer of fat on the skin side, which renders and crisps up during cooking. Make sure to score the skin lightly with a knife to help the fat render more effectively.

Barbecue Chile Lime Chicken

 **Preparation time** 2 MINUTES |  **Cooking time** 15 MINUTES |  **Servings** 1 | ★★★★★ **Ratings**

Ingredients

1 chicken breast

1 tbsp. oil

1 tbsp. Spiceology Chile Lime Seasoning

Directions

1. Preheat your grill to medium heat.
2. Brush the chicken breast with oil, ensuring it is evenly coated.
3. Sprinkle the Chile Lime Seasoning over both sides of the chicken breast, pressing it gently into the meat.
4. Place the seasoned chicken breast on the preheated grill.
5. Cook the chicken for about 6-8 minutes per side, or until the internal temperature reaches 165°F (74°C) and the juices run clear.
6. While grilling, you can baste the chicken with additional barbecue sauce or marinade for extra flavor, if desired.
7. Once cooked, remove the chicken breast from the grill and let it rest for a few minutes.
8. Slice the Barbecue Chile Lime Chicken and serve.

Tips: Serve the chicken breast with your favorite barbecue sides, such as corn on the cob, coleslaw, or grilled vegetables, for a delicious and well-rounded meal.

Barbecue Grilled Buffalo Chicken

 **Preparation time** 5 MINUTES |  **Cooking time** 2 HOURS |  **Servings** 6 | ★★★★★ **Ratings**

Ingredients

5 chicken breasts, boneless and skinless
2 tbsp. homemade BBQ rub
1 cup homemade Cholula Buffalo sauce

Directions

1. Preheat your grill to medium-high heat.
2. Sprinkle the homemade BBQ rub evenly over both sides of the chicken breasts, pressing it gently into the meat.
3. Place the seasoned chicken breasts on the preheated grill.
4. Grill the chicken for about 6-8 minutes per side, or until the internal temperature reaches 165°F (74°C) and the juices run clear.
5. While grilling, baste the chicken breasts with the homemade Cholula Buffalo sauce, using a brush or spoon to coat them generously.
6. Continue grilling for another 1-2 minutes per side to caramelize the sauce and enhance the flavor.
7. Once cooked, remove the chicken breasts from the grill and let them rest for a few minutes.
8. Serve the Barbecue Grilled Buffalo Chicken with additional Cholula Buffalo sauce on the side for dipping.

Tips: For a spicier version, add a pinch of cayenne pepper or a few dashes of hot sauce to the home-made BBQ rub or Buffalo sauce.

Roasted Tuscan Thighs

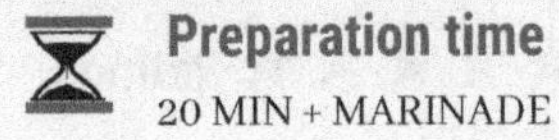
Preparation time
20 MIN + MARINADE

Cooking time
40-60 MINUTES

Servings
4

Ingredients

3 cups Tuscan seasoning per thigh
3 tbsp extra virgin olive oil, roasted garlic flavor
8 chicken thighs, bone-in, skin-on

Directions

1. Preheat your oven to 425°F (220°C).
2. In a small bowl, combine the Tuscan seasoning and roasted garlic-flavored olive oil to create a paste.
3. Rub the Tuscan seasoning paste all over the chicken thighs, ensuring they are evenly coated.
4. Place the seasoned chicken thighs on a baking sheet or in a roasting pan, skin side up.
5. Roast the thighs in the preheated oven for about 35-40 minutes or until the internal temperature reaches 165°F (74°C) and the skin is crispy and golden brown.
6. Remove the roasted Tuscan thighs from the oven and let them rest for a few minutes before serving.

Tips: If you don't have Tuscan seasoning readily available, you can make your own blend using a combination of dried herbs such as rosemary, thyme, oregano, basil, and garlic powder.

Traditional Thanksgiving Turkey

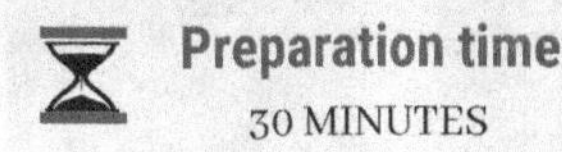
Preparation time
30 MINUTES

Cooking time
1 H 30 MINUTES

Servings
2-4

Ratings

Ingredients

1 (18-20lb) turkey
½ lb. butter, softened
8 sprigs thyme
6 cloves garlic, minced
1 sprig rosemary, roughly chopped

Directions

1. Preheat your oven to 325°F (165°C).
2. Rinse the turkey thoroughly, inside and out, then pat it dry with paper towels.
3. In a small bowl, combine the softened butter, minced garlic, and chopped rosemary. Mix well to incorporate the flavors.
4. Carefully separate the skin from the turkey breast, starting at the neck opening, being careful not to tear it. Spread the butter mixture evenly between the skin and the breast meat, using your hands to gently massage it in.
5. Stuff the cavity of the turkey with the thyme sprigs for added aroma and flavor.
6. Place the prepared turkey on a rack in a roasting pan, breast side up. Tent the turkey loosely with aluminum foil.
7. Roast the turkey in the preheated oven, allowing approximately 13 minutes per lb. for cooking time. Baste the turkey with its own juices every 30 minutes.
8. Remove the foil during the last hour of cooking to allow the skin to brown and become crispy.
9. To ensure the turkey is cooked thoroughly, insert a meat thermometer into the thickest part of the thigh without touching the bone. The internal temperature should reach 165°F (74°C).
10. Once cooked, remove the turkey from the oven and let it rest for 20-30 minutes before carving. This allows the juices to redistribute and the meat to become tender.

Tips: If desired, you can stuff the turkey cavity with your favorite stuffing mix or aromatics such as onions, celery, and citrus fruits.

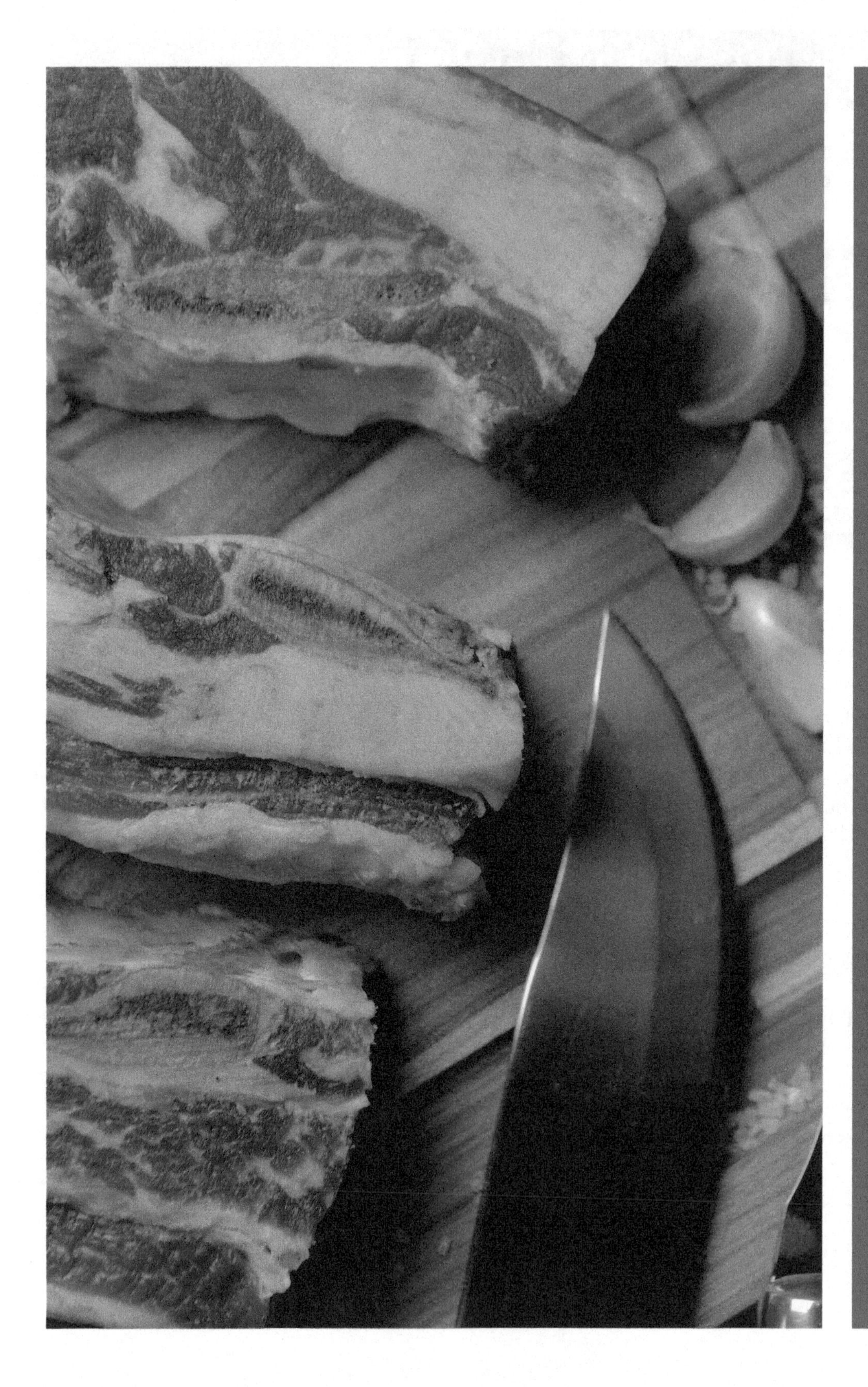

PORK

Recommended Sauces for Pork

Carolina Gold Mustard Sauce:

A sweet and slightly spicy yellow mustard sauce that pairs perfectly with pork. Mix yellow mustard, apple cider vinegar, honey, ketchup, Worcestershire sauce, garlic powder, onion powder, smoked paprika, black pepper, and optional chili powder. Store in the refrigerator.

Sweet and Spicy Chipotle Sauce:

A sauce that combines sweet and spicy flavors with the smoky taste of chipotle. Mix ketchup, apple cider vinegar, brown sugar, minced chipotle peppers, molasses, Worcestershire sauce, garlic powder, onion powder, smoked paprika, salt, and pepper. Blend and store in the refrigerator.

Orange Cranberry Sauce:

A sweet and fruity sauce with the fresh burst of orange. Cook fresh cranberries with orange juice, sugar, orange zest, and a splash of lemon. Cook until the cranberries soften and the sauce thickens. Let cool before serving.

Beer Barbecue Sauce:

A rich and savory sauce with a touch of beer. Sauté onions and garlic, add ketchup, apple cider vinegar, brown sugar, beer, mustard, Worcestershire sauce, soy sauce, paprika, chili powder, and salt. Simmer until the sauce thickens.

Mango Jalapeno Sauce:

A tropical sauce with a hint of spiciness. Blend fresh mango, jalapeno pepper, lime juice, fresh cilantro, garlic powder, onion powder, salt, and pepper. Store in the refrigerator to allow the flavors to develop.

Simple Smoked Baby Back Ribs

 **Preparation time** 25 MINUTES |  **Cooking time** 4-6 HOURS |  **Servings** 4-8 | 

Ingredients

2 (2- or 3-pound) racks baby back ribs
2 tbsp. yellow mustard
1 batch Not-Just-for-Pork Rub

Directions

1. Preheat your smoker to 225°F (107°C).
2. Remove the membrane from the back of each rack of baby back ribs. This can be done by loosening the membrane with a butter knife and then gripping it with a paper towel to pull it off.
3. Brush a thin layer of yellow mustard on both sides of the ribs. This will help the rub adhere and add a subtle tangy flavor.
4. Generously season the ribs with the Not-Just-for-Pork Rub, making sure to coat both sides evenly. You can adjust the amount of rub according to your taste preferences.
5. Place the seasoned ribs in the smoker, bone side down. Close the smoker and let them smoke for approximately 4 to 5 hours, or until the meat is tender and has reached the desired level of smokiness.
6. Every hour or so, spritz the ribs with apple juice or a mixture of apple juice and cider vinegar to keep them moist and enhance the flavor.
7. Towards the end of the cooking time, you can brush the ribs with your favorite barbecue sauce, if desired. This will add a sweet and sticky glaze to the ribs.
8. Once the ribs are done, remove them from the smoker and let them rest for a few minutes. This allows the juices to redistribute and makes the meat even more tender.
9. Cut the racks into individual ribs and serve them hot.

Tips: Choose high-quality baby back ribs for the best flavor and tenderness.

Maple-Smoked Pork Chops

 **Preparation time** 10 MINUTES |  **Cooking time** 55 MINUTES |  **Servings** 4 | ★★★★ **Ratings**

Ingredients

4 (8-ounce) pork chops, bone-in or boneless (I use boneless)
Salt Freshly ground black pepper

Directions

1. Preheat your smoker or grill to a medium heat, around 225°F to 250°F.
2. Season the pork chops generously with salt and freshly ground black pepper on both sides.
3. Place the pork chops on the smoker or grill, ensuring they are evenly spaced apart.
4. Close the lid and smoke the pork chops for about 1.5 to 2 hours, or until the internal temperature reaches 145°F.
5. Optional: During the last 30 minutes of smoking, you can brush the pork chops with a maple glaze made by combining maple syrup, Dijon mustard, and a pinch of cayenne pepper.
6. Once cooked, remove the pork chops from the smoker or grill and let them rest for 5 minutes before serving.
7. Serve the maple-smoked pork chops hot with your favorite sides or additional maple glaze for dipping.

Tips: Consider brining the pork chops for a few hours before smoking. Brining helps to enhance the moisture and flavor of the meat. You can use a simple brine solution of water, salt, sugar, and any desired herbs or spices.

Apple-Smoked Pork Tenderloin

 **Preparation time** 15 MINUTES |  **Cooking time** 4-5 HOURS |  **Servings** 4-6 |  Ratings

Ingredients

2 (1-pound) pork tenderloins
1 batch Not-Just-for-Pork Rub

Directions

1. Preheat your smoker or grill to a medium heat, around 225°F to 250°F.
2. Generously season the pork tenderloins with the Not-Just-for-Pork Rub, ensuring they are coated on all sides.
3. Place the seasoned tenderloins on the smoker or grill, directly over the heat source.
4. Add some apple wood chips or chunks to the smoker or grill to infuse the pork with a delicious smoky and fruity flavor. Close the lid.
5. Smoke the pork tenderloins for approximately 1.5 to 2 hours, or until the internal temperature reaches 145°F.
6. Remove the tenderloins from the smoker or grill and let them rest for 5 minutes before slicing.
7. Slice the tenderloins into medallions and serve them hot with your favorite sides.

Tips: Baste with apple juice: During the smoking process, you can baste the tenderloins with apple juice to add moisture and a subtle fruity sweetness.

Barbecued Tenderloin

 **Preparation time** 5 MINUTES |  **Cooking time** 30 MINUTES |  **Servings** 4-6 | ★★★★★ **Ratings**

Ingredients

2 (1-pound) pork tenderloins
1 batch Sweet and Spicy Cinnamon Rub

Directions

1. Preheat your grill to medium-high heat.
2. Rub the pork tenderloins with the Sweet and Spicy Cinnamon Rub, ensuring they are evenly coated on all sides.
3. Place the tenderloins on the grill and cook for about 15-20 minutes, turning occasionally, until the internal temperature reaches 145°F.
4. While grilling, you can baste the tenderloins with your favorite barbecue sauce to add flavor and moisture. Brush the sauce on during the last 5 minutes of cooking.
5. Once cooked, remove the tenderloins from the grill and let them rest for 5 minutes before slicing.
6. Slice the tenderloins into medallions and serve them warm.

Tips: Allowing the cooked tenderloins to rest before slicing will help retain their juices and ensure a moist and tender result.

Wow-Pork Tenderloin

 **Preparation time** 15 MINUTES |  **Cooking time** 3 HOURS |  **Servings** 4 | ★★★ **Ratings**

Ingredients

1 pork tenderloin
¼ cup BBQ sauce
3 tbsp. dry rub

Directions

1. Preheat your grill to medium-high heat.
2. Season the pork tenderloin with the dry rub, ensuring it is coated on all sides.
3. Place the seasoned tenderloin on the grill and cook for about 20-25 minutes, turning occasionally, until the internal temperature reaches 145°F.
4. Brush the BBQ sauce onto the tenderloin during the last 5 minutes of cooking, allowing it to caramelize and create a flavorful glaze.
5. Remove the tenderloin from the grill and let it rest for 5 minutes before slicing.
6. Slice the tenderloin into medallions and serve it warm.

Tips: Choose a dry rub that complements the flavors of the BBQ sauce. You can use a pre-made dry rub or create your own by combining spices like paprika, brown sugar, garlic powder, salt, and pepper.

Pork Butt

 **Preparation time** 10 MINUTES |  **Cooking time** 3 H 10 MINUTES |  **Servings** 10 | ★★★ **Ratings**

Ingredients

8 lbs. pork butt
Salt

Directions

1. Preheat your smoker or grill to a temperature of 225°F.
2. Rinse the pork butt under cold water and pat it dry with paper towels.
3. Generously season the pork butt with salt, making sure to cover all sides of the meat.
4. Place the seasoned pork butt on the smoker or grill, fat side up.
5. Close the lid and cook the pork butt for approximately 1.5 to 2 hours per pound, or until the internal temperature reaches 195-205°F. This slow and low cooking method will help tenderize the meat and render the fat.
6. If using a smoker, you can add wood chips or chunks of your choice to enhance the smoky flavor. Popular wood options for pork include hickory, apple, or cherry.
7. During the cooking process, you can periodically spritz the pork butt with apple juice or cider vinegar to keep it moist and add extra flavor.
8. Once the pork butt reaches the desired internal temperature, remove it from the smoker or grill and let it rest for 30 minutes to an hour before shredding.
9. Shred the pork butt using two forks or meat claws, discarding any excess fat.
10. Serve the tender and flavorful pulled pork as desired, such as in sandwiches, tacos, or alongside your favorite BBQ sides.

Tips: For additional flavor, you can create a dry rub using spices like paprika, garlic powder, onion powder, brown sugar, and cayenne pepper. Apply the rub to the pork butt before seasoning it with salt.

Wood Pellet Pork Tenderloin

 **Preparation time** 7 MINUTES |  **Cooking time** 1 H 30 MINUTES |  **Servings** 5 |  **Ratings**

Ingredients

1 Cup of Teriyaki Sauce
1 Pork tenderloin GMG Pork Rub

Directions

1. Preheat your wood pellet grill to a temperature of 350°F.
2. Season the pork tenderloin generously with the GMG Pork Rub, ensuring it is evenly coated on all sides.
3. Place the seasoned pork tenderloin directly on the grill grates and close the lid.
4. Cook the pork tenderloin for about 20-25 minutes, or until it reaches an internal temperature of 145°F.
5. While the pork is cooking, heat the teriyaki sauce in a small saucepan over medium heat until it starts to simmer.
6. Once the pork tenderloin reaches the desired internal temperature, brush it with the teriyaki sauce, covering all sides.
7. Continue cooking the pork tenderloin for an additional 5 minutes, allowing the sauce to caramelize and create a flavorful glaze.
8. Remove the pork tenderloin from the grill and let it rest for a few minutes before slicing.
9. Slice the pork tenderloin into medallions and serve with additional teriyaki sauce on the side.

Tips: If you prefer a sweeter flavor, you can add a tablespoon of honey or brown sugar to the teriyaki sauce before heating it.

Smoked Avocado Pork Ribs

 **Preparation time** 20 MINUTES |  **Cooking time** 4 HOURS |  **Servings** 5 | ★★ **Ratings**

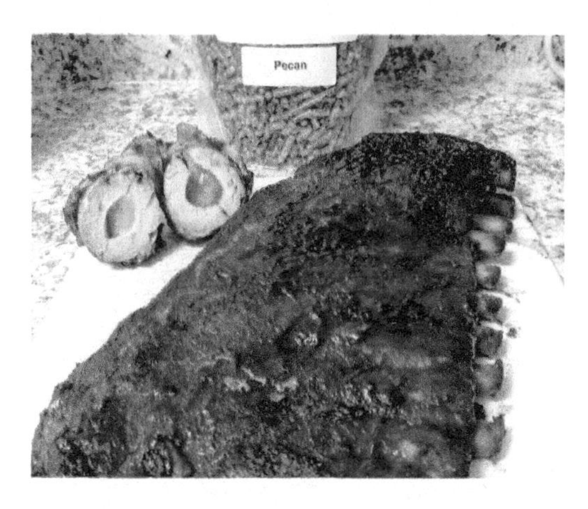

Ingredients

2 lbs. of pork spareribs
1 cup of avocado oil
1 tsp of garlic powder
1 tsp of onion powder
1 tsp of sweet pepper flakes
Salt and pepper, to taste

Directions

1. Preheat your smoker or wood pellet grill to a temperature of 225°F.
2. In a small bowl, mix together the garlic powder, onion powder, sweet pepper flakes, salt, and pepper to create a dry rub.
3. Rub the dry rub mixture evenly onto both sides of the pork spareribs, ensuring they are well coated.
4. Place the seasoned pork spareribs on the smoker or grill grates, bone-side down.
5. Close the lid and let the ribs smoke for approximately 3-4 hours, or until they reach an internal temperature of 195°F. The meat should be tender and easily pull away from the bone.
6. While the ribs are smoking, prepare the avocado oil baste. In a small saucepan, heat the avocado oil over low heat until warm.
7. Once the ribs have reached the desired temperature, baste them with the warm avocado oil, using a brush to coat the ribs evenly.
8. Close the lid and continue smoking the ribs for an additional 30 minutes to allow the oil to infuse and create a delicious glaze.
9. Remove the smoked avocado pork ribs from the smoker or grill and let them rest for a few minutes before serving.
10. Slice the ribs between the bones and serve them hot, accompanied by your favorite BBQ sauce or additional dry rub, if desired.

Tips: For a smokier flavor, use wood pellets or chips such as hickory, apple, or cherry.

Smoked Honey-Garlic Pork Chops

 **Preparation time** 15 MINUTES |  **Cooking time** 1 HOUR |  **Servings** 4 | ★★★ **Ratings**

Ingredients

¼ cup of lemon juice freshly squeezed
¼ cup honey (preferably a darker honey)
3 cloves garlic, minced
2 Tbs soy sauce (or tamari sauce)
Salt and pepper to taste
24 ounces of boneless center-cut pork chops

Directions

1. In a small bowl, combine the lemon juice, honey, minced garlic, and soy sauce. Stir well to ensure the honey is fully dissolved.
2. Season the pork chops with salt and pepper on both sides.
3. Preheat your smoker or wood pellet grill to a temperature of 225°F.
4. Place the seasoned pork chops on the smoker or grill grates.
5. Brush the honey-garlic mixture over the pork chops, coating them evenly.
6. Close the lid and smoke the pork chops for approximately 1-1.5 hours, or until they reach an internal temperature of 145°F.
7. Halfway through the smoking process, you can baste the pork chops with any remaining honey-garlic mixture for added flavor.
8. Once the pork chops reach the desired temperature, remove them from the smoker or grill and let them rest for a few minutes before serving.
9. Serve the smoked honey-garlic pork chops hot, garnished with fresh herbs or a drizzle of the remaining sauce from the smoker.

Tips: Choose thick-cut pork chops for juicier and more flavorful results.

Big Island Pork Kabobs

 **Preparation time** 24 HOURS |  **Cooking time** 15 MINUTES |  **Servings** 6 | ★★ **Ratings**

Ingredients

3 lbs. of pork tenderloin
3 cups of margarita mix
3 cloves of garlic, minced
2 large bell peppers
4 lbs. of whole mushrooms
¼ cup of softened butter
4 tsp. of lime juice
1 tsp. of sugar
3 tbsp. of minced parsley

Directions

1. Cut the pork tenderloin into 1-inch cubes and place them in a large bowl.
2. In a separate bowl, combine the margarita mix and minced garlic. Pour the mixture over the pork cubes, ensuring they are fully coated. Cover the bowl and marinate in the refrigerator for at least 1 hour, or overnight for best results.
3. Preheat your grill to medium-high heat.
4. While the grill is heating, cut the bell peppers into 1-inch pieces and clean the mushrooms.
5. In a small bowl, mix together the softened butter, lime juice, sugar, and minced parsley to create a basting sauce.
6. Thread the marinated pork cubes onto skewers, alternating with bell pepper pieces and mushrooms.
7. Place the kabobs on the preheated grill and cook for about 10-15 minutes, turning occasionally and basting with the prepared sauce.
8. Cook until the pork is cooked through and reaches an internal temperature of 145°F.
9. Remove the kabobs from the grill and let them rest for a few minutes before serving.
10. Serve the Big Island pork kabobs hot, garnished with additional minced parsley if desired.

Tips: Soak wooden skewers in water for at least 30 minutes before threading them with the ingredients. This helps prevent them from burning on the grill.

Asian Pork Sliders

 **Preparation time** 24 HOURS |  **Cooking time** 15 MINUTES |  **Servings** 8 | ★★ **Ratings**

Ingredients

2 lbs. of ground pork
1 cup of diced green onion
2 tsp. of garlic powder
2 tbsp. of soy sauce
2 tsp. of brown sugar
1 cup of shredded lettuce
1 tsp. of cornstarch
Honey-mustard dressing
16 sesame rolls, split

Directions

1. In a large bowl, combine the ground pork, diced green onion, garlic powder, soy sauce, and brown sugar. Mix well to ensure the ingredients are evenly distributed throughout the meat.
2. Form the mixture into small patties, about 2-3 inches in diameter.
3. Preheat a grill or skillet over medium heat.
4. Cook the pork patties for about 4-5 minutes per side, or until they are cooked through and reach an internal temperature of 160°F.
5. While the patties are cooking, prepare the shredded lettuce by tossing it in a bowl with a drizzle of honey-mustard dressing.
6. In a small saucepan, whisk together the cornstarch with a tablespoon of water until it forms a slurry. Heat the mixture over medium heat until it thickens to a glaze-like consistency.
7. Brush the glaze onto the cooked pork patties, coating them evenly.
8. Toast the split sesame rolls on the grill or in a toaster.
9. Assemble the sliders by placing a glazed pork patty on each sesame roll bottom, topping it with a spoonful of shredded lettuce, and adding a drizzle of honey-mustard dressing.
10. Serve the Asian pork sliders immediately while warm.

Tips: Feel free to adjust the seasonings to your taste. You can add more soy sauce for a saltier flavor or increase the amount of brown sugar for added sweetness.

Carolina Pork Ribs

 **Preparation time** 12 HOURS |  **Cooking time** 3 HOURS |  **Servings** 6 | ★★ **Ratings**

Ingredients

2 racks of pork spareribs
½ cup of "Burning' Love" Rub
1 cup of Carolina Basting Sauce
1 cup of Carolina BBQ Sauce

Directions

1. Preheat your grill or smoker to a temperature of 225°F.
2. Season the pork spareribs generously with the "Burning' Love" Rub, ensuring that both sides are coated.
3. Place the seasoned ribs on the grill or smoker and cook them low and slow for approximately 4-5 hours, or until the meat is tender and starts to pull away from the bones.
4. During the last 30 minutes of cooking, baste the ribs with the Carolina Basting Sauce, applying it to both sides and allowing it to caramelize.
5. Once the ribs are cooked to perfection, remove them from the grill or smoker and let them rest for a few minutes.
6. Slice the ribs into individual portions and serve them with a side of Carolina BBQ Sauce for dipping or drizzling.
7. Enjoy the Carolina pork ribs while they're still warm and flavorful.

Tips: For extra tenderness, you can wrap the ribs in foil during the last hour of cooking to help retain moisture.

Bourbon Pork Tenderloin

 **Preparation time** 24 HOURS |  **Cooking time** 1 HOUR |  **Servings** 10 |  **Ratings**

Ingredients

2 cups white sugar
½ cup Jim Beam® Bourbon
2 cups water
2 tsp. vanilla extract
3 to 4 lbs. pork tenderloin
2 tsp. black pepper
2 tsp. garlic powder
2 tbsp. salt

Directions

1. In a large mixing bowl, combine the white sugar, Bourbon, water, and vanilla extract. Stir until the sugar is dissolved and the mixture is well combined.
2. Place the pork tenderloin in a resealable plastic bag and pour the marinade over it. Seal the bag and refrigerate for at least 4 hours, or preferably overnight, to allow the flavors to infuse into the meat.
3. Preheat your grill to medium-high heat.
4. In a small bowl, mix together the black pepper, garlic powder, and salt. Remove the pork tenderloin from the marinade and pat it dry with paper towels. Rub the seasoning mixture all over the pork, ensuring that it is evenly coated.
5. Place the pork tenderloin on the preheated grill and cook for about 15-20 minutes, turning occasionally, until the internal temperature reaches 145°F (63°C). Use a meat thermometer to ensure proper doneness.
6. Remove the pork from the grill and let it rest for a few minutes before slicing.
7. Slice the pork tenderloin into medallions and serve it hot.
8. Optionally, you can brush some additional Bourbon on the cooked pork tenderloin for added flavor.
9. Enjoy the delicious and flavorful Bourbon-infused pork tenderloin!

Tips: If you prefer a sweeter glaze, you can brush the pork tenderloin with a mixture of Bourbon and brown sugar during the last few minutes of grilling.

Sweet & Savory Bacon Wrapped Dates

 **Preparation time** 30 MINUTES |  **Cooking time** 30 MINUTES |  **Servings** 16 | ★★★★ **Ratings**

Ingredients

1 lb. thick-sliced bacon, cut in half
1 lb. pitted dates
4 ounces gorgonzola cheese
32 toothpicks

Directions

1. Preheat your oven to 375°F (190°C) and line a baking sheet with parchment paper.
2. Take a pitted date and stuff it with a small amount (about ½ teaspoon) of gorgonzola cheese.
3. Wrap the stuffed date with a half-slice of bacon and secure it with a toothpick, making sure the bacon completely wraps around the date.
4. Repeat the process with the remaining dates, cheese, and bacon.
5. Place the bacon-wrapped dates on the prepared baking sheet, spacing them out evenly.
6. Bake in the preheated oven for about 15-20 minutes or until the bacon is crispy and cooked to your desired level of doneness.
7. Remove the baking sheet from the oven and transfer the bacon-wrapped dates to a serving platter.
8. Allow the dates to cool slightly before serving, as the cheese filling may be hot.
9. Serve the sweet and savory bacon-wrapped dates as an appetizer or party snack. They can be enjoyed warm or at room temperature.

Tips: If you prefer a milder cheese flavor, you can substitute gorgonzola cheese with cream cheese or another type of soft cheese.

Wood Pellet Grilled Bacon

 **Preparation time** 30 MINUTES |  **Cooking time** 25 MINUTES |  **Servings** 6 |  **Ratings**

Ingredients

1 lb. thick-cut bacon

Directions

1. Preheat your wood pellet grill to a medium-high temperature, around 375°F (190°C).
2. Arrange the bacon slices in a single layer on a grill rack or a grilling pan.
3. Place the rack or pan with the bacon on the preheated grill.
4. Close the lid of the grill and let the bacon cook for about 10-15 minutes, or until it reaches your desired level of crispness. Flip the bacon slices halfway through the cooking time.
5. Keep a close eye on the bacon to prevent it from burning. Adjust the grill temperature if needed.
6. Once the bacon is cooked to your liking, carefully remove it from the grill using tongs or a spatula and transfer it to a paper towel-lined plate to drain excess grease.
7. Allow the bacon to cool for a few minutes before serving.

Tips: Use thick-cut bacon for grilling, as it holds up better to the heat and produces a meatier texture.

Wood Pellet Grilled Pork Chops

 **Preparation time** 20 MINUTES |  **Cooking time** 10 MINUTES |  **Servings** 6 | ★★★★ **Ratings**

Ingredients

6 thick-cut pork chops
BBQ rub of your choice

Directions

1. Preheat your wood pellet grill to a medium-high temperature, around 375°F (190°C).
2. Season both sides of the pork chops generously with the BBQ rub, ensuring even coverage.
3. Place the seasoned pork chops directly on the grill grates, arranging them in a single layer.
4. Close the lid of the grill and let the pork chops cook for about 6-8 minutes per side, or until they reach an internal temperature of 145°F (63°C) for medium-rare or 160°F (71°C) for medium, as recommended by the USDA.
5. Use an instant-read meat thermometer to check the doneness of the pork chops. Insert the thermometer into the thickest part of the chop without touching the bone.
6. Once the pork chops reach the desired temperature, remove them from the grill and let them rest for a few minutes before serving.
7. Serve the wood pellet grilled pork chops hot with your favorite side dishes or sauces.

Tips: Remember to let the grilled pork chops rest for a few minutes before cutting into them. This allows the juices to redistribute and ensures a moist and tender result.

Wood Pellet Blackened Pork Chops

 **Preparation time** 5 MINUTES |  **Cooking time** 20 MINUTES |  **Servings** 6 | ★★★★★ **Ratings**

Ingredients

6 pork chops
¼ cup blackening seasoning
Salt and pepper to taste

Directions

1. Preheat your wood pellet grill to a high temperature, around 450°F (230°C).
2. Season both sides of the pork chops with salt, pepper, and the blackening seasoning, ensuring even coverage.
3. Place the seasoned pork chops directly on the grill grates, arranging them in a single layer.
4. Close the lid of the grill and let the pork chops cook for about 4-5 minutes per side, or until they reach an internal temperature of 145°F (63°C) for medium-rare or 160°F (71°C) for medium, as recommended by the USDA.
5. Use an instant-read meat thermometer to check the doneness of the pork chops. Insert the thermometer into the thickest part of the chop without touching the bone.
6. Once the pork chops reach the desired temperature, remove them from the grill and let them rest for a few minutes before serving.
7. Serve the wood pellet blackened pork chops hot with your favorite side dishes or sauces.

Tips: Ensure that your wood pellet grill is properly preheated to achieve the desired sear and char on the pork chops.

Wood Pellet Grilled Shredded Pork Tacos

 **Preparation time** 15 MINUTES |  **Cooking time** 7 HOURS |  **Servings** 8 | ★★★★★ **Ratings**

Ingredients

5 lb. pork shoulder, bone-in
3 tbsp brown sugar
1 tbsp salt
1 tbsp garlic powder
1 tbsp paprika
1 tbsp onion powder
¼ tbsp cumin
1 tbsp cayenne pepper

Directions

1. Preheat your wood pellet grill to a temperature of 225°F (107°C).
2. In a small bowl, mix together the brown sugar, salt, garlic powder, paprika, onion powder, cumin, and cayenne pepper to create a dry rub.
3. Pat the pork shoulder dry with paper towels and then generously coat it with the dry rub, ensuring all sides are evenly covered.
4. Place the seasoned pork shoulder directly on the grill grates, close the lid, and let it smoke for approximately 6-8 hours or until the internal temperature reaches 195°F (90°C). This low and slow cooking method will result in tender and juicy shredded pork.
5. Monitor the temperature of the pork shoulder using a meat thermometer to ensure it reaches the desired doneness.
6. Once the pork shoulder is fully cooked and tender, remove it from the grill and let it rest for about 15 minutes.
7. Use two forks to shred the pork, discarding any excess fat or bones.
8. Serve the wood pellet grilled shredded pork in warm tortillas, and garnish with your favorite toppings such as salsa, diced onions, cilantro, and lime juice.
9. Enjoy the delicious and flavorful wood pellet grilled shredded pork tacos!

Tips: Use wood pellets that complement the pork, such as hickory or apple, to enhance the smoky flavor.

Wood Pellet Togarashi Pork Tenderloin

 **Preparation time** 5 MINUTES |  **Cooking time** 25 MINUTES |  **Servings** 6 |  **Ratings**

Ingredients

1 Pork tenderloin
½ tbsp kosher salt
¼ cup Togarashi seasoning

Directions

1. Preheat your wood pellet grill to a temperature of 450°F (232°C) for high heat grilling.
2. Season the pork tenderloin with kosher salt, making sure to coat all sides evenly.
3. Generously sprinkle the Togarashi seasoning over the pork tenderloin, ensuring it is well coated.
4. Place the seasoned pork tenderloin directly on the grill grates and close the lid.
5. Grill the pork tenderloin for about 15-20 minutes, or until the internal temperature reaches 145°F (63°C), using a meat thermometer to check for doneness.
6. Once cooked, remove the pork tenderloin from the grill and let it rest for about 5 minutes to allow the juices to redistribute.
7. Slice the pork tenderloin into medallions and serve hot.

Tips: Togarashi is a Japanese spice blend that typically includes ingredients like chili pepper, orange peel, sesame seeds, and other spices. You can find Togarashi seasoning at specialty grocery stores or online. If unavailable, you can make your own Togarashi seasoning by combining chili flakes, sesame seeds, dried orange peel, and other desired spices.

Sweet & Spicy Pork Kabobs

 **Preparation time** 24 HOURS |  **Cooking time** 10 MINUTES |  **Servings** 6 | ★★★★ **Ratings**

Ingredients

2 lbs. boneless pork, cut into 1-inch cubes
¾ cup olive oil
1 tbsp. Worcestershire sauce
2 tsp. black pepper
¾ cup cider vinegar
¼ cup sugar
1 tsp. dried thyme
1 tbsp. oregano
½ tsp. cayenne
1 tsp. salt
2 cloves garlic, minced
4 tbsp. lemon juice

Directions

1. In a bowl, whisk together olive oil, Worcestershire sauce, black pepper, cider vinegar, sugar, dried thyme, oregano, cayenne, salt, minced garlic, and lemon juice to make the marinade.
2. Place the pork cubes in a sealable bag or a shallow dish, and pour the marinade over them. Make sure the pork is evenly coated. Seal the bag or cover the dish and refrigerate for at least 2 hours or overnight for best results.
3. Preheat your grill to medium-high heat.
4. Remove the pork cubes from the marinade, reserving the marinade for basting.
5. Thread the pork cubes onto skewers, leaving a little space between each piece.
6. Place the pork skewers on the preheated grill and cook for about 4-5 minutes on each side, or until the pork is cooked through and nicely charred. Baste the pork with the reserved marinade during grilling.
7. Once cooked, remove the skewers from the grill and let them rest for a few minutes.
8. Serve the sweet and spicy pork kabobs hot, and you can garnish with additional fresh herbs if desired.

Tips: Serve the pork kabobs with your favorite dipping sauce or alongside grilled vegetables and rice for a complete meal.

Simple Pork Tenderloin

 **Preparation time** 15 MINUTES |  **Cooking time** 20 MINUTES |  **Servings** 4-6 | 

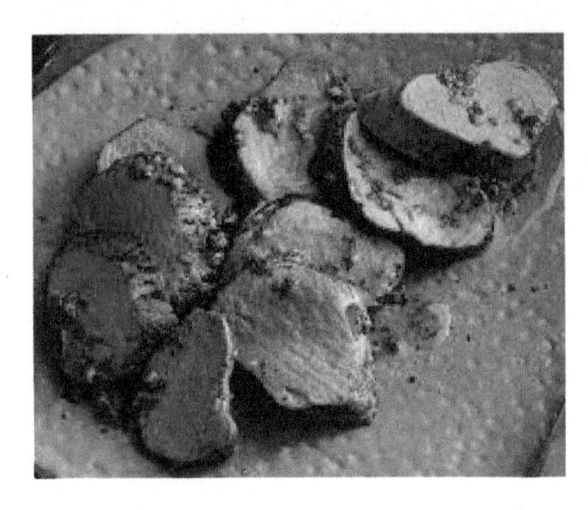

Ingredients

2 Pork Tenderloins (12-15 oz. each)
6 tbsp. melted butter
6 tbsp. hot sauce, Louisiana style
Cajun seasoning, as needed

Directions

1. Preheat your grill to medium-high heat.
2. Season the pork tenderloins with Cajun seasoning, rubbing it evenly over the surface of the meat.
3. In a small bowl, mix together the melted butter and hot sauce.
4. Place the seasoned pork tenderloins on the preheated grill and cook for about 15-20 minutes, turning occasionally, or until the internal temperature reaches 145°F (63°C).
5. During the last few minutes of cooking, brush the butter and hot sauce mixture over the pork tenderloins, ensuring they are evenly coated.
6. Remove the pork tenderloins from the grill and let them rest for about 5 minutes before slicing.
7. Slice the tenderloins into medallions and serve hot.

Tips: Use an instant-read meat thermometer to check the internal temperature of the pork tenderloins for doneness. The recommended safe internal temperature for pork is 145°F (63°C).

Roasted Ham

 **Preparation time** 15 MINUTES |  **Cooking time** 2 H 15 MINUTES |  **Servings** 4 | ★★ **Ratings**

Ingredients

2 tbsp. Dijon mustard
¼ cup horseradish
1 bottle BBQ Apricot Sauce

Directions

1. Preheat your oven to the temperature indicated on the packaging of the ham.
2. In a small bowl, mix together the Dijon mustard and horseradish to create a glaze.
3. Place the ham on a roasting rack or in a shallow roasting pan.
4. Brush the mustard-horseradish glaze all over the surface of the ham, coating it evenly.
5. Pour the BBQ Apricot Sauce over the ham, spreading it evenly.
6. Cover the ham loosely with aluminum foil to prevent it from drying out.
7. Roast the ham in the preheated oven according to the instructions on the packaging, usually about 15-20 minutes per pound. Baste the ham with the pan juices every 30 minutes.
8. About 15 minutes before the estimated cooking time is complete, remove the foil and continue roasting to allow the ham to brown and caramelize.
9. Check the internal temperature of the ham with a meat thermometer to ensure it has reached a safe temperature. The recommended internal temperature for cooked ham is 145°F (63°C).
10. Once the ham is fully cooked, remove it from the oven and let it rest for a few minutes before slicing and serving.

Tips: Serve the roasted ham with your favorite side dishes, such as mashed potatoes, roasted vegetables, or a fresh salad, for a complete and delicious meal.

Cajun Doubled-Smoked Ham

 **Preparation time** 20 MINUTES |  **Cooking time** 4 TO 5 HOURS |  **Servings** 10-12 |  **Ratings**

Ingredients

1 (5- or 6-pound) bone-in smoked ham
1 batch Cajun Rub
3 tbsp. honey

Directions

1. Preheat your smoker to a temperature of 225°F (107°C) according to the manufacturer's instructions.
2. Remove the ham from its packaging and pat it dry with paper towels.
3. Apply the Cajun Rub all over the surface of the ham, ensuring it is evenly coated. Gently press the rub into the meat to help it adhere.
4. Place the ham in the smoker and close the lid. Smoke the ham at 225°F (107°C) for approximately 4-5 hours, or until the internal temperature reaches 140°F (60°C).
5. During the last 30 minutes of smoking, brush the surface of the ham with honey to create a sweet glaze. Repeat the brushing every 10 minutes until the cooking time is complete.
6. Once the ham reaches the desired internal temperature and has a nice caramelized glaze, remove it from the smoker.
7. Let the ham rest for about 15-20 minutes before carving to allow the juices to redistribute.
8. Slice the ham and serve it warm. You can serve it as is or with additional sauce or glaze if desired.

Tips: If you prefer a spicier flavor, you can add some cayenne pepper or hot sauce to the Cajun Rub.

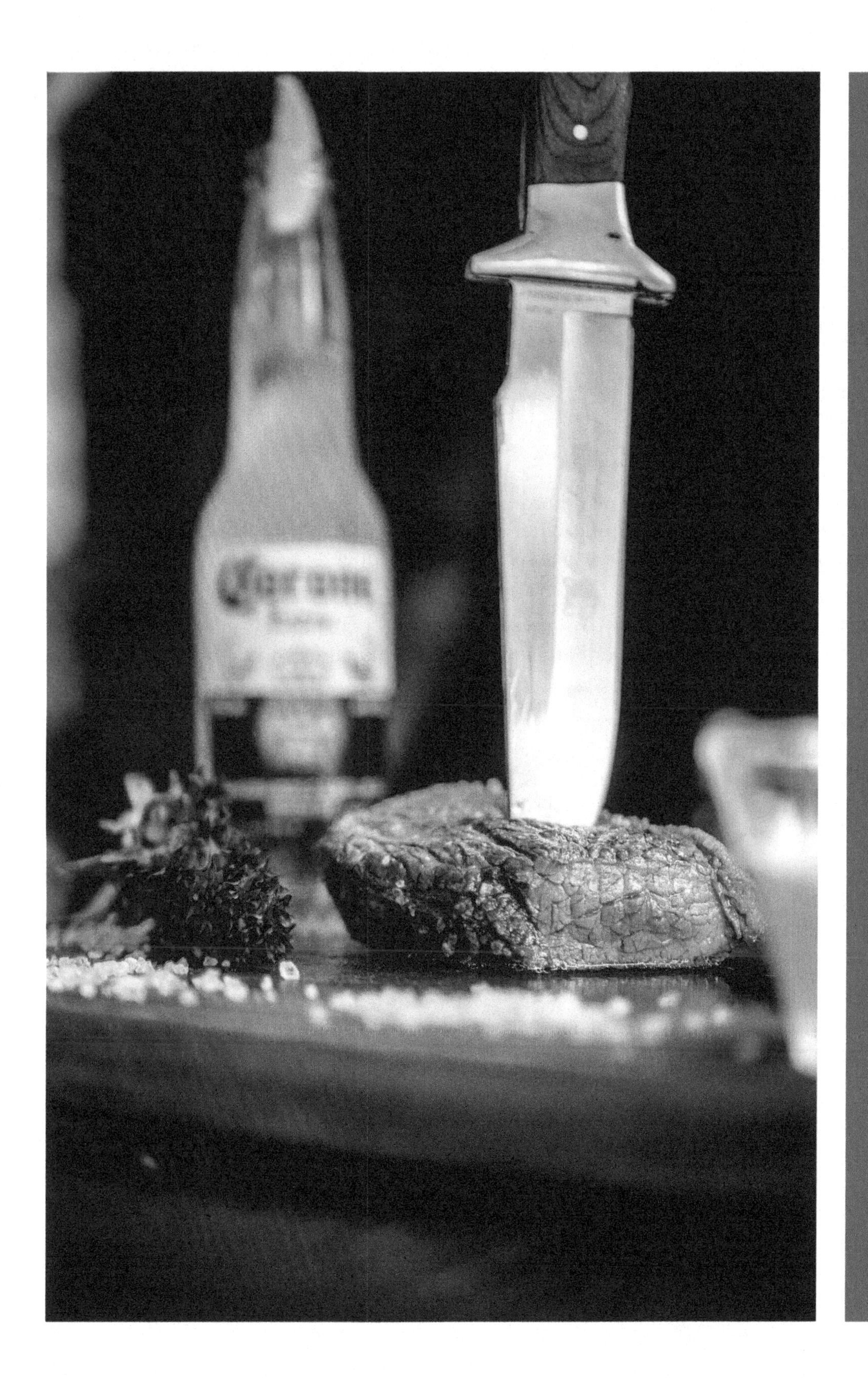

BEEF

Recommended Sauces for Beef

Classic Barbecue Sauce:

A sweet, smoky, and slightly spicy sauce that pairs perfectly with beef. You can prepare it by combining ketchup, brown sugar, apple cider vinegar, mustard, Worcestershire sauce, soy sauce, and spices like paprika, garlic powder, and cayenne pepper.

Chimichurri Sauce:

A fresh and flavorful sauce of Argentine origin. Mix chopped fresh parsley, minced garlic, olive oil, red wine vinegar, lemon juice, red chili flakes, and salt. This sauce adds a touch of freshness and acidity to beef.

Green Peppercorn Sauce:

A rich and creamy sauce with a distinctive green peppercorn flavor. You can prepare it by sautéing chopped shallots in butter, then adding cream, beef broth, brined green peppercorns, and a splash of Cognac. Cook the sauce until it slightly thickens and serve it with beef.

Mushroom Sauce:

A rich and savory sauce with mushrooms that pairs well with the robust flavor of beef. You can prepare it by sautéing sliced fresh mushrooms with butter and garlic, then adding beef broth, cream, and chopped parsley. Cook the sauce until the mushrooms are tender and the consistency is creamy.

Chili Sauce:

A spicy and flavorful sauce for those who enjoy bold taste. You can prepare it by mixing minced hot peppers, minced garlic, apple cider vinegar, brown sugar, lemon juice, olive oil, and salt. Adjust the amount of peppers according to your spice tolerance.

Garlic Butter Grilled Steak

 **Preparation time** 15 MINUTES |  **Cooking time** 25 MINUTES |  **Servings** 4 | ★ **Ratings**

Ingredients

3 tbsp. of unsalted butter
4 cloves of garlic
1 tbsp. of chopped parsley
1 tbsp. of olive oil
4 strip steaks
Salt and pepper

Directions

1. In a small saucepan, melt the butter over medium heat. Add the minced garlic and cook for 1-2 minutes until fragrant and lightly golden. Remove from heat.
2. Stir in the chopped parsley and set aside.
3. Preheat your grill to medium-high heat.
4. Brush the steaks with olive oil and season generously with salt and pepper on both sides.
5. Place the steaks on the preheated grill and cook for about 4-6 minutes per side, depending on the desired doneness. For medium-rare, aim for an internal temperature of 135°F (57°C). Adjust the cooking time accordingly for your preferred doneness.
6. During the last couple of minutes of grilling, baste the steaks with the garlic butter sauce on both sides, using a brush or spoon.
7. Remove the steaks from the grill and let them rest for a few minutes before serving.
8. Serve the Garlic Butter Grilled Steaks hot, and you can drizzle any remaining garlic butter sauce over the top for extra flavor.

Tips: Use high-quality steak cuts like ribeye, strip steak, or tenderloin for the best results.

BBQ Shredded Beef Burger

 **Preparation time** 10 MINUTES |  **Cooking time** 5 H 10 MINUTES |  **Servings** 4 | ★★ **Ratings**

Ingredients

3 lbs. of boneless chuck roast
Salt, to taste
Pepper, to taste
2 tbsp. of minced garlic
1 cup of chopped onion
28 oz. of barbecue sauce
6 buns

Directions

1. Season the chuck roast generously with salt and pepper on all sides.
2. Preheat your grill or smoker to medium-low heat (around 250°F or 120°C).
3. Place the seasoned chuck roast on the grill and cook it low and slow for about 4-5 hours, or until the meat is tender and easily shreds. You can use indirect heat for better results.
4. In a skillet, heat some oil over medium heat and sauté the minced garlic and chopped onion until they become fragrant and lightly golden.
5. Remove the cooked chuck roast from the grill and let it rest for a few minutes. Then, using two forks, shred the meat into bite-sized pieces.
6. Add the shredded beef to the skillet with the sautéed garlic and onion. Pour in the barbecue sauce and stir well to coat the meat evenly.
7. Simmer the mixture over low heat for another 10-15 minutes, allowing the flavors to meld together.
8. Toast the buns on the grill until lightly golden.
9. Spoon the BBQ shredded beef onto the bottom half of each bun. Add additional barbecue sauce if desired.
10. Top with the other half of the bun and serve the BBQ shredded beef burgers hot.

Tips: If you don't have a grill or smoker, you can slow cook the chuck roast in the oven at a low temperature (around 250°F or 120°C) until tender.

Beef Tenderloin

 **Preparation time** 10 MINUTES |  **Cooking time** 1 H 20 MINUTES |  **Servings** 12 | ★★ **Ratings**

Ingredients

1 (5-lbs.) beef tenderloin, trimmed
Kosher salt, as required
¼ cup olive oil
Freshly ground black pepper, as required

Directions

1. Preheat your grill to medium-high heat or set up a two-zone fire for indirect grilling.
2. Season the beef tenderloin generously with kosher salt on all sides, allowing it to come to room temperature for about 30 minutes.
3. Drizzle the olive oil over the tenderloin and rub it evenly to coat the meat.
4. Sprinkle freshly ground black pepper all over the tenderloin, pressing it gently to adhere.
5. Place the tenderloin on the grill over direct heat and sear each side for about 2-3 minutes, or until nicely browned.
6. Move the tenderloin to the cooler side of the grill (indirect heat) and continue grilling with the lid closed. Cook until the internal temperature reaches your desired level of doneness:

   For rare: 120-125°F (49-52°C) - For medium-rare: 130-135°F (54-57°C) - For medium: 140-145°F (60-63°C)

   Note: These temperatures are for reference and it's recommended to use a meat thermometer for accuracy.
7. Once the tenderloin reaches your preferred temperature, remove it from the grill and let it rest for about 10-15 minutes to allow the juices to redistribute.
8. Slice the beef tenderloin into thick slices and serve immediately.

Tips: It's important to season the tenderloin generously with salt to enhance the flavor.

Whole Smoked Bologna Roll

 **Preparation time** 10 MINUTES |  **Cooking time** 4 H 20 MINUTES |  **Servings** 12 | 

Ingredients

1 whole beef bologna roll (3 lbs, 1.4 kgs)
2 tbsp. freshly cracked black pepper
¾ cup brown sugar
¼ cup yellow mustard

Directions

1. Preheat your smoker to a temperature of 225°F (107°C) using your preferred wood chips or chunks for smoking.
2. Remove any packaging or casing from the bologna roll and place it on a clean surface.
3. In a small bowl, combine the black pepper and brown sugar, then mix well.
4. Using a brush or your hands, evenly spread the yellow mustard all over the surface of the bologna roll.
5. Sprinkle the black pepper and brown sugar mixture over the mustard-coated bologna roll, making sure to cover all sides.
6. Place the bologna roll on the smoker grate and close the lid.
7. Smoke the bologna roll for approximately 2 to 3 hours, or until it reaches an internal temperature of 160°F (71°C).
8. Once the bologna roll is fully cooked, remove it from the smoker and let it rest for a few minutes before slicing.
9. Slice the smoked bologna roll into thick slices and serve as desired.

Tips: Make sure to maintain a consistent temperature of 225°F (107°C) throughout the smoking process for even cooking.

Fully Loaded Beef Nachos

Preparation time
10 MINUTES

Cooking time
25 MINUTES

Servings
6

★ **Ratings**

Ingredients

1 lb (0.45 kg) ground beef
1 large bag of tortilla chips
1 green bell pepper, seeded and diced
½ cup sliced scallions
½ cup diced red onion
3 cups shredded cheddar cheese
Sour cream, guacamole, and salsa for serving

Directions

1. Preheat your oven to 375°F (190°C).
2. In a skillet over medium heat, cook the ground beef until browned and cooked through. Drain any excess fat.
3. Spread the tortilla chips in a single layer on a large baking sheet or oven-safe dish.
4. Sprinkle the cooked ground beef evenly over the tortilla chips.
5. Distribute the diced green bell pepper, sliced scallions, and diced red onion on top of the ground beef.
6. Sprinkle the shredded cheddar cheese evenly over the nachos, covering all the toppings.
7. Place the baking sheet or dish in the preheated oven and bake for about 10-15 minutes, or until the cheese is melted and bubbly.
8. Remove the nachos from the oven and let them cool slightly.
9. Serve the fully loaded beef nachos with sour cream, guacamole, and salsa on the side for dipping.
10. Enjoy the delicious nachos while they're still warm and cheesy!

Tips: Make sure to use a baking sheet or dish that is large enough to hold all the nachos in a single layer to ensure even melting of the cheese.

Beef Shoulder Clod

 **Preparation time** 10 MINUTES |  **Cooking time** 12-16 HOURS |  **Servings** 16-20 | ★ **Ratings**

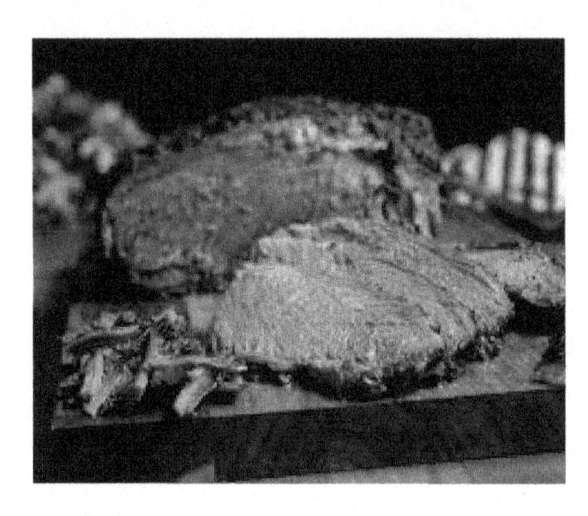

Ingredients

½ cup sea salt
½ cup freshly ground black pepper
1 tbsp. red pepper flakes
1 tbsp. minced garlic
1 tbsp. cayenne pepper
1 tbsp. smoked paprika
1 (13-15 pound) beef shoulder clod

Directions

1. In a bowl, combine the sea salt, black pepper, red pepper flakes, minced garlic, cayenne pepper, and smoked paprika to make the spice rub.
2. Pat the beef shoulder clod dry with paper towels to remove any excess moisture.
3. Rub the spice mixture all over the beef shoulder clod, ensuring it is evenly coated.
4. Preheat your smoker or grill to a temperature of 225°F (107°C).
5. Place the seasoned beef shoulder clod on the smoker or grill, fat side up.
6. Close the lid and smoke or grill the beef shoulder clod for about 8-10 hours, or until the internal temperature reaches 195-205°F (90-96°C). This slow and low cooking process will help tenderize the meat and develop a rich smoky flavor.
7. Remove the beef shoulder clod from the smoker or grill and let it rest for about 20-30 minutes to allow the juices to redistribute.
8. Slice the beef shoulder clod against the grain into thin slices.
9. Serve the smoked beef shoulder clod as a main dish, and you can pair it with your favorite barbecue sauce, sides, and accompaniments.

Tips: This recipe is ideal for larger cuts of beef, such as the shoulder clod, which benefit from low and slow cooking methods to achieve optimal tenderness.

Smoked & Pulled Beef

 **Preparation time** 10 MINUTES |  **Cooking time** 6 HOURS |  **Servings** 6 | ★ **Ratings**

Ingredients

4 lb. beef sirloin tip roast
½ cup BBQ rub
2 bottles of amber beer
1 bottle barbecue sauce

Directions

1. Preheat your smoker to a temperature of 225°F (107°C).
2. Rub the beef sirloin tip roast with the BBQ rub, making sure to coat it evenly on all sides.
3. Place the seasoned roast on the smoker and close the lid.
4. Smoke the beef sirloin tip roast for approximately 1.5 to 2 hours per pound, or until the internal temperature reaches about 200°F (93°C). This slow cooking process will make the meat tender and flavorful.
5. While the roast is smoking, pour the bottles of amber beer into a spray bottle.
6. Every hour or so, spray the roast with the beer to keep it moist and enhance the flavors.
7. Once the roast reaches the desired internal temperature, remove it from the smoker and let it rest for about 30 minutes to an hour.
8. After the resting period, use two forks or your hands to shred the beef into smaller pieces.
9. Place the shredded beef in a large bowl and add the barbecue sauce. Mix well to coat the meat evenly with the sauce.
10. You can serve the smoked and pulled beef on its own as a main dish or use it to make sandwiches or tacos.
11. Serve with additional barbecue sauce on the side, if desired.

Tips: Choose a beef sirloin tip roast that is well-marbled for the best flavor and tenderness.

Wood Pellet Smoked Beef Jerky

 **Preparation time** 15 MINUTES |  **Cooking time** 5 HOURS |  **Servings** 10 | 

Ingredients

3 lb. sirloin steaks, sliced into ¼-inch thickness
2 cups soy sauce
½ cup brown sugar
1 cup pineapple juice
2 tbsp. sriracha
2 tbsp. red pepper flakes
2 tbsp. hoisin sauce
2 tbsp. onion powder
2 tbsp. rice wine vinegar
2 tbsp. minced garlic

Directions

1. In a bowl, combine soy sauce, brown sugar, pineapple juice, sriracha, red pepper flakes, hoisin sauce, onion powder, rice wine vinegar, and minced garlic. Stir well to ensure all ingredients are thoroughly mixed.
2. Place the sliced sirloin steaks in a resealable plastic bag or a shallow dish.
3. Pour the marinade over the steak slices, making sure they are fully submerged. Seal the bag or cover the dish and refrigerate for at least 4 hours or overnight to marinate. The longer it marinates, the more flavor the jerky will have.
4. Preheat your smoker to a temperature of 180°F (82°C).
5. Remove the marinated steak slices from the bag or dish, allowing any excess marinade to drip off.
6. Place the steak slices on the smoker racks, making sure they are not touching each other for even smoking.
7. Smoke the beef jerky at 180°F (82°C) for about 4 to 6 hours, or until it reaches your desired level of dryness and chewiness. Rotate the racks or flip the jerky slices occasionally for even smoking.
8. Once smoked, remove the beef jerky from the smoker and let it cool completely.
9. Store the cooled beef jerky in an airtight container or resealable bags. It can be kept at room temperature for a few weeks or refrigerated for longer shelf life.

Tips: When slicing the sirloin steaks, aim for consistent thickness to ensure even cooking and drying.

Reverse Seared Flank Steak

 **Preparation time** 10 MINUTES |  **Cooking time** 10 MINUTES |  **Servings** 2 | ★★★★★ **Ratings**

Ingredients

1.5 lb. flank steak

1 tbsp. salt

½ tbsp. onion powder

¼ tbsp. garlic powder

½ tbsp. coarsely ground black pepper

Directions

1. Preheat your grill to indirect heat. If using a charcoal grill, arrange the coals on one side of the grill to create a hot zone and a cooler zone. If using a gas grill, light only half of the burners and leave the other half off to create a two-zone setup.
2. Season the flank steak on all sides with salt, onion powder, garlic powder, and coarsely ground black pepper. Ensure the steak is evenly coated with the seasoning.
3. Place the seasoned flank steak on the cooler side of the grill, away from direct heat. Close the lid and allow the steak to cook indirectly for about 30-40 minutes or until the internal temperature reaches around 100°F (38°C) for medium-rare. Use a meat thermometer to monitor the temperature.
4. While the steak is cooking, you can prepare any accompanying sauces or sides.
5. Once the steak reaches the desired temperature, remove it from the grill and set it aside.
6. Increase the heat on your grill to high or prepare a separate grill or cast-iron skillet for direct high heat cooking.
7. Sear the flank steak on the hot side of the grill or in the hot skillet for about 1-2 minutes per side until you achieve a nicely charred crust.
8. Transfer the seared steak to a cutting board and let it rest for 5-10 minutes to allow the juices to redistribute.
9. Slice the flank steak against the grain into thin strips to maximize tenderness.
10. Serve the reverse-seared flank steak hot and enjoy!

Tips: Use a meat thermometer to ensure the desired level of doneness. For medium-rare, aim for an internal temperature of around 130-135°F (54-57°C).

Smoked Midnight Brisket

 **Preparation time** 15 MINUTES |  **Cooking time** 12 MINUTES |  **Servings** 6 | ★ **Ratings**

Ingredients

1 tbsp Worcestershire sauce

1 tbsp Barbecue beef rub

1 tbsp Barbecue chicken rub

1 tbsp Barbecue Blackened Saskatchewan rub

5 lb flat-cut brisket

1 cup beef broth

Directions

1. Preheat your smoker to a temperature of 225°F (107°C). You can use wood chips or chunks of your choice for smoking, such as hickory or oak.
2. In a small bowl, combine the Worcestershire sauce, barbecue beef rub, barbecue chicken rub, and barbecue Blackened Saskatchewan rub to make a flavorful dry rub.
3. Rub the dry rub mixture all over the brisket, ensuring all sides are well coated. Allow the brisket to sit at room temperature for about 30 minutes to allow the flavors to penetrate the meat.
4. Place the seasoned brisket on the smoker grates, fat side up. Close the smoker lid and let the brisket smoke for several hours, maintaining a steady temperature of 225°F (107°C). The cooking time will vary depending on the size of the brisket, but you can estimate about 1.5 hours per pound.
5. After a few hours of smoking, pour the beef broth into a foil pan or a drip pan placed underneath the brisket to catch the drippings. This will help keep the brisket moist during the cooking process.
6. Continue smoking the brisket until it reaches an internal temperature of around 195°F (90°C) to 205°F (96°C). The meat should be tender and easily pull apart with a fork. You can also test for doneness by probing the brisket with a meat thermometer. It should slide in and out with little resistance.
7. Once the brisket is done, carefully remove it from the smoker and transfer it to a cutting board. Tent the brisket loosely with aluminum foil and let it rest for at least 30 minutes to an hour. This allows the juices to redistribute and the meat to become even more tender.
8. After the resting period, slice the smoked brisket against the grain into thin slices for serving. Serve with your favorite barbecue sauce or on a platter alongside sides like coleslaw, cornbread, or baked beans.

Tips: Letting the brisket rest after cooking is crucial for ensuring juicy and tender meat. Do not skip this step.

Prime Rib Roast

 **Preparation time** 5 MINUTES |  **Cooking time** 4 HOURS |  **Servings** 10 |  **Ratings**

Ingredients

7 lb bone-in prime rib roast

Barbecue prime rib rub (amount as per your preference)

Directions

1. Preheat your smoker or grill to indirect heat at a temperature of 225°F (107°C). You can use wood chips or chunks of your choice for smoking, such as mesquite or cherry.
2. Trim any excess fat from the prime rib roast, leaving a thin layer for added flavor and moisture.
3. Generously season the entire surface of the roast with the barbecue prime rib rub. Make sure to coat all sides of the meat, pressing the rub into the surface for better adherence.
4. Place the seasoned prime rib roast on the grill grates, bone side down, and close the lid. Allow the roast to smoke for several hours, maintaining a consistent temperature of 225°F (107°C). The cooking time will vary depending on the size of the roast and your desired level of doneness, but you can estimate about 20 minutes per lb. for medium-rare.
5. Monitor the internal temperature of the roast using a meat thermometer inserted into the thickest part of the meat, away from the bone. For medium-rare, aim for an internal temperature of 130°F (54°C). Remember, the temperature will rise a few degrees during the resting period.
6. Once the desired internal temperature is reached, remove the prime rib roast from the grill and tent it loosely with aluminum foil. Let it rest for at least 20-30 minutes to allow the juices to redistribute and the meat to become more tender.
7. After the resting period, slice the prime rib roast into thick, juicy slices and serve. The meat should be pink in the center with a beautiful crust on the outside.
8. Serve the prime rib roast with your favorite side dishes, such as roasted potatoes, Yorkshire pudding, horseradish sauce, and au jus.

Tips: Choose a high-quality prime rib roast with good marbling for the best flavor and tenderness. Letting the roast come to room temperature for about 30 minutes before smoking helps with even cooking.

Smoked Longhorn Cowboy Tri-Tip

 **Preparation time** 15 MINUTES |  **Cooking time** 4 HOURS |  **Servings** 7 | ★★★★ **Ratings**

Ingredients

3 lb tri-tip roast
1/8 cup ground coffee
¼ cup Barbecue beef rub

Directions

1. Preheat your smoker or grill to indirect heat at a temperature of 225°F (107°C). You can use wood chips or chunks of your choice for smoking, such as oak or hickory.
2. Pat the tri-tip roast dry with paper towels to remove any excess moisture.
3. In a small bowl, combine the ground coffee and barbecue beef rub.
4. Generously season the entire surface of the tri-tip roast with the coffee and rub mixture. Make sure to coat all sides of the meat, pressing the mixture into the surface for better adherence.
5. Place the seasoned tri-tip roast on the grill grates, fat side up, and close the lid. Allow the roast to smoke for about 1.5 to 2 hours, or until the internal temperature reaches 130°F (54°C) for medium-rare. The cooking time may vary depending on the thickness of the roast.
6. Monitor the internal temperature of the roast using a meat thermometer inserted into the thickest part of the meat.
7. Once the desired internal temperature is reached, remove the tri-tip roast from the grill and tent it loosely with aluminum foil. Let it rest for about 10-15 minutes to allow the juices to redistribute.
8. After the resting period, slice the tri-tip roast against the grain into thin slices. The roast should have a pink center with a smoky crust on the outside.
9. Serve the smoked Longhorn Cowboy tri-tip with your favorite sides, such as grilled vegetables, cornbread, or a fresh salad.

Tips: Remember to slice the tri-tip against the grain to ensure tenderness.

Teriyaki Beef Jerky

 **Preparation time** 15 MINUTES |  **Cooking time** 5 HOURS |  **Servings** 10 | ★★★★ **Ratings**

Ingredients

3 cups soy sauce
2 cups brown sugar
3 garlic cloves
2-inch ginger knob, peeled and chopped
1 tbsp sesame oil
4 lb beef (skirt steak)

Directions

1. In a blender or food processor, combine soy sauce, brown sugar, garlic cloves, chopped ginger, and sesame oil. Blend until you have a smooth marinade.
2. Trim any excess fat from the beef and slice it into thin strips, about ¼ inch thick. Make sure to slice against the grain for tender jerky.
3. Place the beef strips in a large resealable plastic bag or a glass container with a tight-fitting lid.
4. Pour the teriyaki marinade over the beef, making sure all the strips are evenly coated. Seal the bag or container and refrigerate for at least 4 hours or overnight, allowing the flavors to penetrate the meat.
5. Preheat your oven to the lowest temperature setting, typically around 170°F (77°C).
6. Line a baking sheet with aluminum foil or use a wire rack placed on top of a baking sheet to allow air circulation during the drying process.
7. Remove the marinated beef strips from the bag or container, shaking off any excess marinade. Arrange the strips in a single layer on the prepared baking sheet or wire rack.
8. Place the baking sheet or wire rack in the preheated oven and leave the door slightly ajar to allow moisture to escape.
9. Let the beef strips dry in the oven for 4-6 hours, or until they become firm and dry to the touch. You can check for doneness by bending a strip, which should crack but not break.
10. Once the beef jerky is dried to your desired texture, remove it from the oven and let it cool completely.
11. Store the teriyaki beef jerky in an airtight container or resealable bags. It can be kept at room temperature for up to 2 weeks, or refrigerated for longer shelf life.

Tips: For a stronger ginger flavor, grate the ginger instead of chopping it.

Smoked Ribeye Steaks

 **Preparation time** 15 MINUTES |  **Cooking time** 35 MINUTES |  **Servings** 1 | ★ **Ratings**

Ingredients

2-inch-thick ribeye steaks
Steak rub of choice

Directions

1. Preheat your smoker to a temperature of 225°F (107°C). Use your preferred type of wood for smoking, such as mesquite, hickory, or oak, to add flavor to the steaks.
2. Remove the ribeye steaks from the refrigerator and let them come to room temperature for about 30 minutes. This will help them cook more evenly.
3. Season the steaks generously with your favorite steak rub. Make sure to coat all sides of the steaks, pressing the rub into the meat.
4. Once the smoker is preheated, place the ribeye steaks directly on the grill grates or on a smoking rack. Leave enough space between the steaks for proper air circulation.
5. Close the smoker and let the steaks smoke for approximately 1 to 1.5 hours, depending on your desired level of doneness. Use a meat thermometer to monitor the internal temperature of the steaks.

   For medium-rare, cook until the steaks reach an internal temperature of 130°F (54°C).

   For medium, cook until the steaks reach an internal temperature of 135°F (57°C).

   Adjust the cooking time accordingly if you prefer your steaks more well done.
6. Once the steaks have reached your desired level of doneness, remove them from the smoker and let them rest for about 5 minutes. This allows the juices to redistribute within the meat.
7. Serve the smoked ribeye steaks hot, either as they are or with your favorite steak sauce or compound butter on top.
8. Enjoy the tender, flavorful smoked ribeye steaks!

Tips: For a more pronounced smoky flavor, you can add wood chips or chunks to the smoker throughout the cooking process.

Smoked Tri-Tip with Java Chophouse Seasoning

 **Preparation time** 10 MINUTES |  **Cooking time** 90 MINUTES |  **Servings** 4 | ★★ **Ratings**

Ingredients

2 tbsp. olive oil
2 tbsp. Java Chophouse seasoning
3-lb. tri-tip roast, fat cap and silver skin removed

Directions

1. Preheat your smoker to a temperature of 225°F (107°C). Use your preferred type of wood, such as oak or hickory, for smoking to enhance the flavor of the tri-tip.
2. In a small bowl, mix together the olive oil and Java Chophouse seasoning to create a paste.
3. Rub the mixture evenly all over the tri-tip roast, making sure to coat all sides.
4. Place the seasoned tri-tip directly on the smoker's grill grates or on a smoking rack. Ensure there is enough space for proper air circulation.
5. Close the smoker and let the tri-tip smoke for approximately 2 to 2.5 hours, or until it reaches your desired level of doneness. Use a meat thermometer to monitor the internal temperature.
   For medium-rare, cook until the tri-tip reaches an internal temperature of 130°F (54°C).
   For medium, cook until the tri-tip reaches an internal temperature of 135°F (57°C).
   Adjust the cooking time accordingly if you prefer your tri-tip more well done.
6. Once the tri-tip reaches the desired internal temperature, remove it from the smoker and let it rest for about 10 minutes. This allows the juices to redistribute within the meat.
7. Slice the smoked tri-tip across the grain into thin slices for serving.
8. Serve the smoked tri-tip hot and enjoy its flavorful and tender meat.

Tips: Letting the tri-tip rest after smoking is essential to retain its juiciness. Cover it loosely with foil during the resting period to keep it warm. Consider marinating the tri-tip in the Java Chophouse seasoning paste for a few hours or overnight before smoking to enhance the flavor even more.

Deli-Style Roast Beef

 **Preparation time** 15 MINUTES |  **Cooking time** 4 HOURS |  **Servings** 2 |  Ratings

Ingredients

4-lb. round-bottomed roast
1 tbsp. coconut oil (or oil of your choice)
¼ tbsp. garlic powder
¼ tbsp. onion powder
¼ tbsp. dried thyme
¼ tbsp. dried oregano
½ tbsp. paprika
½ tbsp. salt
½ tbsp. black pepper

Directions

1. Preheat your oven to 325°F (165°C).
2. In a small bowl, combine the garlic powder, onion powder, dried thyme, dried oregano, paprika, salt, and black pepper. Mix well to create a spice rub.
3. Pat the round-bottomed roast dry with paper towels.
4. Heat the coconut oil in a large skillet over medium-high heat.
5. Rub the spice mixture all over the roast, coating it evenly.
6. Place the seasoned roast in the hot skillet and sear it on all sides until browned. This step helps seal in the juices and adds flavor to the meat.
7. Transfer the seared roast to a roasting pan or a baking dish with a rack.
8. Insert a meat thermometer into the thickest part of the roast, making sure it doesn't touch the bone if present.
9. Place the roasting pan in the preheated oven and roast the beef until it reaches your desired level of doneness. The internal temperature should be:

   125°F (52°C) for rare - 135°F (57°C) for medium-rare - 145°F (63°C) for medium

   Adjust the cooking time accordingly based on your preference. Keep in mind that the roast's temperature will rise a few degrees during resting.
10. Once the roast reaches the desired temperature, remove it from the oven and cover it loosely with foil. Allow it to rest for about 15 minutes. This resting period allows the juices to redistribute throughout the meat, resulting in a juicier and more tender roast.
11. After resting, slice the roast beef thinly across the grain for optimal tenderness and texture.
12. Serve the deli-style roast beef as desired, such as in sandwiches, wraps, or alongside your favorite sides.

Tips: For added flavor, you can marinate the roast in the spice rub overnight in the refrigerator before cooking. This allows the flavors to penetrate the meat more deeply.

Perfect Roast Prime Ribs

 **Preparation time** 15 MINUTES |  **Cooking time** 4-5 HOURS |  **Servings** 4-6 | ★★★★ **Ratings**

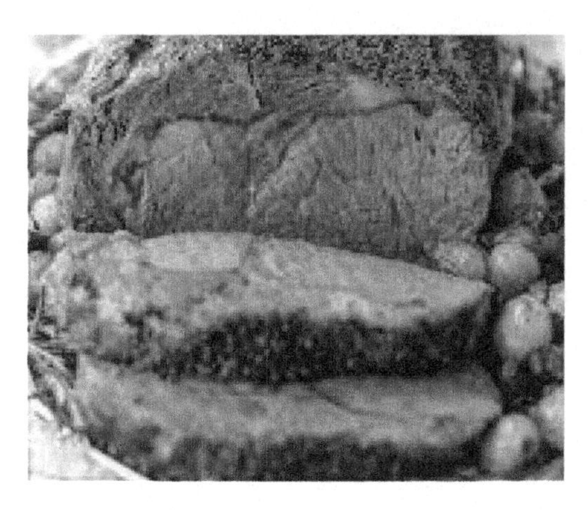

Ingredients

1 (3-bone) rib roast
Salt
Freshly ground black pepper
1 garlic clove, minced

Directions

1. Preheat your oven to 450°F (230°C).
2. Place the rib roast on a cutting board and generously season it with salt and freshly ground black pepper. Make sure to season all sides of the roast, including the fatty side.
3. Rub the minced garlic evenly over the surface of the roast, pressing it into the meat.
4. Place the seasoned rib roast on a rack in a roasting pan, bone-side down. This helps promote even cooking and allows the heat to circulate around the meat.
5. Insert a meat thermometer into the thickest part of the roast, making sure it doesn't touch the bone.
6. Transfer the roasting pan to the preheated oven and roast the prime rib at 450°F (230°C) for 15 minutes to sear the exterior and lock in the juices.
7. After the initial searing, reduce the oven temperature to 325°F (165°C) and continue roasting the prime rib. Estimate about 15 minutes of cooking time per lb. for medium-rare doneness. Adjust the cooking time based on your desired level of doneness and the size of your roast. Use the following internal temperature guide:

   125°F (52°C) for rare - 135°F (57°C) for medium-rare - 145°F (63°C) for medium

   Keep in mind that the internal temperature will rise a few degrees during resting.
8. Once the desired internal temperature is reached, remove the prime rib from the oven and cover it loosely with foil. Allow it to rest for at least 15 minutes. This resting period allows the juices to redistribute and the roast to become more tender and juicy.
9. After resting, carve the prime rib into thick slices, cutting against the grain. Serve it with your favorite sides and enjoy!

Tips: Using a meat thermometer is crucial for achieving the desired level of doneness. Make sure to insert it into the thickest part of the meat, away from the bone.

Braised Short Ribs

 **Preparation time** 25 MINUTES |  **Cooking time** 4 HOURS |  **Servings** 2-4 | ★★★★ **Ratings**

Ingredients

4 beef short ribs
Salt
Freshly ground black pepper
½ cup beef broth

Directions

1. Preheat your oven to 325°F (165°C).
2. Season the beef short ribs generously with salt and freshly ground black pepper on all sides.
3. Heat a large oven-safe pot or Dutch oven over medium-high heat. Add a small amount of oil to the pot and sear the short ribs until they develop a brown crust on all sides. This helps to lock in the flavor.
4. Once the short ribs are nicely seared, remove them from the pot and set them aside.
5. Pour the beef broth into the pot, scraping the bottom to release any browned bits (this adds flavor to the sauce).
6. Return the short ribs to the pot, placing them in a single layer.
7. Cover the pot with a lid and transfer it to the preheated oven.
8. Allow the short ribs to braise in the oven for about 2.5 to 3 hours, or until they become tender and easily fall off the bone.
9. Check the short ribs occasionally during the cooking process and add more beef broth if needed to prevent them from drying out.
10. Once the short ribs are tender, remove them from the pot and let them rest for a few minutes before serving.
11. Optionally, you can strain the braising liquid and reduce it on the stovetop to create a flavorful sauce to drizzle over the short ribs.
12. Serve the braised short ribs with your favorite side dishes, such as mashed potatoes, roasted vegetables, or creamy polenta.

Tips: It's essential to sear the short ribs before braising them. This step adds flavor and helps to create a caramelized crust on the meat.

Smoked Italian Meatballs

 **Preparation time** 10 MINUTES |  **Cooking time** 30 MINUTES |  **Servings** 8 | ★ **Ratings**

Ingredients

1 lb. ground beef
1 lb. Italian sausage
½ cup Italian breadcrumbs
1 tsp. dry mustard
½ cup grated Parmesan cheese
1 tsp. Italian seasoning
1 jalapeno, finely chopped
2 eggs
1 tsp. salt
1 onion, finely chopped
2 tsp. garlic powder
½ tsp. smoked paprika
1 tsp. oregano
1 tsp. crushed red pepper
1 tbsp. Worcestershire sauce

Directions

1. In a large mixing bowl, combine the ground beef and Italian sausage. Mix them together until well combined.
2. Add the breadcrumbs, dry mustard, grated Parmesan cheese, Italian seasoning, finely chopped jalapeno, eggs, salt, finely chopped onion, garlic powder, smoked paprika, oregano, crushed red pepper, and Worcestershire sauce to the meat mixture.
3. Use your hands or a spoon to thoroughly mix all the ingredients together until well combined. Ensure that all the seasonings and ingredients are evenly distributed throughout the mixture.
4. Preheat your smoker to a temperature of 225°F (107°C).
5. Shape the meat mixture into small meatballs, about 1 to 1.5 inches in diameter. You can adjust the size according to your preference.
6. Place the meatballs on a baking sheet lined with parchment paper or a wire rack.
7. Once the smoker is preheated, place the meatballs directly on the smoker racks or use a perforated pan or smoker tray to prevent them from falling through the grates.
8. Close the smoker lid and smoke the meatballs at 225°F (107°C) for approximately 2 to 3 hours, or until they reach an internal temperature of 160°F (71°C).
9. Remove the smoked meatballs from the smoker and let them rest for a few minutes before serving.
10. Serve the smoked Italian meatballs as an appetizer, or use them in pasta dishes, sandwiches, or as a topping for pizza.
11. Enjoy the smoky and flavorful Italian meatballs!

Tips: If you don't have a smoker, you can also bake the meatballs in the oven at 350°F (175°C) for approximately 20 to 25 minutes, or until they are cooked through and reach an internal temperature of 160°F (71°C).

Blackened Saskatchewan Tomahawk Steak

 **Preparation time** 5 MINUTES |  **Cooking time** 10 MINUTES |  **Servings** 4 | ★ **Ratings**

Ingredients

2 (40 oz) tomahawk steaks
4 tbsp. butter
4 tbsp. blackened Saskatchewan rub

Directions

1. Preheat your grill or smoker to high heat for direct grilling or set up for two-zone cooking.
2. Pat dry the tomahawk steaks with paper towels to remove any excess moisture.
3. Rub the steaks all over with the blackened Saskatchewan rub, ensuring they are well coated on all sides.
4. Allow the steaks to sit at room temperature for about 30 minutes to allow the flavors to penetrate the meat.
5. If using a grill, make sure the grates are clean and lightly oiled to prevent sticking. If using a smoker, ensure it is at the desired temperature.
6. Place the tomahawk steaks directly over the hot coals or on the hot side of the grill. Sear them for about 3-4 minutes per side to achieve a nice crust.
7. Once both sides are nicely seared, move the steaks to the indirect heat side of the grill or smoker. Close the lid and continue cooking until the desired internal temperature is reached. For medium-rare, cook until the internal temperature reaches 130°F (54°C). Adjust the cooking time according to your preferred doneness.
8. During the last few minutes of cooking, place a tablespoon of butter on top of each steak and allow it to melt and baste the meat.
9. Remove the steaks from the grill or smoker and let them rest for about 5-10 minutes to allow the juices to redistribute.
10. Serve the blackened Saskatchewan tomahawk steaks as a centerpiece for your meal. You can slice them before serving or serve them whole for a dramatic presentation.
11. Enjoy the flavorful and juicy tomahawk steaks with your favorite side dishes.

Tips: Make sure to use a high-quality blackened Saskatchewan rub for the best flavor.

Wood pellet BBQ Brisket

Preparation time
20 MINUTES

Cooking time
9 HOURS

Servings
8-12

Ratings

Ingredients

1 (12-14 lb) whole packer brisket
Wood pellet beef rub, as needed

Directions

1. Preheat your smoker to 225°F (107°C) using wood pellets of your choice.
2. Trim any excessive fat from the brisket, leaving a thin layer for flavor and moisture.
3. Apply a generous amount of wood pellet beef rub to all sides of the brisket, ensuring it is evenly coated. Massage the rub into the meat for better flavor penetration.
4. Place the brisket directly on the smoker grates, fat side up, and close the lid.
5. Maintain a steady temperature of 225°F (107°C) throughout the smoking process. Use a digital meat thermometer to monitor the internal temperature of the brisket.
6. Smoke the brisket for about 1.5 hours per pound, or until the internal temperature reaches around 195°F (90°C) for a tender and juicy brisket. This can take anywhere from 10-14 hours depending on the size of the brisket and the consistency of your smoker.
7. At around 160°F (71°C) internal temperature, you can choose to wrap the brisket in butcher paper or aluminum foil to help retain moisture and accelerate the cooking process. This step, known as the Texas crutch, can help prevent the brisket from drying out.
8. Once the brisket reaches the desired internal temperature, remove it from the smoker and let it rest for at least 30 minutes to an hour. This allows the juices to redistribute and the meat to become even more tender.
9. Carefully slice the brisket against the grain into thin or thick slices, depending on your preference.
10. Serve the wood pellet BBQ brisket with your favorite barbecue sauce and sides such as coleslaw, baked beans, or cornbread.
11. Enjoy the smoky and flavorful wood pellet BBQ brisket!

Tips: Letting the brisket rest after cooking is crucial for a moist and tender result. Wrap it in foil or butcher paper and place it in a cooler or insulated container to retain heat.

BBQ Meatloaf

 **Preparation time** 25 MINUTES |  **Cooking time** 1 H 30 MINUTES |  **Servings** 4 | ★ **Ratings**

Ingredients

1 ½ lbs. ground beef
1/3 cup ketchup
2 tsp. Worcestershire sauce
1 large egg
1 cup soft breadcrumbs
1 cup chopped onions
½ tsp. salt, to taste
¼ tsp. ground black pepper, to taste
Barbecue sauce for glaze

Directions

1. Preheat your oven to 375°F (190°C).
2. In a large mixing bowl, combine the ground beef, ketchup, Worcestershire sauce, egg, breadcrumbs, chopped onions, salt, and black pepper. Mix well using your hands or a spoon until all the ingredients are evenly incorporated.
3. Transfer the mixture to a greased loaf pan and shape it into a loaf shape.
4. Bake the meatloaf in the preheated oven for approximately 45-60 minutes, or until it reaches an internal temperature of 160°F (71°C).
5. Remove the meatloaf from the oven and drain any excess grease.
6. Brush the top of the meatloaf with barbecue sauce to glaze it.
7. Return the meatloaf to the oven and bake for an additional 5-10 minutes, or until the barbecue sauce forms a sticky glaze on top.
8. Remove the meatloaf from the oven and let it rest for a few minutes before slicing.
9. Slice the BBQ meatloaf into thick slices and serve with additional barbecue sauce on the side, if desired.
10. Enjoy the flavorful and moist BBQ meatloaf!

Tips: Serve the BBQ meatloaf with your favorite sides like mashed potatoes, roasted vegetables, or a side salad.

Blackened Steak

 **Preparation time** 10 MINUTES |  **Cooking time** 60 MINUTES |  **Servings** 4 | ★★ **Ratings**

Ingredients

2 steaks, each about 40 ounces (such as ribeye or New York strip)
4 tbsp. blackened rub (store-bought or homemade)
4 tbsp. unsalted butter

Directions

1. Preheat your grill or stovetop cast-iron skillet to high heat.
2. Pat the steaks dry with paper towels to remove any excess moisture.
3. Rub the blackened rub evenly on all sides of the steaks, pressing it into the meat to adhere.
4. Place the steaks on the hot grill or skillet and cook for about 4-5 minutes per side for medium-rare, or adjust the cooking time to your desired level of doneness.
5. While the steaks are cooking, melt the butter in a small saucepan or microwave-safe bowl.
6. Once the steaks are done, remove them from the heat and let them rest for a few minutes to allow the juices to redistribute.
7. Drizzle the melted butter over the steaks, allowing it to melt and coat the surface.
8. Slice the blackened steaks against the grain into thick slices.
9. Serve the steak slices hot, and you can also spoon any remaining butter from the pan over the top for extra flavor.
10. Enjoy the juicy and flavorful blackened steak!

Tips: Allow the steaks to rest after cooking to ensure that the juices are evenly distributed and the meat remains tender. Serve the blackened steak with your favorite side dishes, such as roasted potatoes, grilled vegetables, or a fresh salad

Traeger New York Strip

 **Preparation time** 5 MINUTES |  **Cooking time** 15 MINUTES |  **Servings** 6 | ★ **Ratings**

Ingredients

3 New York strip steaks
Salt and pepper to taste

Directions

1. Preheat your Traeger grill to the desired temperature (around 400°F or your preferred grilling temperature).
2. Season the New York strip steaks generously with salt and pepper on both sides, ensuring even coverage.
3. Place the steaks directly on the grill grates and close the lid.
4. Grill the steaks for about 4-6 minutes per side for medium-rare, or adjust the cooking time to your desired level of doneness. Remember to flip the steaks only once during cooking to promote a nice sear.
5. Use an instant-read meat thermometer to check the internal temperature. For medium-rare, the temperature should read around 135°F (57°C).
6. Once the steaks reach the desired temperature, remove them from the grill and let them rest for a few minutes to allow the juices to redistribute.
7. Slice the New York strip steaks against the grain into thick slices.
8. Serve the grilled steaks hot and enjoy the juicy and flavorful Traeger New York Strip!

Tips: Make sure to preheat your Traeger grill for about 15 minutes before placing the steaks on the grates to ensure proper heat distribution.

Barbecue Beef Short Rib Lollipop

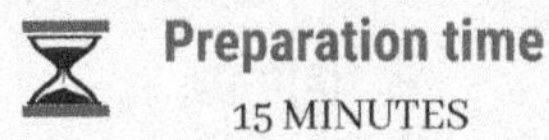  

Preparation time	Cooking time	Servings	★★★ Ratings
15 MINUTES	3 HOURS	4	

Ingredients

4 beef short rib lollipops
BBQ rub of your choice
BBQ sauce for glazing

Directions

1. Preheat your grill to medium-high heat or around 350-400°F (175-200°C).
2. Season the beef short rib lollipops generously with the BBQ rub, coating all sides of the meat.
3. Place the seasoned short rib lollipops on the grill grates and close the lid. Cook for about 3-4 minutes per side to sear and develop grill marks.
4. Once the short rib lollipops have seared on both sides, reduce the heat to low or move them to an indirect grilling zone.
5. Continue cooking the lollipops over low heat for about 1 to 1 ½ hours, or until they reach your desired level of tenderness. You can use a meat thermometer to check the internal temperature. For medium-rare, it should read around 145°F (63°C), while medium to medium-well will be higher.
6. During the last 10-15 minutes of cooking, brush the lollipops with your favorite BBQ sauce to glaze them and add extra flavor.
7. Once cooked to your liking, remove the beef short rib lollipops from the grill and let them rest for a few minutes before serving.
8. Serve the barbecue beef short rib lollipops hot, accompanied by additional BBQ sauce if desired.

Tips: Beef short rib lollipops can be prepped in advance by applying the BBQ rub and letting them marinate in the refrigerator for a few hours or overnight. Experiment with different BBQ rubs and sauces to find your preferred flavor profile.

Grilled Butter Basted Steak

 **Preparation time** 10 MINUTES |  **Cooking time** 40 MINUTES |  **Servings** 2 | ★ **Ratings**

Ingredients

2 steaks, each about 16 ounces, 1 ½-inch thick (such as ribeye or strip steak)

Rib rub of your choice

2 tsp. Dijon mustard

2 tbsp. Worcestershire sauce

4 tbsp. butter, unsalted, melted

Directions

1. Preheat your grill to medium-high heat.
2. Season the steaks with the rib rub, coating all sides evenly.
3. In a small bowl, whisk together the Dijon mustard and Worcestershire sauce.
4. Place the seasoned steaks on the grill and cook for about 4-5 minutes per side for medium-rare, or adjust the cooking time based on your desired doneness.
5. During the last few minutes of grilling, baste the steaks with the melted butter using a brush. Continuously baste the steaks with the butter, flipping them and basting the other side as well. This will help enhance the flavor and keep the steaks juicy.
6. Remove the steaks from the grill and let them rest for a few minutes before serving to allow the juices to redistribute.
7. Serve the grilled butter basted steaks hot, with any remaining butter on top for added richness.

Tips: If you prefer a charred crust on your steaks, you can sear them over high heat for a couple of minutes on each side before moving to medium-high heat for the remaining cooking time.

Mediterranean Meatballs

 **Preparation time** 15 MINUTES |  **Cooking time** 35 MINUTES |  **Servings** 8 | ★★★★ **Ratings**

Ingredients

Pepper, to taste
Salt, to taste
1 tsp. vinegar
2 tbsp. olive oil
2 eggs
1 chopped onion
1 soaked slice of bread
½ tsp. cumin
1 tbsp. chopped basil
1 ½ tbsp. chopped parsley
2 ½ lbs. ground beef

Directions

1. Preheat your oven to 375°F (190°C).
2. In a large mixing bowl, combine the ground beef, chopped onion, soaked bread (squeeze out any excess liquid), eggs, cumin, chopped basil, chopped parsley, salt, and pepper. Mix well until all the ingredients are evenly incorporated.
3. Shape the meat mixture into meatballs of your desired size. You can make them small or larger, depending on your preference.
4. Heat olive oil in a skillet over medium heat. Once the oil is hot, add the meatballs in batches and brown them on all sides. This step adds flavor and texture to the meatballs.
5. Transfer the browned meatballs to a baking dish and drizzle them with vinegar.
6. Place the baking dish in the preheated oven and bake for about 20-25 minutes or until the meatballs are cooked through and browned.
7. Once cooked, remove the meatballs from the oven and let them rest for a few minutes before serving.
8. Serve the Mediterranean meatballs as a main dish with your choice of sides, such as rice, couscous, or a salad. They also work well as an appetizer or can be served with pita bread and tzatziki sauce for a Mediterranean-inspired meal.

Tips: If you prefer, you can pan-fry the meatballs instead of baking them. Simply cook them in a skillet with olive oil until browned and cooked through.

Greek Meatballs

 **Preparation time** 10 MINUTES |  **Cooking time** 40 MINUTES |  **Servings** 6 | ★★★★ **Ratings**

Ingredients

Pepper, to taste
Salt, to taste
2 chopped green onions
1 tbsp. almond flour
2 eggs
½ lb. ground pork
2 ½ lbs. ground beef

Directions

1. In a large mixing bowl, combine the ground pork, ground beef, chopped green onions, almond flour, eggs, salt, and pepper. Mix well until all the ingredients are evenly incorporated.
2. Shape the mixture into meatballs of your desired size. You can make them small or larger, depending on your preference.
3. Heat a skillet or grill pan over medium heat. Once hot, add the meatballs in batches and cook them until browned on all sides and cooked through. Make sure to cook them evenly and avoid overcrowding the pan.
4. Remove the cooked meatballs from the pan and transfer them to a serving dish.
5. Serve the Greek meatballs as an appetizer, main dish, or in pita bread as gyro-style sandwiches.
6. You can also serve them with tzatziki sauce, a Greek yogurt and cucumber sauce, for added flavor and freshness.

Tips: For added Greek flavor, you can incorporate other traditional Mediterranean ingredients into the meatball mixture, such as chopped fresh mint, oregano, or crumbled feta cheese.

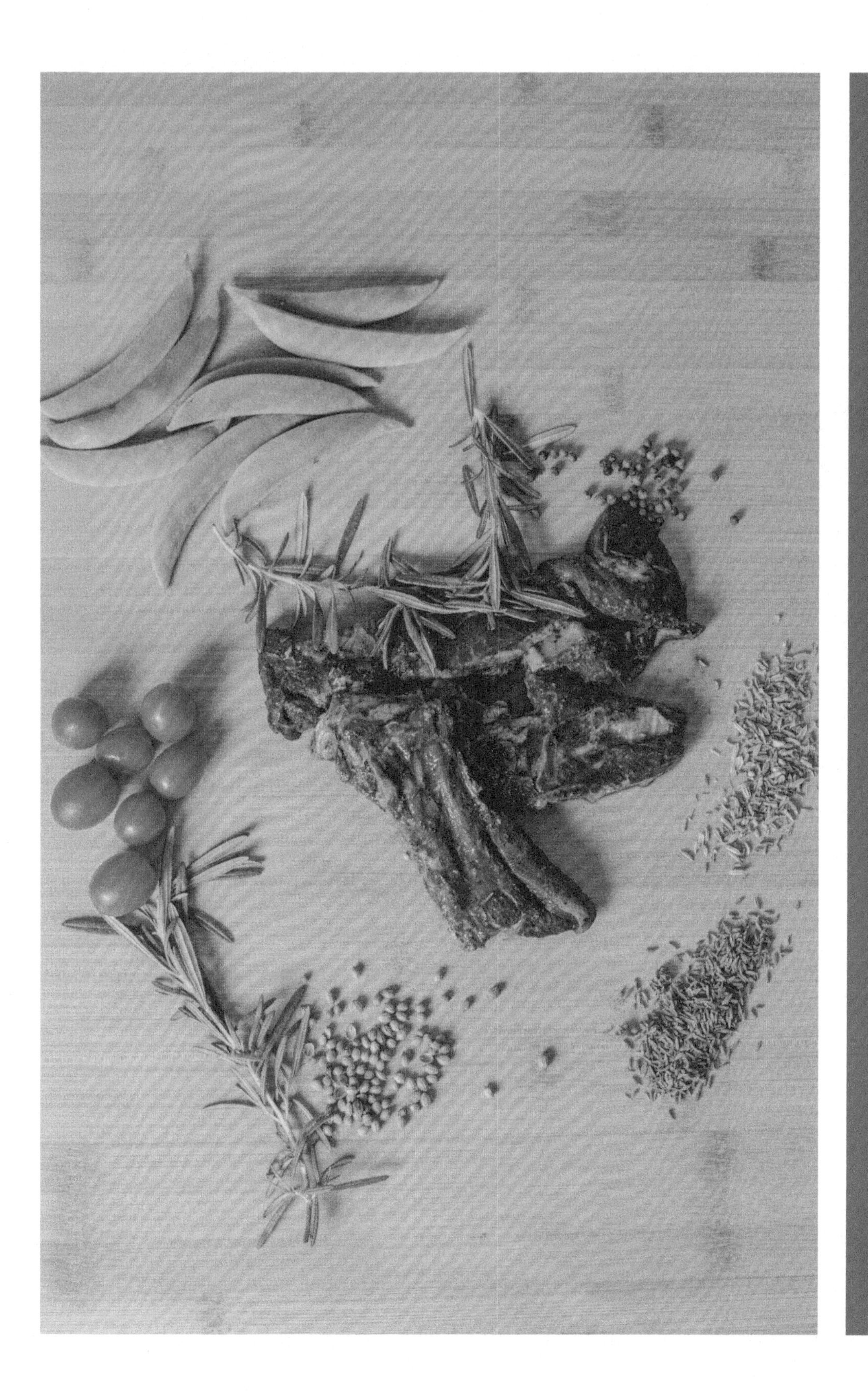

LAMB

Recommended Sauces for Lamb

Mint Yogurt Sauce:
Mix Greek yogurt with chopped fresh mint leaves, lemon juice, minced garlic, salt, and pepper. Add a touch of honey for sweetness, if desired.

Tomato Chili Sauce:
Blend ripe tomatoes with fresh red chilies (or chili powder), minced garlic, red wine vinegar, olive oil, salt, and pepper. Add a pinch of sugar for a slightly sweet flavor, if preferred.

Garlic Yogurt Sauce:
Combine Greek yogurt with minced garlic, lemon juice, chopped fresh parsley, salt, and pepper. You can also drizzle in some olive oil for a smoother consistency.

Mint BBQ Sauce:
Prepare a traditional BBQ sauce and add finely chopped fresh mint leaves for a fresh and aromatic twist. You can also add a dash of chili for extra heat.

Chimichurri Sauce:
Blend fresh parsley, minced garlic, olive oil, red wine vinegar, chopped red chili pepper, salt, and pepper. This vibrant and spicy sauce is perfect for dressing grilled lamb.

Seasoned Lamb Shoulder

 **Preparation time** 15 MINUTES |  **Cooking time** 5 HOURS |  **Servings** 6 | ★★★★ **Ratings**

Ingredients

1 (5-pound) bone-in lamb shoulder, trimmed
3-4 tbsp. Moroccan seasoning
2 tbsp. olive oil
1 cup water
¼ cup apple cider vinegar

Directions

1. Preheat your grill or smoker to a medium-high heat, around 300-325°F (150-163°C).
2. In a small bowl, combine the Moroccan seasoning and olive oil to create a paste. Mix well until the seasoning is evenly incorporated into the oil.
3. Rub the Moroccan seasoning paste all over the trimmed lamb shoulder, ensuring that it is evenly coated on all sides.
4. Place the seasoned lamb shoulder on the grill or smoker, fat side up. Close the lid and let it cook for about 3-4 hours, or until the internal temperature reaches around 160°F (71°C).
5. While the lamb is cooking, prepare a basting mixture by combining water and apple cider vinegar in a bowl.
6. Every hour, baste the lamb shoulder with the water and vinegar mixture to keep it moist and enhance the flavors.
7. Once the lamb shoulder reaches the desired internal temperature, remove it from the grill or smoker and let it rest for about 10-15 minutes.
8. Slice the lamb shoulder against the grain into thin slices and serve it hot.

Tips: For a more intense flavor, marinate the lamb shoulder with the Moroccan seasoning paste overnight in the refrigerator before cooking.

Leg of Lamb

 **Preparation time** 15 MINUTES |  **Cooking time** 3 HOURS |  **Servings** 6 |  **Ratings**

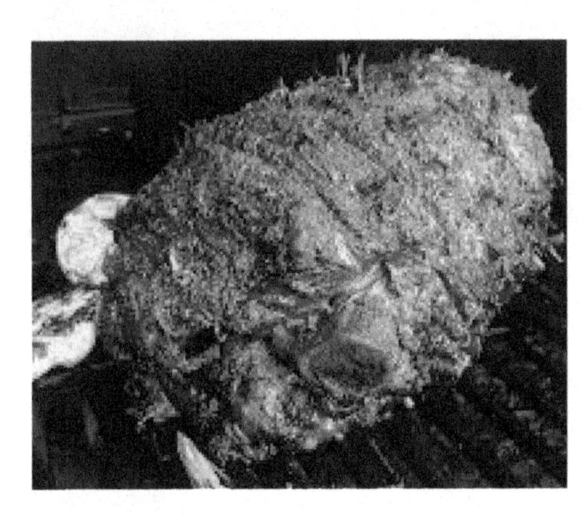

Ingredients

1 leg of lamb, boneless
4 garlic cloves, minced
2 tbsp. salt
1 tbsp. black pepper, freshly ground
2 tbsp. oregano
1 tbsp. thyme
2 tbsp. olive oil

Directions

1. Preheat your grill or oven to a medium-high heat, around 375°F (190°C).
2. In a small bowl, combine the minced garlic, salt, black pepper, oregano, thyme, and olive oil. Mix well to create a paste.
3. Using your hands or a basting brush, rub the garlic and herb paste all over the leg of lamb, ensuring that it is evenly coated.
4. If using a grill, place the lamb directly on the grates. If using an oven, place the lamb on a roasting rack set inside a roasting pan.
5. Cook the leg of lamb for about 20-25 minutes per pound, or until the internal temperature reaches 135°F (57°C) for medium-rare doneness. Adjust the cooking time based on your desired level of doneness.
6. Remove the leg of lamb from the heat source and let it rest for about 10-15 minutes. This allows the juices to redistribute and the meat to become more tender.
7. Slice the leg of lamb against the grain into thin slices and serve it hot.

Tips: Serve the leg of lamb with roasted potatoes, grilled vegetables, or a fresh salad for a delicious meal.

Simple Grilled Lamb Chops

 **Preparation time** 10 MINUTES |  **Cooking time** 6 MINUTES |  **Servings** 6 | ★★★ **Ratings**

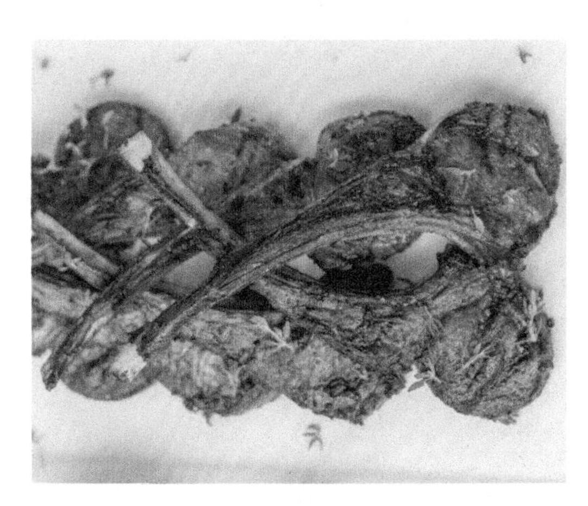

Ingredients

¼ cup distilled white vinegar
2 tbsp. salt
½ tbsp. black pepper
1 tbsp. garlic, minced
1 onion, thinly sliced
2 tbsp. olive oil
2 lbs. lamb chops

Directions

1. In a small bowl, combine the white vinegar, salt, black pepper, minced garlic, and thinly sliced onion. Mix well to create a marinade.
2. Place the lamb chops in a shallow dish or a resealable plastic bag. Pour the marinade over the lamb chops, ensuring that they are fully coated. Cover the dish or seal the bag and refrigerate for at least 1 hour, or overnight for maximum flavor.
3. Preheat your grill to medium-high heat.
4. Remove the lamb chops from the marinade and discard the marinade.
5. Drizzle the olive oil over the lamb chops and rub it evenly on both sides.
6. Place the lamb chops on the preheated grill and cook for about 4-5 minutes per side for medium-rare, or adjust the cooking time according to your desired level of doneness.
7. Once cooked to your liking, remove the lamb chops from the grill and let them rest for a few minutes.
8. Serve the grilled lamb chops hot, garnished with fresh herbs if desired.

Tips: For extra tenderness, allow the lamb chops to come to room temperature before grilling.

Spicy Chinese Cumin Lamb Skewers

 **Preparation time** 20 MINUTES |  **Cooking time** 6 MINUTES |  **Servings** 10 |  **Ratings**

Ingredients

1 lb. lamb shoulder, cut into ½-inch pieces
10 skewers
2 tbsp. ground cumin
2 tbsp. red pepper flakes
1 tbsp. salt

Directions

1. Preheat your grill to medium-high heat.
2. In a bowl, combine the ground cumin, red pepper flakes, and salt. Mix well to create a spice blend.
3. Thread the lamb shoulder pieces onto the skewers, evenly distributing the meat.
4. Sprinkle the spice blend over the lamb skewers, ensuring that all sides are coated.
5. Place the skewers on the preheated grill and cook for about 8-10 minutes, turning occasionally, until the lamb is cooked to your desired doneness.
6. Once cooked, remove the skewers from the grill and let them rest for a few minutes before serving.
7. Serve the spicy Chinese cumin lamb skewers hot as an appetizer or main dish. They pair well with a side of steamed rice or a fresh salad.

Tips: if using wooden skewers, make sure to soak them in water for about 30 minutes before threading the lamb to prevent them from burning on the grill.

Garlic & Rosemary Grilled Lamb Chops

 **Preparation time** 10 MINUTES |  **Cooking time** 20 MINUTES |  **Servings** 4 | ★★ **Ratings**

Ingredients

2 lbs. lamb loin, thick-cut
4 garlic cloves, minced
1 tbsp. fresh chopped rosemary leaves
1 tbsp. kosher salt
½ tbsp. black pepper
Zest of 1 lemon
¼ cup olive oil

Directions

1. In a small bowl, combine the minced garlic, chopped rosemary, kosher salt, black pepper, lemon zest, and olive oil. Mix well to create a marinade.
2. Place the lamb chops in a shallow dish and pour the marinade over them. Ensure that the lamb chops are evenly coated. Cover the dish and let it marinate in the refrigerator for at least 1 hour, or overnight for best results.
3. Preheat your grill to medium-high heat.
4. Remove the lamb chops from the marinade and discard any excess marinade. Allow the lamb chops to come to room temperature for about 15 minutes before grilling.
5. Place the lamb chops on the preheated grill and cook for about 4-5 minutes per side, or until they reach your desired level of doneness. For medium-rare, the internal temperature should be around 145°F (63°C).
6. Once cooked, transfer the lamb chops to a plate and let them rest for a few minutes before serving.
7. Serve the garlic and rosemary grilled lamb chops hot, garnished with additional fresh rosemary if desired. They pair well with a side of roasted vegetables or a fresh salad.

Tips: If using a gas grill, preheat the grill with the lid closed for about 10-15 minutes before grilling the lamb chops.

Wood Pellet Grilled Lamb Loin Chops

 **Preparation time** 10 MINUTES |  **Cooking time** 10 MINUTES |  **Servings** 6 | ★★ **Ratings**

Ingredients

2 tbsp. herbs de Provence
1 ½ tbsp. olive oil
2 garlic cloves, minced
2 tbsp. lemon juice
5 ounces lamb loin chops
Salt and black pepper to taste

Directions

1. In a small bowl, combine the herbs de Provence, olive oil, minced garlic, and lemon juice. Mix well to create a marinade.
2. Place the lamb loin chops in a shallow dish and pour the marinade over them. Make sure the chops are evenly coated. Cover the dish and refrigerate for at least 30 minutes to allow the flavors to meld.
3. Preheat your grill or grill pan to medium-high heat.
4. Remove the lamb loin chops from the marinade and season them with salt and black pepper to taste.
5. Place the chops on the preheated grill or grill pan and cook for about 3-4 minutes per side for medium-rare doneness. Adjust the cooking time according to your preference and the thickness of the chops.
6. Once cooked to your desired level, remove the lamb loin chops from the grill and let them rest for a few minutes before serving.
7. Serve the lamb loin chops hot, garnished with fresh herbs if desired. They pair well with roasted potatoes, grilled vegetables, or a side salad.

Tips: For extra flavor, you can brush the chops with the remaining marinade during grilling.

Smoked Lamb Shoulder

 **Preparation time** 30 MINUTES |  **Cooking time** 3 HOURS |  **Servings** 7 | ★★★ **Ratings**

Ingredients

5 lbs. lamb shoulder
1 cup cider vinegar
2 tbsp. oil
2 tbsp. kosher salt
2 tbsp. black pepper, freshly ground
1 tbsp. dried rosemary
For the Spritz:
1 cup apple cider vinegar
1 cup apple juice

Directions

1. In a small bowl, mix together the cider vinegar, oil, kosher salt, black pepper, and dried rosemary to create a marinade.
2. Place the lamb shoulder in a large resealable plastic bag or a shallow dish and pour the marinade over it. Ensure that the lamb is coated evenly with the marinade.
3. Cover the dish or seal the bag and let the lamb marinate in the refrigerator for at least 2 hours or overnight for more flavor penetration.
4. Preheat your smoker to a temperature of 225°F (107°C), using your choice of wood chips or chunks for smoking.
5. Remove the lamb shoulder from the marinade and discard any excess marinade.
6. Place the lamb shoulder on the smoker rack and close the lid.
7. Smoke the lamb shoulder at 225°F (107°C) for approximately 6-8 hours, or until the internal temperature reaches 195°F (90°C) and the meat is tender.
8. During the smoking process, you can spritz the lamb shoulder every hour with a mixture of apple cider vinegar and apple juice to keep it moist and add flavor.
9. Once the lamb shoulder reaches the desired temperature, remove it from the smoker and let it rest for about 15-20 minutes.
10. Slice or shred the smoked lamb shoulder, and it is ready to be served.
11. Serve the smoked lamb shoulder as a main dish, accompanied by your favorite sides, such as roasted vegetables, mashed potatoes, or a fresh salad.

Tips: Monitoring the Internal Temperature: While smoking, it's essential to use a meat thermometer to monitor the internal temperature of the lamb shoulder. Aim for an internal temperature of 195°F (90°C) for tender and fully cooked meat.

Smoked Lamb Meatballs

 **Preparation time** 30 MINUTES |  **Cooking time** 1 HOUR |  **Servings** 20 | ★★ **Ratings**

Ingredients

1 lb. ground lamb shoulder
3 garlic cloves, finely diced
3 tbsp. shallot, diced
1 tbsp. salt
1 egg
½ tbsp. pepper
½ tbsp. cumin
½ tbsp. smoked paprika
¼ tbsp. red pepper flakes
¼ tbsp. cinnamon
¼ cup panko breadcrumbs

Directions

1. In a large mixing bowl, combine the ground lamb shoulder, diced garlic, diced shallot, salt, egg, pepper, cumin, smoked paprika, red pepper flakes, cinnamon, and panko breadcrumbs.
2. Mix the ingredients together until well combined. Use your hands to ensure even distribution of the seasonings.
3. Form the mixture into meatballs of your desired size. You can make them small for appetizers or larger for main courses.
4. Preheat your smoker to a temperature of around 225°F (107°C) and set it up for indirect heat smoking.
5. Place the lamb meatballs on the smoker grate and close the lid.
6. Smoke the meatballs for approximately 1 to 1.5 hours, or until they reach an internal temperature of 160°F (71°C).
7. Once cooked, remove the meatballs from the smoker and let them rest for a few minutes before serving.
8. Serve the smoked lamb meatballs as an appetizer, in sandwiches, or as part of a main dish. They can be enjoyed on their own or with your favorite dipping sauce.

Tips: For added flavor, you can mix in some fresh herbs like mint or parsley into the meatball mixture. If the mixture feels too wet and sticky, add a little more breadcrumbs to help bind it together.

Spicy & Tangy Lamb Shoulder

 **Preparation time** 30 MINUTES |  **Cooking time** 5¾ HOURS |  **Servings** 6 | 

Ingredients

1 (5-lb.) bone-in lamb shoulder, trimmed
3-4 tbsp. Moroccan seasoning
2 tbsp. olive oil
1 cup water
¼ cup apple cider vinegar

Directions

1. Preheat your smoker to a temperature of 225°F (107°C) and set it up for indirect heat smoking.
2. Rub the lamb shoulder with Moroccan seasoning, ensuring all sides are well coated. Allow the lamb shoulder to sit at room temperature for about 30 minutes to let the flavors penetrate.
3. In a small bowl, combine the olive oil, water, and apple cider vinegar. This will serve as a spritz mixture to keep the lamb moist during the smoking process.
4. Place the lamb shoulder on the smoker grate and close the lid. Maintain the smoker temperature at 225°F (107°C).
5. Smoke the lamb shoulder for approximately 5-6 hours, or until it reaches an internal temperature of 195°F (90°C) and is tender and easily shredded. Use a meat thermometer to check for doneness.
6. Every hour during the smoking process, open the smoker and spritz the lamb shoulder with the olive oil, water, and apple cider vinegar mixture to keep it moist and add extra flavor.
7. Once the lamb shoulder is fully smoked and tender, remove it from the smoker and let it rest for about 20 minutes. This allows the juices to redistribute and the flavors to settle.
8. Slice or shred the smoked lamb shoulder as desired and serve it hot.

Tips: For a richer flavor, marinate the lamb shoulder in the Moroccan seasoning and olive oil mixture overnight in the refrigerator before smoking.

Cheesy Lamb Burgers

 **Preparation time** 15 MINUTES |  **Cooking time** 20 MINUTES |  **Servings** 4 | ★ **Ratings**

Ingredients

2 lb. ground lamb

1 cup Parmigiano-Reggiano cheese, grated

Salt, to taste

Freshly ground black pepper, to taste

Directions

1. In a large mixing bowl, combine the ground lamb and grated Parmigiano-Reggiano cheese. Season with salt and freshly ground black pepper according to your taste preferences.
2. Gently mix the ingredients together until well combined, being careful not to overmix as it can result in dense burgers.
3. Divide the lamb mixture into equal portions and shape them into burger patties. You can adjust the size of the patties to your liking.
4. Preheat your grill or stovetop griddle to medium-high heat. Make sure the cooking surface is well greased to prevent sticking.
5. Place the lamb burger patties on the grill or griddle and cook for about 4-6 minutes per side, or until they reach your desired level of doneness. Lamb is typically cooked to medium-rare or medium for the best flavor and juiciness.
6. Once cooked, remove the lamb burgers from the heat and let them rest for a few minutes to allow the juices to redistribute.
7. Serve the cheesy lamb burgers on buns or lettuce wraps, topped with your favorite condiments and garnishes. You can also add additional cheese, sliced tomatoes, lettuce, or caramelized onions for extra flavor.
8. Enjoy the cheesy lamb burgers while they're still hot and juicy!

Tips: For added meltiness, you can place a slice of cheese, such as cheddar or Swiss, on top of the lamb burgers during the last minute of cooking.

Lamb Breast

 **Preparation time** 30 MINUTES |  **Cooking time** 2 H 40 MINUTES |  **Servings** 2 | ★★★ **Ratings**

Ingredients

1 (2-pound) trimmed bone-in lamb breast
½ cup white vinegar
¼ cup yellow mustard
½ cup BBQ rub

Directions

1. Preheat your smoker or grill to a temperature of 225°F (107°C) for low and slow cooking.
2. In a small bowl, combine the white vinegar and yellow mustard to create a marinade.
3. Place the lamb breast in a large resealable bag or a shallow dish and pour the marinade over it. Make sure the lamb is well coated with the marinade. Allow it to marinate in the refrigerator for at least 2 hours, or overnight for maximum flavor.
4. Remove the lamb breast from the marinade and pat it dry with paper towels.
5. Sprinkle the BBQ rub evenly over all sides of the lamb breast, ensuring good coverage.
6. Place the lamb breast on the smoker or grill, bone side down. Close the lid and smoke or grill for about 3-4 hours, or until the internal temperature reaches 180°F (82°C) and the meat is tender.
7. To achieve a smoky flavor, you can add wood chips or chunks to the smoker or grill during the cooking process. Use woods like hickory, apple, or cherry for a delicious aroma.
8. Once cooked, remove the lamb breast from the smoker or grill and let it rest for about 10 minutes before slicing.
9. Slice the lamb breast into individual portions or serve it as a whole. The meat should be tender and juicy, with a flavorful crust from the BBQ rub.
10. Serve the lamb breast with your favorite side dishes, such as roasted vegetables, mashed potatoes, or a fresh salad.

Tips: For a crispy exterior, you can finish the lamb breast on high heat for a few minutes after smoking or grilling to achieve a nice char.

Braised Lamb

 **Preparation time** 30 MINUTES |  **Cooking time** 3 H 20 MINUTES |  **Servings** 4 | ★★★ **Ratings**

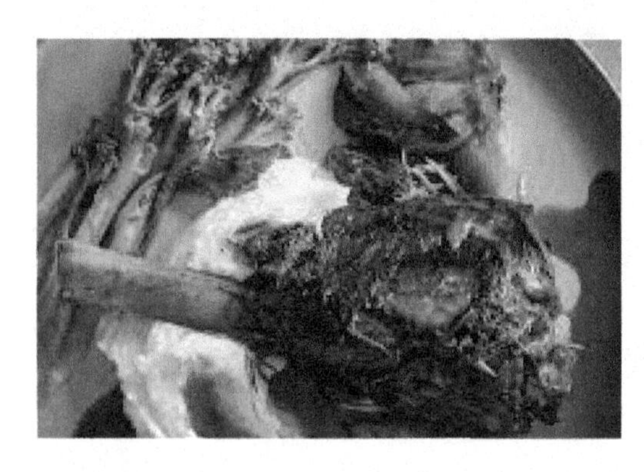

Ingredients

4 lamb shanks

Prime rib rub (or your preferred seasoning blend)

1 cup red wine

1 cup beef broth

2 sprigs thyme

2 sprigs rosemary

Directions

1. Preheat your oven to 325°F (163°C).
2. Season the lamb shanks generously with the prime rib rub or your preferred seasoning blend. Make sure to coat all sides of the shanks.
3. Heat a large, oven-safe pot or Dutch oven over medium-high heat. Add a little oil to the pot and sear the lamb shanks until they are well browned on all sides. This will help to develop rich flavors.
4. Once the lamb shanks are browned, remove them from the pot and set them aside temporarily.
5. Pour the red wine into the pot and use a wooden spoon or spatula to scrape up any browned bits from the bottom. Let the wine simmer for a minute or two to cook off some of the alcohol.
6. Add the beef broth to the pot, along with the thyme and rosemary sprigs. Stir to combine.
7. Return the lamb shanks to the pot, nestling them into the liquid. The liquid should come up about halfway up the sides of the shanks.
8. Cover the pot with a lid and transfer it to the preheated oven. Allow the lamb shanks to braise for about 2 to 2 ½ hours, or until the meat is tender and easily pulls away from the bone.
9. Check the lamb shanks occasionally during the cooking process and baste them with the cooking liquid to keep them moist.
10. Once the lamb shanks are cooked to your desired tenderness, remove them from the pot and let them rest for a few minutes.
11. Strain the cooking liquid from the pot, discarding the herbs and any solids. You can reduce the cooking liquid on the stovetop to create a flavorful sauce if desired.
12. Serve the braised lamb shanks with the reduced cooking liquid as a sauce, along with your favorite side dishes such as mashed potatoes, roasted vegetables, or a salad.

Tips: Feel free to add other aromatics such as garlic, onions, or carrots to the braising liquid for additional depth of flavor.

Grilled Leg of Lambs Steaks

 **Preparation time** 5 MINUTES |  **Cooking time** 10 MINUTES |  **Servings** 4 | ★★★ **Ratings**

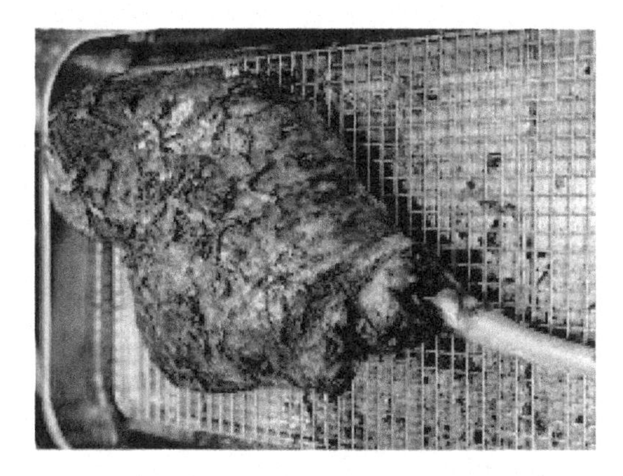

Ingredients

4 lamb steaks, bone-in
¼ cup olive oil
4 garlic cloves, minced
1 tbsp. rosemary, freshly chopped
Salt and black pepper to taste

Directions

1. In a small bowl, whisk together the olive oil, minced garlic, chopped rosemary, salt, and black pepper.
2. Place the lamb steaks in a shallow dish or zip-top bag. Pour the marinade over the steaks, making sure they are well coated. Allow the steaks to marinate in the refrigerator for at least 1 hour, or overnight for maximum flavor.
3. Preheat your grill to medium-high heat.
4. Remove the lamb steaks from the marinade, letting any excess drip off. Discard the remaining marinade.
5. Place the lamb steaks on the preheated grill and cook for about 4-6 minutes per side, or until they reach your desired level of doneness. The cooking time may vary depending on the thickness of the steaks and your preferred level of doneness.
6. Use a meat thermometer to check the internal temperature of the steaks. For medium-rare, the temperature should reach around 135°F (57°C). For medium, aim for 145°F (63°C). Keep in mind that the temperature will rise a few degrees as the steaks rest.
7. Once cooked to your liking, remove the lamb steaks from the grill and let them rest for a few minutes. This allows the juices to redistribute and ensures a tender and juicy steak.
8. Serve the grilled leg of lamb steaks with your favorite side dishes, such as roasted vegetables, couscous, or a fresh salad.

Tips: For best results, let the lamb steaks marinate in the refrigerator for at least 1 hour or overnight. This allows the flavors to penetrate the meat and enhances the overall taste. Before grilling, make sure to preheat your grill to medium-high heat. This ensures proper cooking and creates those desirable grill marks on the steaks.

Wine Braised Lamb Shank

 **Preparation time** 30 MINUTES |  **Cooking time** 10 HOURS |  **Servings** 2 | ★ **Ratings**

Ingredients

2 (1¼-lb.) lamb shanks
1-2 cups water
¼ cup brown sugar
1/3 cup rice wine
1/3 cup soy sauce
1 tbsp. dark sesame oil
4 (1½x½-inch) orange zest strips
2 (3-inch long) cinnamon sticks
1½ tsp. Chinese five-spice powder

Directions

1. Preheat your oven to 325°F (160°C).
2. In a large Dutch oven or oven-safe pot, heat some oil over medium-high heat. Add the lamb shanks and brown them on all sides, about 5-7 minutes per side.
3. In a separate bowl, whisk together the water, brown sugar, rice wine, soy sauce, dark sesame oil, orange zest strips, cinnamon sticks, and Chinese five-spice powder.
4. Pour the mixture over the browned lamb shanks in the pot.
5. Cover the pot with a lid and transfer it to the preheated oven.
6. Braise the lamb shanks in the oven for about 2-2.5 hours, or until the meat is tender and easily pulls away from the bone.
7. Remove the pot from the oven and carefully transfer the lamb shanks to a serving platter. Tent them with foil to keep them warm.
8. Place the pot with the braising liquid on the stovetop over medium heat. Simmer the liquid until it thickens slightly and reduces, about 10-15 minutes.
9. Strain the liquid to remove any solids and skim off any excess fat.
10. Serve the lamb shanks drizzled with the reduced braising liquid.

Tips: Make sure to use an oven-safe pot or Dutch oven that can withstand the oven temperature.

Lamb Leg With Salsa

 **Preparation time** 30 MINUTES |  **Cooking time** 1 H 30 MINUTES |  **Servings** 6 | ★★ **Ratings**

Ingredients

6 cloves garlic, peeled and sliced
1 leg of lamb
Salt and pepper to taste
2 tbsp. fresh rosemary, chopped
Olive oil
3 cups salsa

Directions

1. Preheat the oven to 325°F (165°C).
2. Make small incisions in the lamb leg and insert the sliced garlic into the incisions.
3. Season the lamb leg with salt, pepper, and chopped rosemary, rubbing them all over the meat.
4. Heat a large oven-safe skillet or roasting pan over medium-high heat. Add a drizzle of olive oil.
5. Sear the lamb leg on all sides until nicely browned, about 4-5 minutes per side.
6. Remove the lamb leg from the skillet and place it on a roasting rack in the same skillet or roasting pan.
7. Pour the salsa over the lamb leg, covering it evenly.
8. Place the skillet or roasting pan in the preheated oven and roast the lamb leg for about 2-3 hours, or until the meat is tender and cooked to your desired doneness.
9. Remove the lamb leg from the oven and let it rest for about 10-15 minutes before carving.
10. Serve the lamb leg with the salsa spooned over the top. Enjoy!

Tips: If the salsa is too chunky, you can blend it in a food processor or blender for a smoother consistency.

Morrocan Kebabs

 **Preparation time** 20 MINUTES |  **Cooking time** 30 MINUTES |  **Servings** 2 | ★★★ **Ratings**

Ingredients

1 cup onions, finely diced
1 tbsp. fresh mint, finely diced
1 tsp. paprika
1 tsp. salt
½ tsp. ground coriander
¼ tsp. ground cinnamon
Pita Bread
2 cloves garlic, minced
3 tbsp. cilantro leaves, finely diced
1 tbsp. ground cumin
1 ½ lbs. ground lamb

Directions

1. In a mixing bowl, combine the diced onions, fresh mint, paprika, salt, ground coriander, ground cinnamon, minced garlic, diced cilantro leaves, and ground cumin. Mix well to ensure all the ingredients are evenly incorporated.
2. Add the ground lamb to the bowl and gently mix with your hands until the spice mixture is evenly distributed throughout the meat.
3. Divide the lamb mixture into equal portions and shape them into elongated kebab patties or cylinders around skewers.
4. Preheat your grill or grill pan over medium heat.
5. Place the kebabs on the grill and cook for about 4-5 minutes per side, or until they are cooked through and nicely charred on the outside.
6. While the kebabs are grilling, warm the pita bread on the grill for a minute or two on each side.
7. Once the kebabs are cooked, remove them from the grill and let them rest for a few minutes.
8. Serve the Moroccan kebabs with the warmed pita bread, and you can also include additional accompaniments like tzatziki sauce, hummus, or a fresh salad.
9. Enjoy the flavorful and aromatic Moroccan kebabs!

Tips: Soak wooden skewers in water for about 30 minutes before using them to prevent them from burning on the grill.

Grilled Lamb Sandwiches

 **Preparation time** 5 MINUTES |  **Cooking time** 50 MINUTES |  **Servings** 6 |  **Ratings**

Ingredients

1 (4 lbs) boneless lamb
1 cup raspberry vinegar
2 tbsp. olive oil
1 tbsp. chopped fresh thyme
2 cloves garlic, pressed
¼ tsp. salt, to taste
¼ tsp. ground pepper
Sliced bread

Directions

1. In a mixing bowl, combine the raspberry vinegar, olive oil, chopped fresh thyme, pressed garlic cloves, salt, and ground pepper. Stir well to create a marinade.
2. Place the boneless lamb in a large resealable plastic bag and pour the marinade over it. Seal the bag tightly and refrigerate for at least 4 hours, or overnight if possible, to allow the flavors to penetrate the meat.
3. Preheat your grill to medium-high heat.
4. Remove the lamb from the marinade and discard the excess marinade.
5. Place the lamb on the preheated grill and cook for about 10-12 minutes per side, or until it reaches your desired level of doneness. Use a meat thermometer to ensure it reaches an internal temperature of at least 145°F (63°C) for medium-rare.
6. Once cooked, remove the lamb from the grill and let it rest for a few minutes to allow the juices to redistribute. Then, slice the lamb into thin pieces.
7. Toast the sliced bread on the grill or in a toaster until it is lightly golden and crispy.
8. Assemble the grilled lamb sandwiches by placing the sliced lamb onto the toasted bread.
9. You can add additional toppings or condiments of your choice, such as lettuce, tomato, cucumber, red onion, or a spread like tzatziki sauce or hummus.
10. Serve the grilled lamb sandwiches warm and enjoy!

Tips: If you prefer a different type of vinegar, you can substitute raspberry vinegar with balsamic vinegar or red wine vinegar.

Lamb Chops

 **Preparation time** 10 MINUTES |  **Cooking time** 12 MINUTES |  **Servings** 6 | ★★★ **Ratings**

Ingredients

6 (6-ounce) lamb chops
3 tbsp. olive oil
Ground black pepper

Directions

1. Preheat your grill or stovetop grill pan to medium-high heat.
2. Season the lamb chops generously with ground black pepper on both sides. You can adjust the amount of pepper according to your taste preference.
3. Drizzle the olive oil over the lamb chops and use your hands or a brush to evenly coat them with the oil.
4. Place the lamb chops on the preheated grill or grill pan. Cook for about 3-4 minutes per side for medium-rare doneness. Adjust the cooking time based on your desired level of doneness.
5. Flip the lamb chops once to ensure even cooking on both sides.
6. Remove the lamb chops from the grill or grill pan and let them rest for a few minutes to allow the juices to redistribute.
7. Serve the lamb chops hot and enjoy as a main dish. They pair well with side dishes like roasted vegetables, mashed potatoes, or a fresh salad.

Tips: Use a meat thermometer to check the internal temperature. For medium-rare, the lamb chops should reach an internal temperature of around 145°F (63°C).

Lamb Ribs Rack

 **Preparation time** 10 MINUTES |  **Cooking time** 2 HOURS |  **Servings** 2 | ★★ **Ratings**

Ingredients

2 tbsp. fresh sage
2 tbsp. fresh rosemary
2 tbsp. fresh thyme
2 peeled garlic cloves
1 tbsp. honey
Black pepper
¼ cup olive oil
1 (1½-pound) trimmed rack of lamb ribs

Directions

1. Preheat your grill to medium-high heat or preheat your oven to 375°F (190°C).
2. In a food processor or blender, combine the fresh sage, rosemary, thyme, peeled garlic cloves, honey, a pinch of black pepper, and olive oil. Blend until you have a smooth marinade.
3. Place the trimmed rack of lamb ribs in a shallow dish or a large resealable bag.
4. Pour the marinade over the lamb ribs, ensuring they are coated on all sides. Massage the marinade into the meat.
5. If using a grill, place the lamb ribs on the preheated grill. Cook for about 15-20 minutes, turning occasionally, or until the internal temperature reaches your desired level of doneness. For medium-rare, the internal temperature should be around 135°F (57°C). If using an oven, place the lamb ribs on a baking sheet and roast for approximately 25-30 minutes or until the internal temperature reaches your desired level of doneness.
6. Remove the lamb ribs from the grill or oven and let them rest for a few minutes to allow the juices to redistribute.
7. Slice the lamb ribs into individual portions and serve hot.
8. Enjoy the flavorful and tender lamb ribs as a delicious main dish. They pair well with roasted potatoes, grilled vegetables, or a fresh salad.

Tips: If grilling, you can brush the lamb ribs with any leftover marinade during the cooking process to enhance the flavor and moisture.

Lamb Shank

 **Preparation time** 10 MINUTES |  **Cooking time** 4 HOURS |  **Servings** 6 | ★ **Ratings**

Ingredients

8 ounces red wine
2 ounces whiskey
2 tbsp. minced fresh rosemary
1 tbsp. minced garlic
Black pepper
6 (1¼-pound) lamb shanks

Directions

1. Preheat your oven to 325°F (163°C).
2. In a small bowl, combine the red wine, whiskey, minced rosemary, minced garlic, and a pinch of black pepper. Mix well to create a marinade.
3. Place the lamb shanks in a large baking dish or a deep oven-safe pot.
4. Pour the marinade over the lamb shanks, ensuring they are coated on all sides. Gently massage the marinade into the meat.
5. Cover the baking dish or pot with foil or a lid.
6. Transfer the dish to the preheated oven and bake for approximately 2 to 2½ hours, or until the lamb shanks are tender and the meat easily pulls away from the bone.
7. Every 30 minutes, baste the lamb shanks with the pan juices to keep them moist and flavorful.
8. Once cooked, remove the lamb shanks from the oven and let them rest for a few minutes to allow the flavors to settle.
9. Serve the lamb shanks hot, either individually or family-style, with a drizzle of the pan juices over the top.
10. Enjoy the succulent and aromatic lamb shanks as a satisfying main dish. They pair well with mashed potatoes, roasted vegetables, or a side of your choice.

Tips: Consider garnishing the dish with fresh rosemary sprigs or a sprinkle of chopped parsley for a vibrant presentation.

Lamb Breast

 **Preparation time** 10 MINUTES |  **Cooking time** 2 H 40 MINUTES |  **Servings** 2 | ★★ **Ratings**

Ingredients

1 (2-pound) trimmed bone-in lamb breast
½ cup white vinegar
¼ cup yellow mustard
½ cup BBQ rub

Directions

1. Preheat your grill or oven to 300°F (150°C) for indirect cooking.
2. Rinse the lamb breast under cold water and pat it dry with paper towels.
3. In a small bowl, combine the white vinegar and yellow mustard. Stir well to create a marinade.
4. Place the lamb breast in a large dish or resealable plastic bag and pour the marinade over it. Ensure the lamb breast is fully coated with the marinade.
5. Allow the lamb breast to marinate in the refrigerator for at least 2 hours or overnight for optimal flavor.
6. Remove the lamb breast from the marinade and discard any excess liquid.
7. Sprinkle the BBQ rub evenly over both sides of the lamb breast, pressing it gently to adhere.
8. Place the lamb breast on the grill or in a roasting pan in the oven, bone-side down.
9. Cook the lamb breast for approximately 3 to 4 hours, or until the internal temperature reaches 160°F (71°C) for medium doneness.
10. If using a grill, maintain a constant temperature of around 300°F (150°C) by adjusting the vents or burners as needed.
11. If using an oven, periodically baste the lamb breast with its own juices to keep it moist and flavorful.
12. Once cooked, remove the lamb breast from the grill or oven and let it rest for 10 to 15 minutes before slicing.
13. Slice the lamb breast against the grain into individual portions.
14. Serve the lamb breast hot, either as the main course or in sandwiches. It pairs well with your favorite BBQ sauce or a side of coleslaw.
15. Enjoy the tender and flavorful lamb breast with its smoky and tangy notes.

Tips: Adjust the cooking time based on the thickness and size of the lamb breast. It should be cooked until the internal temperature reaches your desired level of doneness

Barbecue Grilled Lamb with Sugar Glaze

 **Preparation time** 15 MINUTES |  **Cooking time** 20 MINUTES |  **Servings** 4 |  Ratings

Ingredients

¼ cup sugar
2 tbsp ground ginger
2 tbsp dried tarragon
½ tbsp salt
1 tbsp black pepper, ground
1 tbsp ground cinnamon
1 tbsp garlic powder
Four lamb chops

Directions

1. In a small bowl, combine the sugar, ground ginger, dried tarragon, salt, black pepper, ground cinnamon, and garlic powder. Mix well to create a spice rub.
2. Pat the lamb chops dry with a paper towel and generously coat them on all sides with the spice rub. Press the rub into the meat to ensure it adheres.
3. Preheat your grill to medium-high heat.
4. Place the lamb chops on the preheated grill and cook for approximately 4-5 minutes per side, or until desired doneness is reached. Rotate the chops halfway through cooking to achieve grill marks.
5. While grilling, prepare the sugar glaze by combining 1 tablespoon of the spice rub with 2 tablespoons of water in a small saucepan. Heat over medium heat, stirring constantly, until the sugar has dissolved and the glaze has thickened slightly.
6. Brush the sugar glaze over the lamb chops during the last few minutes of grilling, turning them to evenly coat both sides. Allow the glaze to caramelize and create a flavorful crust.
7. Remove the lamb chops from the grill and let them rest for a few minutes before serving.
8. Serve the barbecue grilled lamb chops hot with your favorite side dishes or accompaniments. They pair well with grilled vegetables, mashed potatoes, or a fresh salad.
9. Enjoy the succulent and flavorful lamb chops with a hint of sweetness from the sugar glaze.

Tips: Letting the lamb chops rest after grilling allows the juices to redistribute, resulting in more tender and flavorful meat.

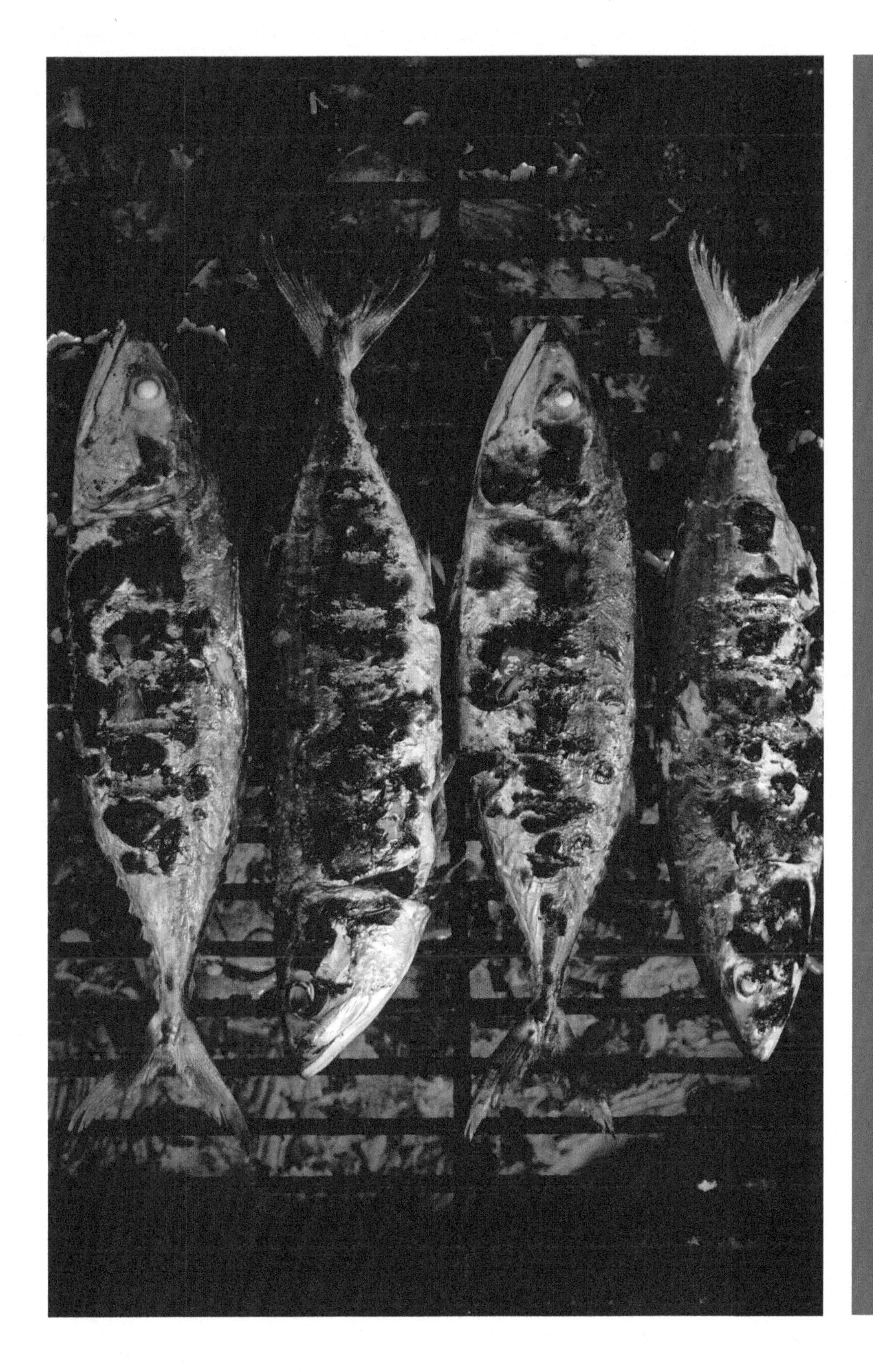

FISH AND SEAFOOD

Recommended Sauces for Fish and Seafood

Honey Mustard Sauce:
Prepare the honey mustard sauce by mixing 2 tablespoons of Dijon mustard, 1 tablespoon of honey, and the juice of half a lemon in a bowl. Add salt and pepper to taste and mix well until the sauce is smooth. Let it chill in the refrigerator for at least 30 minutes before serving.

Tzatziki Sauce:
Make the tzatziki sauce by grating a cucumber and placing it in a colander to remove excess water. In a bowl, mix 1 cup of Greek yogurt, the grated cucumber, 1 minced garlic clove, the juice of half a lemon, 1 tablespoon of olive oil, and 1 tablespoon of chopped fresh mint. Season with salt and pepper to taste and mix well until the sauce is creamy. Let it chill in the refrigerator for at least 1 hour before serving.

Lemon Cream Sauce:
Prepare the lemon cream sauce by mixing ½ cup of sour cream, the juice and zest of 1 lemon, 1 tablespoon of chopped parsley, salt, and pepper in a bowl. Stir well until the sauce is creamy. Taste and adjust the seasoning according to your preference. Let it chill in the refrigerator for at least 30 minutes before serving.

Garlic Butter Sauce:
Make the garlic butter sauce by melting 4 tablespoons of butter in a skillet over medium-low heat. Add 2 minced garlic cloves and cook for 1-2 minutes until the garlic becomes golden and fragrant. Stir in the juice of half a lemon and 1 tablespoon of chopped parsley. Season with salt and pepper to taste. Mix well until the sauce is aromatic. Allow it to cool slightly before serving.

Salsa Verde:
Prepare the salsa verde by placing 1 cup of chopped fresh parsley, 2 minced garlic cloves, 2 anchovy fillets, the juice of 1 lemon, and 2 tablespoons of olive oil in a blender or food processor. Blend until smooth. Season with salt and pepper to taste. Taste and adjust the seasoning according to your preference. Let it chill in the refrigerator for at least 30 minutes before serving.

Barbecue Salmon with Togarashi

 **Preparation time** 5 MINUTES |  **Cooking time** 20 MINUTES |  **Servings** 3 | ★★★★★ **Ratings**

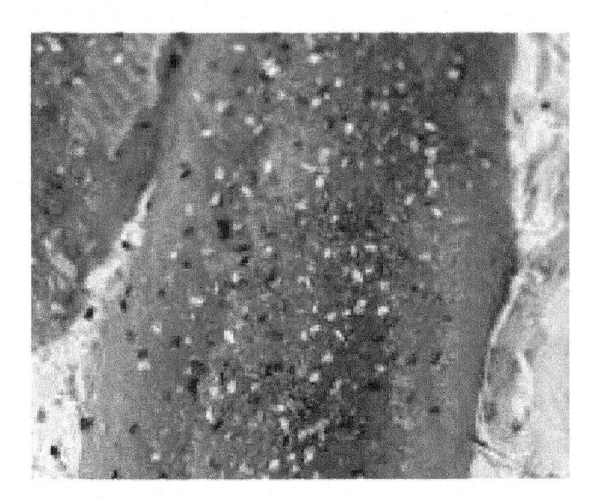

Ingredients

1 salmon fillet
½ tbsp. kosher salt
¼ cup olive oil
1 tbsp. Togarashi seasoning

Directions

1. Preheat your grill to medium-high heat.
2. Pat dry the salmon fillet using a paper towel and place it on a large piece of aluminum foil.
3. Sprinkle the kosher salt evenly over the salmon, ensuring all sides are seasoned.
4. Drizzle the olive oil over the salmon, making sure it is well-coated.
5. Sprinkle the Togarashi seasoning evenly over the salmon, covering the entire surface.
6. Gently wrap the aluminum foil around the salmon, creating a packet that will help keep the fish moist during grilling.
7. Place the salmon packet on the preheated grill and close the lid.
8. Grill the salmon for about 12-15 minutes, or until it reaches an internal temperature of 145°F (63°C) and flakes easily with a fork.
9. Carefully remove the salmon from the grill and let it rest for a few minutes.
10. Open the foil packet and transfer the salmon to a serving dish.
11. Serve hot and enjoy!

Tips: Adjust the grilling time based on the thickness of the salmon fillet. Thicker fillets may require slightly longer cooking times.

Traeger Rockfish

 **Preparation time** 10 MINUTES |  **Cooking time** 20 MINUTES |  **Servings** 6 |  **Ratings**

Ingredients

Six rockfish fillets
¾ tbsp. salt
½ tbsp. garlic powder
6 tbsp. butter
One lemon, sliced
2 tbsp. fresh dill, chopped
½ tbsp. onion powder

Directions

1. Preheat your Traeger grill to 375°F (190°C).
2. Season both sides of the rockfish fillets with salt, garlic powder, and onion powder.
3. Place the seasoned rockfish fillets directly on the grill grates and close the lid.
4. Grill the fish for about 5-7 minutes per side, or until the fillets are opaque and flake easily with a fork.
5. While the rockfish is grilling, melt the butter in a small saucepan over low heat.
6. Add the sliced lemon and chopped dill to the melted butter, stirring well to combine.
7. Brush the butter, lemon, and dill mixture over the grilled rockfish fillets during the last few minutes of cooking.
8. Continue grilling the fish until the butter mixture has slightly caramelized and the fillets are fully cooked.
9. Remove the rockfish from the grill and transfer to a serving platter.
10. Garnish with additional lemon slices and fresh dill, if desired.
11. Serve the Traeger rockfish immediately while it's still hot.

Tips: Rockfish is a delicate fish, so be careful when handling it to avoid breaking the fillets.

Barbecue Grilled Lingcod

 **Preparation time** 10 MINUTES |  **Cooking time** 15 MINUTES |  **Servings** 6 | ★★★★ **Ratings**

Ingredients

2 lbs. lingcod fillets
½ tbsp. white pepper
Lemon wedges
½ tbsp. salt
¼ tbsp. cayenne pepper

Directions

1. Preheat your barbecue grill to medium-high heat.
2. Season both sides of the lingcod fillets with white pepper, salt, and cayenne pepper.
3. Place the seasoned lingcod fillets on the grill grates and close the lid.
4. Grill the fish for about 4-5 minutes per side, or until the fillets are opaque and easily flake with a fork.
5. During the last few minutes of grilling, squeeze some fresh lemon juice over the fillets for added flavor.
6. Remove the lingcod from the grill and transfer to a serving platter.
7. Garnish with lemon wedges for extra tanginess.
8. Serve the barbecue grilled lingcod immediately while it's still hot.

Tips: Make sure the grill grates are clean and well-oiled to prevent the fish from sticking.

Barbecue Smoked Shrimp

 **Preparation time** 10 MINUTES |  **Cooking time** 10 MINUTES |  **Servings** 6 | 

Ingredients

1 lb. tail-on shrimp, uncooked
½ tbsp. onion powder
½ tbsp. garlic powder
4 tbsp. teriyaki sauce
4 tbsp. sriracha mayo
2 tbsp. green onion, minced
½ tbsp. salt

Directions

1. Preheat your barbecue grill or smoker to medium heat.
2. In a bowl, combine the onion powder, garlic powder, and salt.
3. Pat dry the shrimp with paper towels and sprinkle the seasoning mixture evenly over the shrimp.
4. Place the seasoned shrimp on the grill grates or in a smoking pan if using a smoker.
5. Close the lid and cook the shrimp for about 3-4 minutes per side, or until they turn pink and opaque.
6. While the shrimp are cooking, in a small bowl, mix together the teriyaki sauce and sriracha mayo to create a dipping sauce.
7. Once the shrimp are cooked, remove them from the grill and transfer to a serving platter.
8. Drizzle the shrimp with the teriyaki sriracha mayo sauce.
9. Sprinkle minced green onion over the top for added freshness and flavor.
10. Serve the barbecue smoked shrimp immediately while hot.

Tips: Be cautious not to overcook the shrimp as they can become tough and rubbery. Keep a close eye on them while grilling.

Grilled Shrimp Kabobs

 **Preparation time** 5 MINUTES |  **Cooking time** 10 MINUTES |  **Servings** 4 | ★★★★★ **Ratings**

Ingredients

1 lb. colossal shrimp, peeled and deveined
2 tbsp. oil
1/8 tbsp. pepper
½ tbsp. garlic salt
½ tbsp. salt
Six skewers

Directions

1. Preheat your grill to medium-high heat.
2. In a bowl, combine the oil, pepper, garlic salt, and salt. Mix well to create a marinade.
3. Add the peeled and deveined shrimp to the marinade, ensuring they are evenly coated. Let them marinate for about 10-15 minutes.
4. Thread the marinated shrimp onto skewers, piercing through the tail and head ends to keep them secure.
5. Place the shrimp kabobs on the preheated grill and cook for approximately 2-3 minutes per side, or until the shrimp turn pink and opaque.
6. As the shrimp cook, baste them with any remaining marinade to enhance the flavor.
7. Once the shrimp are cooked through, remove them from the grill and transfer to a serving platter.
8. Serve the grilled shrimp kabobs hot as an appetizer or as part of a main course.
9. Optionally, you can garnish with fresh herbs or a squeeze of lemon juice for added freshness.

Tips: Serve the grilled shrimp kabobs with your favorite dipping sauce or alongside a fresh salad, rice, or grilled vegetables for a complete meal. Enjoy the kabobs immediately while they are still hot and flavorful.

Sweet Bacon-Wrapped Shrimp

 **Preparation time** 20 MINUTES |  **Cooking time** 10 MINUTES |  **Servings** 12 | ★★★★ **Ratings**

Ingredients

1 lb. raw shrimp
½ tbsp. salt
¼ tbsp. garlic powder
1 lb. bacon, cut into halves

Directions

1. Preheat your grill to medium-high heat.
2. Peel and devein the shrimp, leaving the tail intact if desired.
3. In a bowl, combine the salt and garlic powder. Mix well.
4. Season the shrimp with the salt and garlic powder mixture, ensuring they are evenly coated.
5. Take a halved strip of bacon and wrap it around each shrimp, securing it with a toothpick if needed. Repeat with the remaining shrimp and bacon.
6. Place the bacon-wrapped shrimp on the preheated grill.
7. Grill the shrimp for about 2-3 minutes per side, or until the bacon is crispy and the shrimp turn pink and opaque.
8. As the shrimp cook, you can baste them with your favorite sweet BBQ sauce for added flavor.
9. Once the bacon-wrapped shrimp are cooked through, remove them from the grill and let them cool slightly.
10. Serve the sweet bacon-wrapped shrimp as an appetizer or as part of a main course.
11. Optionally, you can garnish with chopped parsley or a squeeze of lemon juice for freshness.

Tips: Serve the sweet bacon-wrapped shrimp hot off the grill for the best taste and texture.

Barbecue Spot Prawn Skewers

 **Preparation time** 10 MINUTES |  **Cooking time** 10 MINUTES |  **Servings** 6 | ★★★★★ **Ratings**

Ingredients

2 lbs. spot prawns
2 tbsp. oil
Salt and pepper to taste

Directions

1. Preheat your grill to medium-high heat.
2. Rinse the spot prawns under cold water and pat them dry with a paper towel.
3. In a bowl, toss the spot prawns with oil, salt, and pepper until they are well-coated.
4. Thread the spot prawns onto skewers, making sure to leave a little space between each prawn.
5. Place the prawn skewers on the preheated grill.
6. Grill the prawns for about 2-3 minutes per side, or until they turn pink and opaque.
7. Avoid overcooking the prawns to maintain their tender texture.
8. Once the prawns are cooked through, remove them from the grill and let them cool slightly.
9. Serve the barbecue spot prawn skewers as a flavorful seafood appetizer or as part of a main course.
10. You can squeeze some fresh lemon juice over the prawns before serving for a citrusy touch.
11. Optionally, you can garnish the skewers with chopped parsley or cilantro for added freshness.

Tips: Remember to handle the prawns gently to prevent them from falling apart on the skewers.

Barbecue Bacon-wrapped Scallops

 **Preparation time** 15 MINUTES |  **Cooking time** 20 MINUTES |  **Servings** 8 | ★★★★ **Ratings**

Ingredients

1 lb. sea scallops
½ lb. bacon
Sea salt

Directions

1. Preheat your grill to medium-high heat.
2. Rinse the sea scallops under cold water and pat them dry with a paper towel.
3. Cut the bacon slices in half widthwise so that you have shorter pieces.
4. Wrap each scallop with a half slice of bacon, securing it with a toothpick if needed.
5. Sprinkle sea salt lightly over the wrapped scallops.
6. Place the bacon-wrapped scallops on the preheated grill.
7. Grill the scallops for about 2-3 minutes per side, or until the bacon is crispy and the scallops are opaque.
8. Turn the scallops carefully to ensure even cooking and prevent sticking.
9. Once the bacon is cooked to your desired crispiness and the scallops are fully cooked, remove them from the grill.
10. Let the scallops cool for a few minutes before serving.
11. Serve the barbecue bacon-wrapped scallops as an appetizer or as part of a main course.
12. You can serve them on their own or pair them with a dipping sauce of your choice, such as tartar sauce or a citrus aioli.
13. Garnish with fresh herbs like parsley or chives for added flavor and presentation.

Tips: Choose large sea scallops for grilling, as smaller ones may cook too quickly and become overdone. Make sure the bacon is wrapped tightly around the scallops to prevent it from unraveling during grilling.

Barbecue Lobster Tail

 **Preparation time** 10 MINUTES |  **Cooking time** 15 MINUTES |  **Servings** 2 | ★★★★★ **Ratings**

Ingredients

10 oz lobster tail
¼ tbsp Old Bay seasoning
¼ tbsp Himalayan salt
2 tbsp butter, melted
1 tbsp fresh parsley, chopped

Directions

1. Preheat your grill to medium-high heat.
2. Using kitchen shears, carefully cut the top of the lobster tail shell lengthwise, exposing the meat.
3. Gently pry open the shell and loosen the lobster meat, but keep it attached at the base of the tail.
4. Season the exposed meat with Old Bay seasoning and Himalayan salt, ensuring it is evenly coated.
5. Brush the melted butter over the seasoned lobster meat, making sure to cover it completely.
6. Place the lobster tail on the preheated grill, shell side down.
7. Grill the lobster tail for about 5-6 minutes, or until the meat turns opaque and firm.
8. Carefully remove the lobster tail from the grill and transfer it to a serving plate.
9. Sprinkle fresh parsley over the grilled lobster tail for added flavor and presentation.
10. Serve the barbecue lobster tail immediately while it's still hot.
11. You can enjoy the lobster tail on its own or pair it with lemon wedges and additional melted butter for dipping.
12. Serve the grilled lobster tail as a main course or as part of a seafood feast.

Tips: Use a meat thermometer to check the internal temperature of the lobster meat. It should reach 135°F (57°C) for optimal doneness.

Blackened Salmon

 **Preparation time** 10 MINUTES |  **Cooking time** 20 MINUTES |  **Servings** 4 | ★★★★★ **Ratings**

Ingredients

2 lb. salmon fillet, scaled and deboned
2 tbsp. olive oil
4 tbsp. sweet dry rub
1 tbsp. cayenne pepper
2 cloves garlic, minced

Directions

1. Preheat a cast-iron skillet or grill to high heat.
2. Brush the salmon fillet with olive oil, coating both sides.
3. In a small bowl, mix together the sweet dry rub, cayenne pepper, and minced garlic.
4. Sprinkle the dry rub mixture evenly over both sides of the salmon, pressing it gently to adhere.
5. Place the salmon fillet on the preheated skillet or grill, skin side down.
6. Cook the salmon for about 4-5 minutes per side, or until it is cooked to your desired doneness. The timing may vary depending on the thickness of the fillet.
7. As the salmon cooks, you'll notice the dry rub forming a flavorful crust on the outside of the fish.
8. Carefully flip the salmon using a spatula and continue cooking for another 4-5 minutes on the other side.
9. Remove the blackened salmon from the heat and transfer it to a serving platter.
10. Let the salmon rest for a few minutes before serving to allow the juices to redistribute.
11. Serve the blackened salmon as a main course, garnished with fresh herbs or lemon wedges if desired.
12. Enjoy the flavorful and spicy blackened salmon alongside your favorite side dishes, such as roasted vegetables or a fresh salad.

Tips: Serve the blackened salmon with a squeeze of fresh lemon juice or a drizzle of sauce, such as dill sauce or mango salsa, for additional tang and freshness.

Salmon Cakes

 **Preparation time** 5 MINUTES |  **Cooking time** 25 MINUTES |  **Servings** 4 |  Ratings

Ingredients

1 cup cooked salmon, flaked
½ red bell pepper, chopped
2 eggs, beaten
¼ cup mayonnaise
½ tbsp. dry sweet rub
1 ½ cups breadcrumbs
1 tbsp. mustard
Olive oil

Directions

1. In a mixing bowl, combine the flaked salmon, chopped red bell pepper, beaten eggs, mayonnaise, dry sweet rub, breadcrumbs, and mustard. Mix well until all the ingredients are evenly incorporated.
2. Shape the mixture into patties of your desired size. You can make smaller cakes for appetizers or larger ones for a main course.
3. Heat a skillet or frying pan over medium heat and add enough olive oil to coat the bottom.
4. Once the oil is hot, carefully place the salmon cakes in the pan, leaving space between each cake.
5. Cook the salmon cakes for about 3-4 minutes on each side, or until they are golden brown and crispy. Flip them gently with a spatula to avoid breaking them.
6. Transfer the cooked salmon cakes to a paper towel-lined plate to drain any excess oil.
7. Serve the salmon cakes warm, garnished with fresh herbs or a squeeze of lemon juice if desired.
8. These salmon cakes are versatile and can be enjoyed in various ways. They make a delicious appetizer, can be served on a bun as a burger, or paired with a side salad or steamed vegetables for a complete meal.

Tips: If you prefer a crispier texture, you can refrigerate the formed salmon cakes for about 30 minutes before cooking. This helps them hold their shape better during frying.

Smoked Catfish Recipe

 **Preparation time** 10 MINUTES |  **Cooking time** 5 MINUTES |  **Servings** 3 |  **Ratings**

Ingredients

The Rub:

2 tbsp. paprika

¼ tsp. salt

1 tbsp. garlic powder

1 tbsp. onion powder

½ tbsp. dried thyme

½ tbsp. cayenne

Other ingredients:

2 lbs. fresh catfish fillets

4 tbsp. butter, softened

Directions

1. In a small bowl, combine the paprika, salt, garlic powder, onion powder, dried thyme, and cayenne to make the rub. Mix well to ensure all the spices are evenly incorporated.
2. Preheat your smoker to a temperature of 225°F (107°C).
3. Rinse the catfish fillets under cold water and pat them dry with paper towels.
4. Spread the softened butter evenly over both sides of the catfish fillets.
5. Sprinkle the prepared rub generously over the buttered catfish fillets, ensuring they are well coated on all sides.
6. Place the seasoned catfish fillets directly on the smoker grate, leaving space between them for the smoke to circulate.
7. Close the smoker and let the catfish smoke for approximately 1 to 1 ½ hours, or until the fish is fully cooked and reaches an internal temperature of 145°F (63°C).
8. Once cooked, carefully remove the catfish fillets from the smoker and transfer them to a serving plate.
9. Allow the catfish to rest for a few minutes before serving to enhance the flavors.
10. Serve the smoked catfish hot and enjoy it as a delicious and flavorful seafood dish.

Tips: Leftover smoked catfish can be refrigerated for a few days and enjoyed as a tasty addition to salads, sandwiches, or pasta dishes.

Cajun Smoked Shrimp

 **Preparation time** 10 MINUTES |  **Cooking time** 10 MINUTES |  **Servings** 2 | ★★★★ **Ratings**

Ingredients

2 tbsp. virgin olive oil

½ lemon, juiced

3 cloves garlic, finely minced

2 tbsp. Cajun spice

Salt, to taste

Pounds of shrimp, raw, peeled, deveined

Directions

1. In a bowl, combine the virgin olive oil, lemon juice, minced garlic, Cajun spice, and salt. Mix well to create a marinade.
2. Add the peeled and deveined shrimp to the marinade, ensuring they are coated evenly. Allow the shrimp to marinate for at least 30 minutes to allow the flavors to meld.
3. Preheat your smoker to a temperature of 225°F (107°C).
4. If using wooden skewers, soak them in water for about 30 minutes to prevent them from burning.
5. Thread the marinated shrimp onto the skewers, leaving a small gap between each shrimp.
6. Place the shrimp skewers directly on the smoker grate, ensuring they are spaced apart to allow smoke circulation.
7. Close the smoker and let the shrimp smoke for approximately 20-30 minutes, or until they turn pink and are fully cooked.
8. Once cooked, carefully remove the shrimp skewers from the smoker and transfer them to a serving platter.
9. Serve the Cajun smoked shrimp hot, garnished with fresh herbs or a squeeze of lemon juice if desired.

Tips: Ensure the shrimp are properly peeled and deveined before marinating and smoking.

Citrus Salmon

 **Preparation time** 15 MINUTES |  **Cooking time** 30 MINUTES |  **Servings** 6 | 

Ingredients

2 (1-pound) salmon fillets
Salt and ground black pepper, as required
1 tbsp. seafood seasoning
2 lemons, sliced
2 limes, sliced

Directions

1. Preheat your grill or smoker to medium-high heat.
2. Season the salmon fillets with salt, ground black pepper, and seafood seasoning on both sides. Ensure the seasoning is evenly distributed.
3. Place the salmon fillets on a sheet of aluminum foil or a grilling plank to prevent sticking.
4. Arrange the lemon and lime slices on top of the salmon fillets, creating a layer of citrus slices.
5. Carefully transfer the salmon with the citrus slices onto the preheated grill or smoker.
6. Close the grill or smoker lid and cook the salmon for approximately 10-15 minutes, or until the fish is cooked through and flakes easily with a fork. The cooking time may vary depending on the thickness of the fillets.
7. Once cooked, remove the salmon from the grill or smoker and let it rest for a few minutes.
8. Serve the citrus salmon hot, garnished with additional fresh citrus slices or herbs if desired.

Tips: Adding citrus slices not only infuses the salmon with a refreshing flavor but also helps to keep the fish moist during cooking.

Simple Mahi-Mahi

 **Preparation time** 10 MINUTES |  **Cooking time** 10 MINUTES |  **Servings** 4 | ★★★★ **Ratings**

Ingredients

4 (6-ounce) mahi-mahi fillets
2 tbsp. olive oil
Salt and ground black pepper, as required

Directions

1. Preheat your grill to medium-high heat.
2. Brush the mahi-mahi fillets with olive oil on both sides, ensuring they are well coated.
3. Season the fillets with salt and ground black pepper to taste. Make sure to season both sides evenly.
4. Place the mahi-mahi fillets on the preheated grill, making sure they are not overcrowded.
5. Grill the fish for about 4-6 minutes per side, or until the fish is opaque and easily flakes with a fork. The cooking time may vary depending on the thickness of the fillets.
6. Once cooked, carefully remove the mahi-mahi fillets from the grill and transfer them to a serving platter.
7. Let the fish rest for a few minutes before serving to allow the juices to redistribute.
8. Serve the simple mahi-mahi hot with your favorite side dishes, such as steamed vegetables, rice, or a fresh salad.

Tips: Fresh mahi-mahi fillets are best for this recipe. Look for firm, shiny fillets with a mild oceanic scent.

Sesame Seeds Flounder

 **Preparation time** 15 MINUTES |  **Cooking time** 2½ MINUTES |  **Servings** 4 | ★★★★★ **Ratings**

Ingredients

½ cup sesame seeds, toasted
½ tsp. kosher salt flakes
1 tbsp. canola oil
1 tsp. sesame oil
4 (6-ounce) flounder fillets

Directions

1. In a shallow dish, combine the toasted sesame seeds and kosher salt flakes.
2. In a separate small bowl, mix together the canola oil and sesame oil.
3. Brush both sides of each flounder fillet with the oil mixture.
4. Dredge the oiled fillets in the sesame seed mixture, pressing lightly to ensure the seeds adhere to the fish.
5. Preheat your grill to medium heat.
6. Grease the grill grates with oil to prevent sticking.
7. Place the sesame-coated flounder fillets on the preheated grill.
8. Grill the fish for about 3-4 minutes per side, or until the fillets are cooked through and flake easily with a fork.
9. Remove the flounder fillets from the grill and transfer them to a serving platter.
10. Serve the sesame seeds flounder immediately, garnished with additional toasted sesame seeds if desired.

Tips: Toasting the sesame seeds before coating the fish will enhance their nutty flavor. To toast sesame seeds, heat them in a dry skillet over medium heat for a few minutes until they turn golden brown and become fragrant. Be sure to watch them closely and stir frequently to prevent burning.

Grilled Scallops with Lemony Salsa Verde

 **Preparation time** 15 MINUTES |  **Cooking time** 15 MINUTES |  **Servings** 2 | ★★★★★ **Ratings**

Ingredients

2 tbsp. of vegetable oil (plus more for the grill)
12 large sea scallops, side muscle removed
Kosher salt and ground black pepper
Lemony Salsa Verde (recipe follows)
Lemony Salsa Verde:
½ cup fresh parsley, finely chopped
¼ cup fresh mint leaves, finely chopped
¼ cup fresh basil leaves, finely chopped
2 tbsp. capers, drained and chopped
2 tbsp. lemon juice
2 tbsp. extra-virgin olive oil
1 small garlic clove, minced
Kosher salt and ground black pepper to taste

Directions

1. Preheat your grill to medium-high heat and brush the grates with vegetable oil to prevent sticking.
2. Pat the scallops dry with a paper towel and season them with salt and ground black pepper.
3. Drizzle the vegetable oil over the scallops and gently toss them to coat evenly.
4. Place the scallops on the preheated grill and cook for about 2-3 minutes per side, or until they are opaque and grill marks form.
5. Remove the scallops from the grill and let them rest for a few minutes.

Lemony Salsa Verde:

1. In a small bowl, combine the chopped parsley, mint, basil, capers, lemon juice, olive oil, minced garlic, salt, and pepper. Mix well to combine.
2. Taste and adjust the seasoning if needed.

To serve:

1. Arrange the grilled scallops on a serving platter.
2. Spoon the Lemony Salsa Verde over the top of the scallops, or serve it on the side as a dipping sauce.
3. Garnish with additional fresh herbs if desired.
4. Serve the grilled scallops immediately while they are still warm.

Tips: It's important to remove the side muscle from the scallops before cooking as it can be tough and chewy.

Citrus Soy Squid

 **Preparation time** 15 MINUTES |  **Cooking time** 45 MINUTES |  **Servings** 4 |  **Ratings**

Ingredients

1/3 cup yuzu juice

2 cups water

1 cup mirin

2 lbs. squid tentacles, left whole and 1 inch thick

1 cup soy sauce

Directions

1. In a large bowl, combine the yuzu juice, water, mirin, and soy sauce. Stir well to combine and create the marinade.
2. Add the squid tentacles to the marinade and make sure they are fully submerged. Cover the bowl and let the squid marinate in the refrigerator for at least 30 minutes, or up to 2 hours for more flavor.
3. Preheat your grill to medium-high heat.
4. Remove the squid tentacles from the marinade and gently pat them dry with paper towels. Discard the marinade.
5. Place the squid tentacles on the preheated grill and cook for about 2-3 minutes per side, or until they are opaque and lightly charred.
6. Remove the grilled squid from the heat and transfer them to a serving platter.
7. Serve the citrus soy squid hot as an appetizer or main course.

Tips: Yuzu juice is a citrus fruit commonly used in Japanese cuisine. If you can't find yuzu juice, you can substitute it with a combination of lemon and lime juice for a similar citrus flavor.

Smoked Shrimp

 **Preparation time** 4 H 15 MINUTES |  **Cooking time** 10 MINUTES |  **Servings** 4 | ★★★★ **Ratings**

Ingredients

4 tbsp. olive oil

1 tbsp. Cajun seasoning

2 cloves garlic, minced

1 tbsp. lemon juice

Salt to taste

2 lbs. shrimp, peeled and deveined

Direction

1. Preheat your smoker to a temperature of 225°F (107°C).
2. In a large bowl, combine the olive oil, Cajun seasoning, minced garlic, lemon juice, and salt. Stir well to create the marinade.
3. Add the peeled and deveined shrimp to the marinade, ensuring they are evenly coated. Let the shrimp marinate for about 15-20 minutes to absorb the flavors.
4. If using wooden skewers, soak them in water for 15 minutes to prevent burning.
5. Thread the marinated shrimp onto skewers, leaving a small space between each shrimp.
6. Place the shrimp skewers directly on the smoker grates, ensuring they are not touching each other.
7. Close the smoker and let the shrimp smoke for approximately 20-25 minutes, or until they turn pink and opaque, with a slightly smoky flavor.
8. Check the shrimp occasionally to avoid overcooking. The cooking time may vary depending on the size of the shrimp and the temperature of your smoker.
9. Once the shrimp are cooked, remove them from the smoker and transfer them to a serving platter.
10. Serve the smoked shrimp as an appetizer or main dish. They can be enjoyed on their own or with your favorite dipping sauce.

Tips: Serve the smoked shrimp with lemon wedges and fresh herbs for garnish. They pair well with a variety of dipping sauces like cocktail sauce, remoulade, or garlic aioli.

Cod with Lemon Herb Butter

 **Preparation time** 30 MINUTES |  **Cooking time** 15 MINUTES |  **Servings** 4 | ★ **Ratings**

Ingredients

4 tbsp. butter
1 clove garlic, minced
1 tbsp. tarragon, chopped
1 tbsp. lemon juice
1 tsp. lemon zest
Salt and pepper to taste
1 lb. cod fillet

Direction

1. Preheat your grill to medium-high heat.
2. In a small saucepan, melt the butter over low heat. Add the minced garlic and cook for 1-2 minutes until fragrant.
3. Remove the saucepan from the heat and stir in the chopped tarragon, lemon juice, lemon zest, salt, and pepper. Mix well to combine all the flavors.
4. Place the cod fillet on a sheet of aluminum foil. Season the fish with salt and pepper on both sides.
5. Spread the lemon herb butter mixture evenly over the top of the cod fillet, covering it completely.
6. Carefully wrap the aluminum foil around the cod, creating a packet to enclose the fish and the butter mixture.
7. Place the foil packet on the grill and close the lid. Cook for about 10-12 minutes, or until the cod is opaque and easily flakes with a fork.
8. Carefully remove the foil packet from the grill and open it, being cautious of the hot steam.
9. Transfer the cooked cod fillet to a serving plate. Spoon any remaining melted butter from the foil packet over the fish.
10. Garnish with additional chopped tarragon and lemon slices if desired.
11. Serve the cod with lemon herb butter hot and enjoy!

Tips: Make sure to use fresh tarragon for the best flavor. If you don't have tarragon, you can substitute it with other herbs like dill, parsley, or thyme.

Grilled Tilapia

 **Preparation time** 10 MINUTES |  **Cooking time** 20 MINUTES |  **Servings** 6 | ★ **Ratings**

Ingredients

2 tsp. dried parsley
½ tsp. garlic powder
1 tsp. cayenne pepper
½ tsp. ground black pepper
½ tsp. thyme
½ tsp. dried basil
½ tsp. oregano
3 tbsp. olive oil
½ tsp. lemon pepper
1 tsp. kosher salt
Juice of 1 lemon
6 tilapia fillets
1 ½ tsp. creole seafood seasoning

Directions

1. In a small bowl, combine the dried parsley, garlic powder, cayenne pepper, black pepper, thyme, basil, and oregano. Mix well to create the spice blend.
2. In a separate bowl, whisk together the olive oil, lemon pepper, kosher salt, and lemon juice.
3. Place the tilapia fillets on a large plate or in a shallow dish. Sprinkle both sides of the fillets evenly with the creole seafood seasoning.
4. Drizzle the olive oil and lemon juice mixture over the tilapia fillets, making sure to coat them thoroughly.
5. Rub the spice blend onto both sides of the seasoned tilapia fillets, pressing it gently into the fish to adhere.
6. Preheat your grill to medium-high heat.
7. Lightly oil the grill grates to prevent sticking.
8. Place the seasoned tilapia fillets directly on the grill and close the lid.
9. Grill the tilapia for about 4-5 minutes per side, or until the fish is opaque and flakes easily with a fork.
10. Carefully remove the grilled tilapia from the grill and transfer it to a serving platter.
11. Serve the grilled tilapia hot, garnished with fresh herbs and lemon wedges if desired.

Tips: Tilapia is a delicate fish, so handle it gently to prevent it from breaking apart while grilling. Using a fish spatula or grill basket can help with this.

Grilled Blackened Salmon

 **Preparation time** 15 MINUTES |  **Cooking time** 30 MINUTES |  **Servings** 4 | ★ **Ratings**

Ingredients

4 salmon fillets
Blackened dry rub
Italian seasoning powder

Direction

1. Preheat your grill to medium-high heat.
2. Pat the salmon fillets dry with paper towels to remove any excess moisture.
3. Sprinkle the blackened dry rub generously on both sides of the salmon fillets. Ensure that the fillets are evenly coated with the seasoning.
4. Sprinkle the Italian seasoning powder over the fillets, adding an additional layer of flavor.
5. Lightly oil the grill grates to prevent sticking.
6. Place the seasoned salmon fillets directly on the grill, skin-side down.
7. Close the lid of the grill and cook the salmon for about 4-5 minutes per side, or until the fish is opaque and flakes easily with a fork.
8. Carefully remove the grilled blackened salmon from the grill and transfer it to a serving platter.
9. Allow the salmon to rest for a few minutes before serving.

Tips: Adjust the amount of blackened dry rub and Italian seasoning powder according to your taste preferences. You can use pre-made seasoning blends or create your own by combining spices like paprika, cayenne pepper, garlic powder, onion powder, and dried herbs.

Grilled Herbed Tuna

 **Preparation time** 4 H 15 MINUTES |  **Cooking time** 10 MINUTES |  **Servings** 6 | ★★★★ **Ratings**

Ingredients

6 tuna steaks
1 tbsp. lemon zest
1 tbsp. fresh thyme, chopped
1 tbsp. fresh parsley, chopped
Garlic salt to taste

Direction

1. Preheat your grill to medium-high heat.
2. In a small bowl, combine the lemon zest, fresh thyme, fresh parsley, and garlic salt.
3. Pat the tuna steaks dry with paper towels to remove any excess moisture.
4. Sprinkle the herb mixture evenly over both sides of the tuna steaks, pressing lightly to adhere the herbs.
5. Lightly oil the grill grates to prevent sticking.
6. Place the seasoned tuna steaks on the grill and cook for about 2-3 minutes per side for medium-rare doneness. Adjust the cooking time based on your desired level of doneness. Remember that tuna is best when cooked medium-rare to preserve its tenderness and flavor.
7. Once cooked to your liking, carefully remove the tuna steaks from the grill and transfer them to a serving platter.
8. Allow the tuna steaks to rest for a few minutes before serving. This will help the juices redistribute and ensure a moist and flavorful final result.

Tips: Use fresh herbs for the best flavor. You can substitute or add other herbs like rosemary or basil to customize the herb mixture according to your taste.

Whole Vermillion Snapper

 **Preparation time** 15 MINUTES |  **Cooking time** 25 MINUTES |  **Servings** 6 | ★ **Ratings**

Ingredients

2 rosemary sprigs
4 garlic cloves, chopped (peeled)
1 lemon, thinly sliced
Black pepper
Sea salt
1 vermillion snapper, gutted and scaled

Directions

1. Preheat your grill to medium-high heat.
2. Rinse the vermillion snapper inside and out with cold water and pat it dry with paper towels.
3. Make several shallow cuts on both sides of the snapper to allow the flavors to penetrate.
4. Season the fish generously with sea salt and black pepper, both inside and outside the cavity.
5. Stuff the cavity of the snapper with the chopped garlic cloves, lemon slices, and rosemary sprigs.
6. Lightly oil the grill grates to prevent sticking.
7. Place the vermillion snapper on the grill and cook for about 5-7 minutes per side, depending on the thickness of the fish. The skin should become crispy and the flesh should be opaque and easily flake with a fork.
8. Carefully flip the fish using a spatula or grill tongs to ensure it doesn't fall apart.
9. Once the fish is cooked through and the skin is nicely charred, remove it from the grill and transfer it to a serving platter.
10. Let the vermillion snapper rest for a few minutes before serving to allow the flavors to meld and the juices to redistribute.

Tips: Serve the grilled whole vermillion snapper with your favorite side dishes, such as steamed vegetables, roasted potatoes, or a fresh green salad.

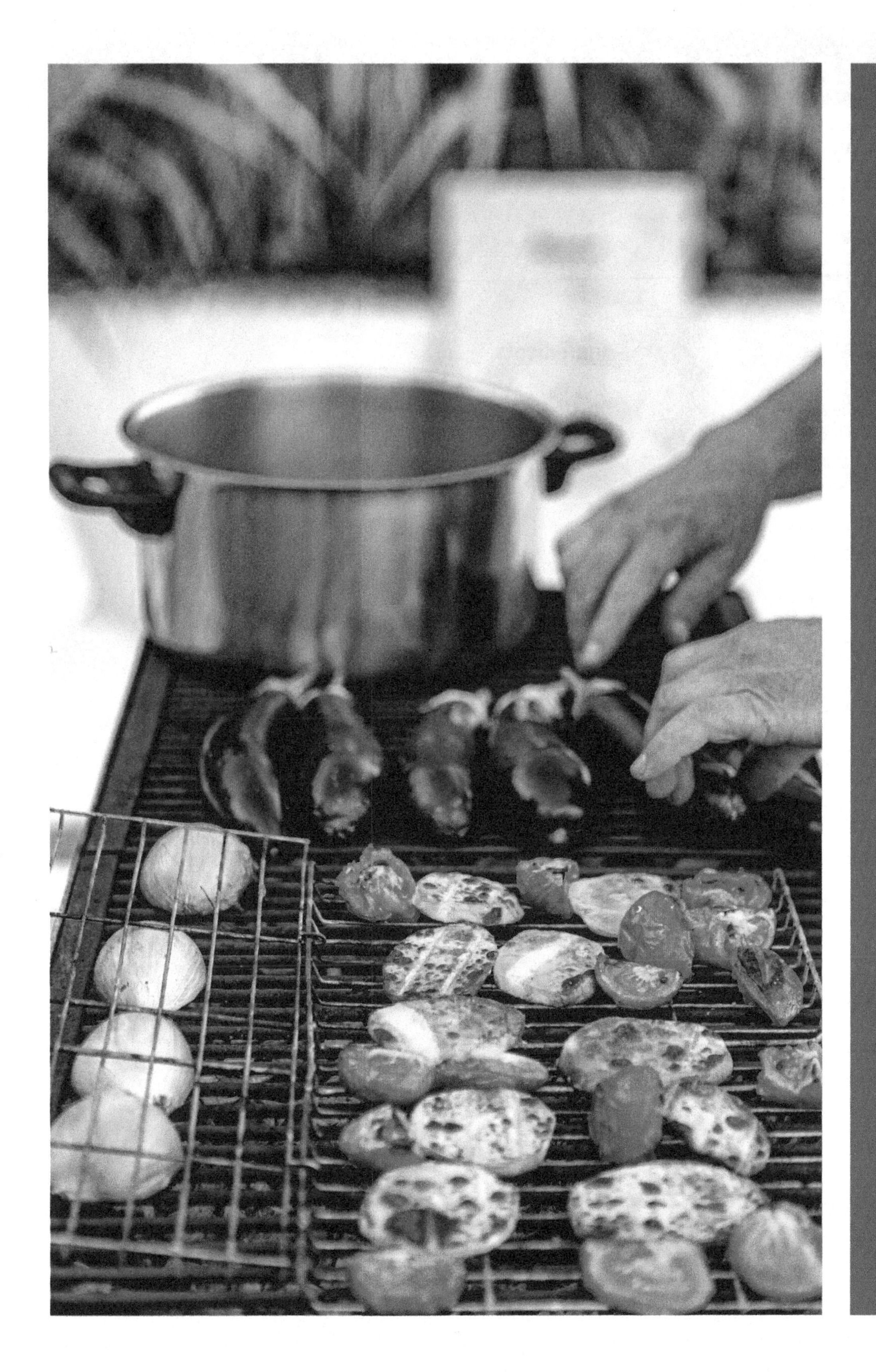

VEGETARIAN

Smoky Grilled Kale Chips

 **Preparation time** 30 MINUTES |  **Cooking time** 20 MINUTES |  **Servings** 4 | ★★★★★ **Ratings**

Ingredients

4 cups kale leaves
Olive oil
Salt to taste

Directions

1. Preheat your grill to medium heat.
2. Wash the kale leaves thoroughly and pat them dry with a paper towel. Remove the tough stems and tear the leaves into bite-sized pieces.
3. Drizzle the kale leaves with olive oil, making sure to coat them evenly. Massage the oil into the leaves to ensure they are well-coated.
4. Sprinkle salt over the kale leaves according to your taste preference. You can also add other seasonings such as garlic powder, paprika, or cayenne pepper for extra flavor if desired.
5. Place the kale leaves directly on the grill grates, ensuring they are spread out in a single layer. Close the grill lid and cook for about 3-5 minutes, or until the leaves start to crisp up and become slightly charred. Keep a close eye on them to prevent burning.
6. Using tongs, carefully flip the kale leaves to the other side and continue grilling for an additional 2-3 minutes, or until they are crispy and slightly browned.
7. Remove the kale chips from the grill and let them cool for a few minutes before serving.

Tips: Enjoy the kale chips immediately for the best texture and taste. They can become soggy if stored for too long.

Sweet Potato Fries

 **Preparation time** 30 MINUTES |  **Cooking time** 40 MINUTES |  **Servings** 4 | ★★★★★ **Ratings**

Ingredients

3 sweet potatoes, sliced into strips
4 tbsp. olive oil
2 tbsp. fresh rosemary, chopped
Salt and pepper to taste

Directions

1. Preheat your grill to medium-high heat.
2. In a large bowl, toss the sweet potato strips with olive oil until well coated.
3. Sprinkle the chopped rosemary over the sweet potatoes and season with salt and pepper to taste. Toss to evenly distribute the seasoning.
4. Place the sweet potato strips directly on the grill grates or in a grill basket.
5. Grill the sweet potato fries for about 15-20 minutes, or until they are tender and lightly browned, flipping them occasionally to ensure even cooking.
6. Once done, remove the sweet potato fries from the grill and transfer them to a serving platter.
7. Serve hot as a delicious and healthy side dish or snack.

Tips: If you don't have fresh rosemary, you can substitute with dried rosemary, but use half the amount.

Barbecue Grilled Zucchini

 **Preparation time** 30 MINUTES |  **Cooking time** 10 MINUTES |  **Servings** 4 |  Ratings

Ingredients

4 zucchinis, sliced into strips
1 tbsp. sherry vinegar
2 tbsp. olive oil
Salt and pepper to taste
2 sprigs of fresh thyme, chopped

Directions

1. Preheat your grill to medium heat.
2. In a bowl, combine the sherry vinegar, olive oil, salt, pepper, and chopped thyme. Mix well to create a marinade.
3. Add the zucchini strips to the marinade and toss until they are evenly coated.
4. Allow the zucchini to marinate for about 10-15 minutes to absorb the flavors.
5. Place the marinated zucchini strips directly on the grill grates or in a grill basket.
6. Grill the zucchini for about 4-5 minutes per side, or until they are tender and slightly charred, flipping them once during cooking.
7. Once done, remove the grilled zucchini from the grill and transfer them to a serving platter.
8. Serve hot as a tasty and healthy side dish or as a delicious addition to salads or sandwiches.

Tips: Serve the grilled zucchini with a squeeze of lemon juice or a sprinkle of grated Parmesan cheese for extra flavor.

Baked Parmesan Mushrooms

 **Preparation time** 15 MINUTES |  **Cooking time** 15 MINUTES |  **Servings** 8 | ★★★★★ **Ratings**

Ingredients

8 mushroom caps
½ cup grated Parmesan cheese
½ tsp. garlic salt
¼ cup mayonnaise
Pinch of paprika
Hot sauce (optional)

Directions

1. Preheat your oven to 375°F (190°C).
2. Place the mushroom caps on a baking sheet lined with parchment paper.
3. In a small bowl, combine the grated Parmesan cheese, garlic salt, mayonnaise, and a pinch of paprika. Mix well until all the ingredients are evenly incorporated.
4. Spoon the Parmesan mixture onto each mushroom cap, spreading it evenly to cover the surface.
5. Optional: If desired, drizzle a few drops of hot sauce over the mushrooms for some extra heat.
6. Bake the mushrooms in the preheated oven for about 15-20 minutes, or until the cheese is melted and golden brown.
7. Remove from the oven and let the mushrooms cool for a few minutes before serving.

Tips: Feel free to add other herbs or spices to the Parmesan mixture, such as chopped parsley or dried oregano, for added flavor.

Roasted Spicy Tomatoes

 **Preparation time** 30 MINUTES |  **Cooking time** 1 H 30 MINUTES |  **Servings** 4 | ★★★★★ **Ratings**

Ingredients

2 lb. large tomatoes, sliced in half
Olive oil
2 tbsp. garlic, chopped
3 tbsp. parsley, chopped
Salt and pepper to taste
Hot pepper sauce

Directions

1. Preheat your oven to 400°F (200°C).
2. Place the tomato halves on a baking sheet lined with parchment paper, cut side up.
3. Drizzle olive oil over the tomatoes, ensuring they are evenly coated.
4. Sprinkle the chopped garlic and parsley over the tomatoes.
5. Season with salt and pepper to taste.
6. If desired, add a few dashes of hot pepper sauce for some spicy kick.
7. Place the baking sheet in the preheated oven and roast the tomatoes for about 25-30 minutes, or until they are tender and slightly caramelized.
8. Remove from the oven and let the roasted tomatoes cool for a few minutes before serving.

Tips: These roasted spicy tomatoes make a delicious side dish or topping for salads, sandwiches, or pasta.

Grilled Corn with Honey & Butter

  |  | Servings 4 | 

Preparation time 30 MINUTES | Cooking time 10 MINUTES | Servings 4 | ★★★★★ Ratings

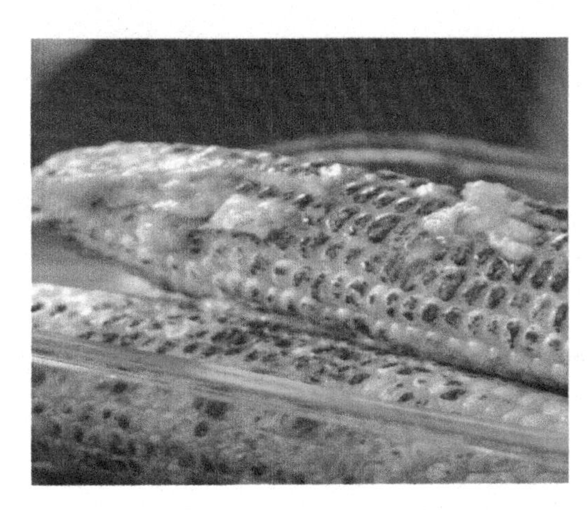

Ingredients

6 pieces of corn, husked
2 tbsp. olive oil
½ cup butter
½ cup honey
1 tbsp. smoked salt
Pepper to taste

Directions

1. Preheat your grill to medium-high heat.
2. Brush the corn with olive oil to coat evenly.
3. Place the corn on the grill and cook, turning occasionally, until the kernels are tender and lightly charred, about 10-12 minutes.
4. While the corn is grilling, prepare the honey butter glaze. In a small saucepan, melt the butter over medium heat.
5. Stir in the honey and smoked salt until well combined. Cook for a few minutes until the mixture is heated through.
6. Remove the corn from the grill and transfer to a serving platter.
7. Brush the corn generously with the honey butter glaze, ensuring each ear is coated.
8. Season with freshly ground pepper to taste.
9. Serve the grilled corn immediately while it is still warm and the glaze is melted and sticky.

Tips: If you prefer a spicier version, add a pinch of cayenne pepper or chili powder to the honey butter glaze.

Grilled Sweet Potato Planks

 **Preparation time** 30 MINUTES |  **Cooking time** 30 MINUTES |  **Servings** 8 |  **Ratings**

Ingredients

5 sweet potatoes, sliced into planks
1 tbsp. olive oil
1 tsp. onion powder
Salt and pepper to taste

Directions

1. Preheat your grill to medium heat.
2. In a large bowl, toss the sweet potato planks with olive oil, onion powder, salt, and pepper. Ensure all the planks are evenly coated with the seasoning.
3. Place the sweet potato planks on the grill grates and cook for about 4-5 minutes per side, or until tender and grill marks appear.
4. Remove the sweet potato planks from the grill and transfer to a serving platter.
5. Serve immediately as a side dish or as a base for other grilled vegetables or meats.

Tips: If you prefer a softer texture, you can wrap the sweet potato planks in foil before grilling.

Roasted Veggies & Hummus

 **Preparation time** 30 MINUTES |  **Cooking time** 20 MINUTES |  **Servings** 4 | ★★★★★ **Ratings**

Ingredients

1 white onion, sliced into wedges
2 cups butternut squash, cubed
2 cups cauliflower, sliced into florets
1 cup mushroom buttons, halved
Olive oil
Salt and pepper to taste
Hummus (store-bought or homemade)

Directions

1. Preheat your oven to 425°F (220°C).
2. Place the sliced onion, butternut squash, cauliflower florets, and mushroom buttons on a baking sheet.
3. Drizzle olive oil over the vegetables and toss to coat them evenly. Sprinkle with salt and pepper to taste.
4. Roast the vegetables in the preheated oven for about 25-30 minutes, or until they are tender and slightly caramelized, stirring once or twice during cooking.
5. Remove the roasted vegetables from the oven and let them cool slightly.
6. Serve the roasted veggies with a side of hummus for dipping. You can arrange them on a platter or individual plates.
7. Enjoy the flavorful combination of roasted veggies and creamy hummus as a healthy and satisfying snack or appetizer.

Tips: Feel free to customize the roasted vegetable selection based on your preferences. You can add or substitute other veggies like bell peppers, carrots, or broccoli.

Barbecue Smoked Mushrooms

 **Preparation time** 15 MINUTES |  **Cooking time** 45 MINUTES |  **Servings** 2 | ★★★★★ **Ratings**

Ingredients

4 cups whole baby portobello mushrooms, cleaned
1 tbsp. canola oil
1 tbsp. onion powder
1 tbsp. garlic, granulated
1 tbsp. salt
1 tbsp. pepper

Directions

1. Preheat your smoker to 225°F (107°C).
2. In a bowl, toss the baby portobello mushrooms with canola oil, onion powder, garlic granules, salt, and pepper until evenly coated.
3. Arrange the seasoned mushrooms on a wire rack or directly on the smoker grates.
4. Place the rack or grates with the mushrooms in the smoker and close the lid.
5. Smoke the mushrooms for approximately 1 to 1.5 hours, or until they have a tender texture and have absorbed the smoky flavors.
6. Remove the smoked mushrooms from the smoker and let them cool slightly before serving.

Tips: Use your preferred wood chips or chunks for smoking, such as hickory, applewood, or mesquite, to add additional flavor to the mushrooms. If you don't have a smoker, you can also achieve a similar result by grilling the mushrooms over indirect heat on a charcoal or gas grill. Just maintain a low and steady temperature for smoking.

Barbecue Grilled Vegetables

 **Preparation time** 5 MINUTES |  **Cooking time** 15 MINUTES |  **Servings** 12 | ★★★★★ **Ratings**

Ingredients

1 veggie tray (assorted vegetables of your choice, such as bell peppers, zucchini, eggplant, onions, mushrooms, etc.)

¼ cup vegetable oil

1-2 tbsp. barbecue veggie seasoning

Directions

1. Preheat your grill to medium-high heat.
2. Wash and prepare the vegetables by cutting them into even-sized pieces, if needed.
3. In a large bowl, combine the vegetable oil and barbecue veggie seasoning. Mix well to create a marinade.
4. Add the vegetables to the bowl and toss them in the marinade until evenly coated.
5. Place the vegetables on the preheated grill, using a grill basket or directly on the grates.
6. Grill the vegetables, turning occasionally, until they are charred and tender. The cooking time will vary depending on the vegetables and their size, but it usually takes about 10-15 minutes.
7. Once the vegetables are cooked to your desired level of tenderness and have nice grill marks, remove them from the grill.
8. Serve the barbecue grilled vegetables as a delicious side dish or as a topping for sandwiches, wraps, or salads.

Tips: Serve the grilled vegetables with your favorite dipping sauce or drizzle them with balsamic glaze or vinaigrette for added flavor.

Roasted Green Beans with Bacon

 **Preparation time** 15 MINUTES |  **Cooking time** 20 MINUTES |  **Servings** 6 | 

Ingredients

1 lb. green beans, trimmed
4 strips bacon, cut into small pieces
4 tbsp. extra virgin olive oil
2 cloves garlic, minced
1 tsp. salt

Directions

1. Preheat your oven to 425°F (220°C).
2. In a large bowl, toss the green beans with olive oil, minced garlic, and salt until well coated.
3. Arrange the green beans in a single layer on a baking sheet.
4. Sprinkle the bacon pieces evenly over the green beans.
5. Place the baking sheet in the preheated oven and roast for about 20-25 minutes, or until the green beans are tender and slightly crispy, and the bacon is cooked and crispy.
6. Remove from the oven and let cool for a few minutes.
7. Serve the roasted green beans with bacon as a delicious side dish or appetizer.

Tips: For extra crispy bacon, you can partially cook the bacon before adding it to the green beans, or cook it separately and sprinkle it over the roasted green beans before serving.

Smoked Watermelon

 **Preparation time** 15 MINUTES |  **Cooking time** 45-90 MINUTES |  **Servings** 5 | ★★★★ **Ratings**

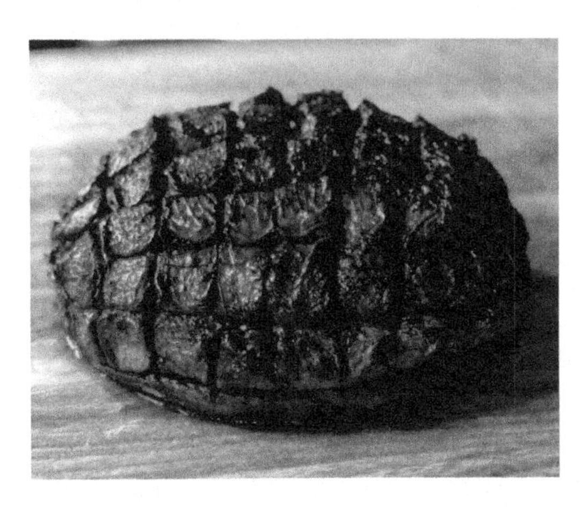

Ingredients

1 small seedless watermelon
Balsamic vinegar
Wooden skewers

Directions

1. Preheat your smoker to 225°F (107°C) using your preferred type of wood for smoking. Fruit woods like apple or cherry work well with watermelon.
2. Cut the watermelon into thick slices, about 1 inch thick.
3. Insert wooden skewers into each watermelon slice for easy handling on the smoker.
4. Place the watermelon slices directly on the smoker grates and close the lid.
5. Smoke the watermelon slices for about 30-45 minutes, or until they develop a light smoky flavor and slightly caramelized edges.
6. Remove the smoked watermelon from the smoker and let it cool for a few minutes.
7. Drizzle balsamic vinegar over the smoked watermelon slices for added flavor.
8. Serve the smoked watermelon as a unique and refreshing appetizer or dessert.

Tips: Make sure to keep an eye on the watermelon while smoking to prevent it from becoming too soft or mushy.

Smoked Mushrooms

 **Preparation time** 20 MINUTES |  **Cooking time** 2 HOURS |  **Servings** 6 | ★★★★ **Ratings**

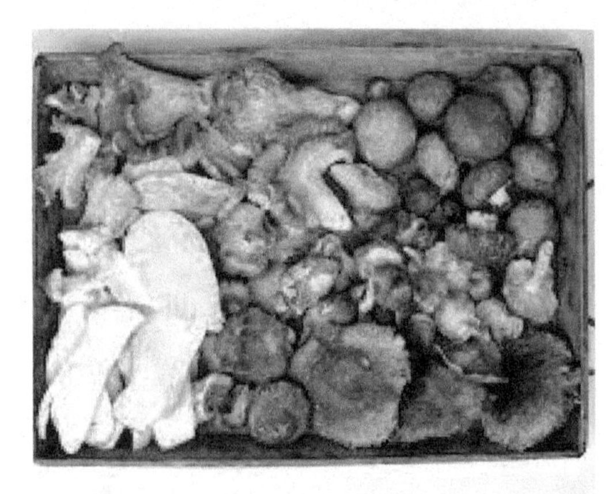

Ingredients

6-12 large Portobello mushrooms
Sea salt
Black pepper
Extra virgin olive oil
Herbs de Provence

Directions

1. Preheat your smoker to 225°F (107°C) using your preferred type of wood for smoking. Fruit woods like apple or cherry work well with mushrooms.
2. Clean the Portobello mushrooms by gently wiping them with a damp cloth to remove any dirt or debris. Remove the stems if desired.
3. Season the mushrooms generously with sea salt, black pepper, and herbs de Provence. Drizzle them with extra virgin olive oil to enhance the flavor and prevent sticking.
4. Place the seasoned mushrooms directly on the smoker grates, gill-side down, to allow the smoke to penetrate the caps.
5. Close the smoker lid and let the mushrooms smoke for about 45-60 minutes, or until they are tender and have absorbed a smoky flavor.
6. Remove the smoked mushrooms from the smoker and let them cool for a few minutes before serving.
7. Serve the smoked mushrooms as a side dish, appetizer, or use them as a flavorful addition to salads, sandwiches, or pasta dishes.

Tips: For added richness, you can brush the mushrooms with melted butter or sprinkle them with grated Parmesan cheese before smoking.

Smoked Cherry Tomatoes

 **Preparation time** 20 MINUTES |  **Cooking time** 1 ½ HOURS |  **Servings** 8-10 | ★★★★ **Ratings**

Ingredients

2 pints of cherry tomatoes

Directions

1. Preheat your smoker to 225°F (107°C) using your preferred type of wood for smoking. Fruit woods like cherry or apple work well with tomatoes.
2. Rinse the cherry tomatoes and pat them dry with a paper towel.
3. Place the cherry tomatoes directly on the smoker grates, making sure they are spread out in a single layer for even smoking.
4. Close the smoker lid and let the tomatoes smoke for about 1-2 hours, or until they develop a slightly wrinkled appearance and a smoky flavor.
5. Remove the smoked cherry tomatoes from the smoker and let them cool before using them in recipes or enjoying them as a flavorful snack.

Tips: You can drizzle the cherry tomatoes with a small amount of olive oil and sprinkle them with salt and pepper before smoking for added flavor.

Smoked & Smashed New Potatoes

 **Preparation time** 5 MINUTES |  **Cooking time** 8 HOURS |  **Servings** 4 | ★★ **Ratings**

Ingredients

1-½ lbs. small new red potatoes or fingerlings
Extra virgin olive oil
Sea salt and black pepper
2 tbsp. softened butter

Directions

1. Preheat your smoker to 225°F (107°C) using your preferred type of wood for smoking. Fruit woods like apple or cherry work well for potatoes.
2. Rinse the potatoes and pat them dry with a paper towel.
3. Drizzle the potatoes with olive oil and sprinkle them with sea salt and black pepper, ensuring they are evenly coated.
4. Place the potatoes directly on the smoker grates and close the lid.
5. Smoke the potatoes for about 1-2 hours, or until they are tender and have a smoky flavor. You can check their doneness by piercing them with a fork.
6. Once the potatoes are smoked, remove them from the smoker and let them cool slightly.
7. Using the back of a fork or a potato masher, gently smash each potato to flatten it slightly.
8. Heat a skillet or griddle over medium heat and add the softened butter. Place the smashed potatoes in the skillet and cook for a few minutes on each side until they are crispy and golden brown.
9. Remove the potatoes from the skillet and serve them hot.

Tips: Feel free to experiment with different types of potatoes for varying flavors and textures.

Smoked Brussels Sprouts

 **Preparation time** 15 MINUTES |  **Cooking time** 45 MINUTES |  **Servings** 6 | ★★★★ **Ratings**

Ingredients

1-½ lbs. Brussels sprouts
2 cloves of garlic, minced
2 tbsp. extra virgin olive oil
Sea salt and cracked black pepper to taste

Directions

1. Preheat your smoker to 225°F (107°C) using your preferred type of wood for smoking. Fruit woods like apple or cherry work well for Brussels sprouts.
2. Trim the ends of the Brussels sprouts and remove any loose outer leaves. Cut larger sprouts in half so that all the pieces are similar in size.
3. In a large mixing bowl, combine the Brussels sprouts, minced garlic, olive oil, sea salt, and cracked black pepper. Toss until the Brussels sprouts are evenly coated with the seasonings.
4. Transfer the Brussels sprouts to a grilling pan or a perforated aluminum foil tray to prevent them from falling through the grates.
5. Place the grilling pan or foil tray directly on the smoker grates and close the lid.
6. Smoke the Brussels sprouts for about 45 minutes to 1 hour, or until they are tender and have a smoky flavor. You can check their doneness by piercing them with a fork.
7. Once the Brussels sprouts are smoked, remove them from the smoker and serve them hot.

Tips: Experiment with different seasonings such as lemon zest, balsamic glaze, or red pepper flakes to customize the flavor profile.

Smoked Tofu

 **Preparation time** 10 MINUTES |  **Cooking time** 1 H 45 MINUTES |  **Servings** 4 |  **Ratings**

Ingredients

400g plain tofu
Sesame oil for brushing

Directions

1. Preheat your smoker to 250°F (120°C) using your preferred type of wood for smoking. Fruit woods like apple or cherry work well for tofu.
2. Drain and pat dry the tofu using paper towels to remove excess moisture.
3. Cut the tofu into slices or cubes of your desired size.
4. Brush each piece of tofu with a thin layer of sesame oil on all sides. This will help to prevent sticking and add flavor.
5. Place the tofu pieces directly on the smoker grates or on a grilling pan.
6. Close the lid of the smoker and smoke the tofu for about 30-40 minutes, or until it develops a smoky flavor and a slightly firmer texture. You can adjust the smoking time based on your preference for a lighter or stronger smoky flavor.
7. Once smoked, remove the tofu from the smoker and let it cool slightly before serving.

Tips: You can marinate the tofu before smoking by combining soy sauce, garlic, ginger, and other seasonings of your choice. This will infuse the tofu with additional flavors.

Shiitake Smoked Mushrooms

 **Preparation time** 15 MINUTES |  **Cooking time** 45 MINUTES |  **Servings** 4-6 | ★★★★★ **Ratings**

Ingredients

4 cups Shiitake mushrooms, stems removed
1 tbsp. canola oil
1 tsp. onion powder
1 tsp. granulated garlic
1 tsp. salt
1 tsp. pepper

Directions

1. Preheat your smoker to 225°F (107°C) using your preferred type of wood for smoking. Hardwoods like oak or hickory work well for mushrooms.
2. In a large bowl, toss the Shiitake mushrooms with canola oil, onion powder, granulated garlic, salt, and pepper until the mushrooms are evenly coated with the seasonings.
3. Place the seasoned mushrooms directly on the smoker grates or on a grilling pan.
4. Close the lid of the smoker and smoke the mushrooms for about 1 to 1 ½ hours, or until they are tender and have developed a smoky flavor.
5. Once smoked, remove the mushrooms from the smoker and let them cool slightly before serving.

Tips: You can adjust the smoking time based on the size and thickness of the mushrooms. Thicker mushrooms may require additional smoking time.

Smoked Baked Beans

 **Preparation time** 15 MINUTES |  **Cooking time** 3 HOURS |  **Servings** 12 | 

Ingredients

1 medium yellow onion, diced
3 jalapenos, seeded and diced
56 oz pork and beans
¾ cup barbeque sauce
½ cup dark brown sugar
¼ cup apple cider vinegar
2 tbsp. Dijon mustard
2 tbsp. molasses

Directions

1. Preheat your smoker to 225°F (107°C) using your preferred type of wood for smoking. Fruitwoods like apple or cherry work well for baked beans.
2. In a large bowl, combine the diced onion, diced jalapenos, pork and beans, barbeque sauce, dark brown sugar, apple cider vinegar, Dijon mustard, and molasses. Mix well to combine all the ingredients.
3. Transfer the bean mixture to a disposable aluminum pan or a cast iron skillet.
4. Place the pan of beans in the smoker and close the lid.
5. Let the beans smoke for about 2-3 hours, stirring occasionally, until they are hot and bubbly, and the flavors have melded together.
6. Remove the smoked baked beans from the smoker and let them cool slightly before serving.

Tips: If you prefer sweeter baked beans, you can increase the amount of brown sugar or molasses.

Smoked Healthy Cabbage

 **Preparation time** 10 MINUTES |  **Cooking time** 2 HOURS |  **Servings** 5 |  **Ratings**

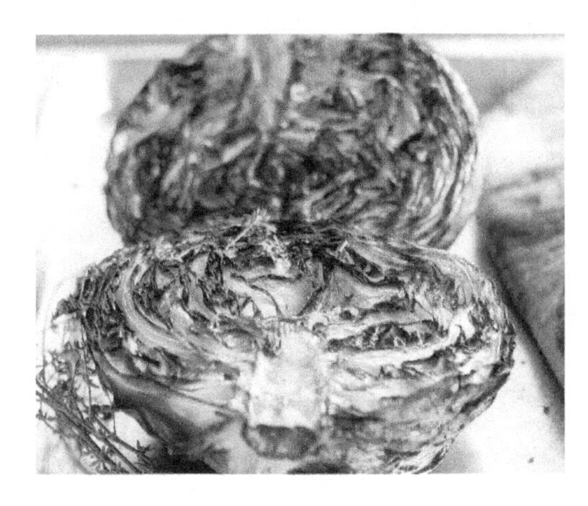

Ingredients

Maple pellets (for smoking)
1 head of cabbage, cored and quartered
4 tbsp. butter
2 tbsp. rendered bacon fat
1 chicken bouillon cube
1 tsp. fresh ground black pepper
1 garlic clove, minced

Directions

1. Preheat your smoker to 225°F (107°C) using maple pellets for a sweet and subtle smoky flavor.
2. In a small saucepan, melt the butter and bacon fat over low heat.
3. Add the minced garlic to the melted butter and bacon fat and cook for about 1 minute until fragrant.
4. Dissolve the chicken bouillon cube in ¼ cup of hot water, then add it to the butter mixture along with the black pepper. Stir well to combine.
5. Place the cabbage quarters on a smoker rack or in a disposable aluminum pan.
6. Pour the butter mixture over the cabbage, making sure to evenly coat each quarter.
7. Place the cabbage in the smoker and close the lid.
8. Smoke the cabbage for approximately 1 to 1 ½ hours, or until it is tender and has a nice smoky flavor. The exact cooking time may vary depending on the size and thickness of the cabbage quarters.
9. Remove the smoked cabbage from the smoker and let it rest for a few minutes before serving.

Tips: If you prefer a vegetarian option, you can omit the bacon fat and use additional butter or olive oil.

Feisty Roasted Cauliflower

 **Preparation time** 15 MINUTES |  **Cooking time** 10 MINUTES |  **Servings** 4 | ★★★★★ **Ratings**

Ingredients

1 cauliflower head, cut into florets
1 tbsp. oil
1 cup grated Parmesan cheese
2 garlic cloves, crushed
½ tsp. pepper
½ tsp. salt
¼ tsp. paprika

Directions

1. Preheat your oven to 425°F (220°C) and line a baking sheet with parchment paper.
2. In a large bowl, combine the cauliflower florets, oil, crushed garlic cloves, pepper, salt, and paprika. Toss well to evenly coat the cauliflower with the seasoning mixture.
3. Spread the seasoned cauliflower in a single layer on the prepared baking sheet.
4. Roast in the preheated oven for about 25-30 minutes, or until the cauliflower is tender and lightly browned, stirring once halfway through.
5. Remove the roasted cauliflower from the oven and sprinkle the grated Parmesan cheese over the top.
6. Return the baking sheet to the oven and roast for an additional 5 minutes, or until the cheese is melted and golden brown.
7. Remove from the oven and let the roasted cauliflower cool slightly before serving.

Tips: Feel free to add other herbs or spices such as thyme, rosemary, or cayenne pepper for added flavor variations.

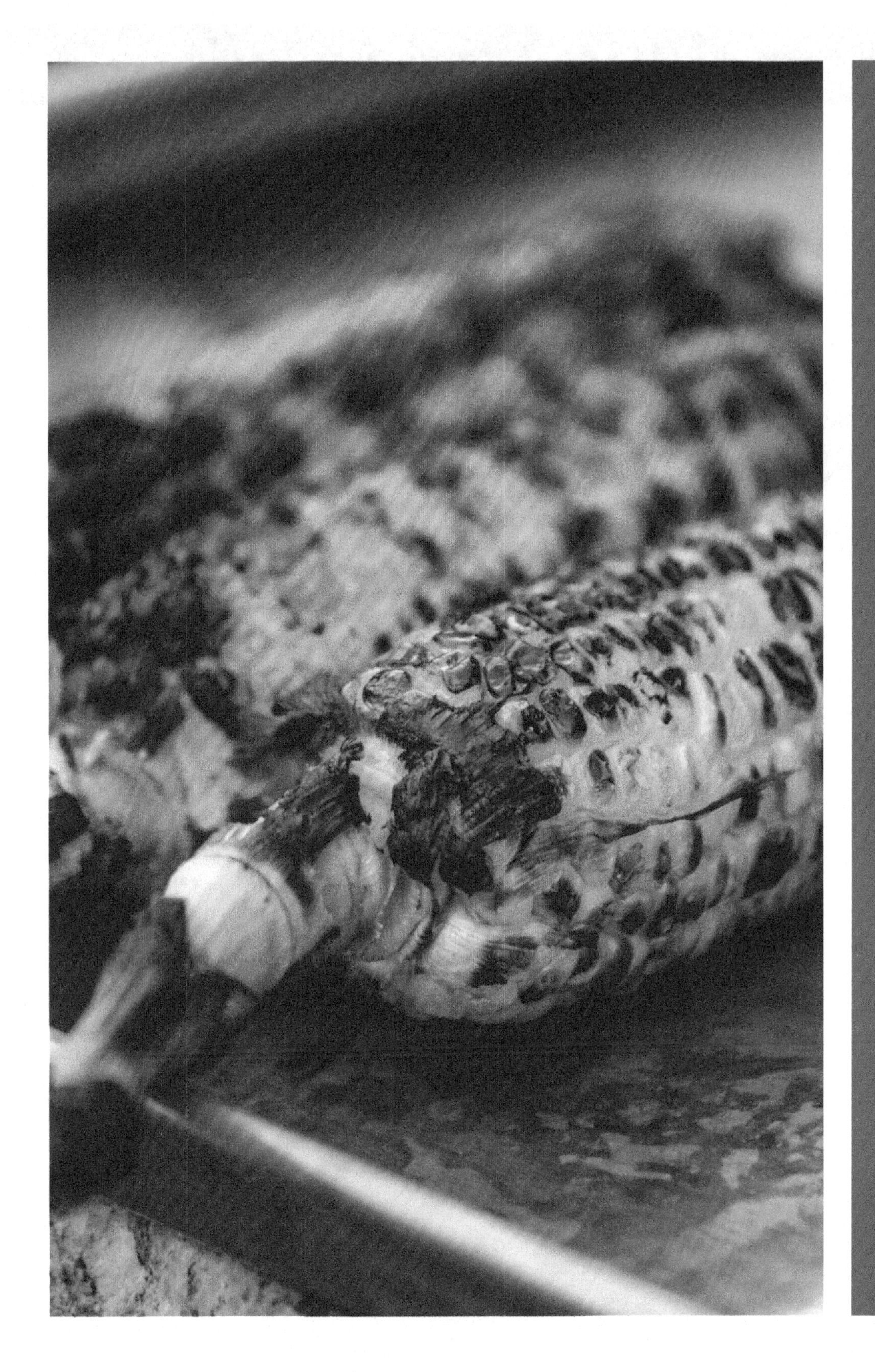

APPETIZER AND SNACKS

Simple Dump Cake

 **Preparation time** 20 MINUTES |  **Cooking time** 60-120 MINUTES |  **Servings** 6-8 | ★★★ **Ratings**

Ingredients

1 box of your chosen cake mix
2 cans of your desired pie filling
1 stick of butter

Directions

1. Preheat the oven to 350°F (180°C) and lightly grease a baking dish.
2. Pour both cans of pie filling into the baking dish.
3. Sprinkle the cake mix evenly over the top of the filling. Do not stir, leave the mix on the surface.
4. Cut the stick of butter into thin slices and distribute them on top of the cake mix.
5. Place the baking dish in the preheated oven and bake for about 30-35 minutes, or until the top is golden brown and crispy.
6. Remove the dish from the oven and let it cool slightly before serving. You can serve the Dump Cake on its own or with a scoop of vanilla ice cream for an extra touch.

Tips: Add a sprinkle of cinnamon or nutmeg for an extra flavor boost.

Spectacular Smoked Peach

 **Preparation time** 20 MINUTES |  **Cooking time** 35-45 MINUTES |  **Servings** 4 | ★★★ **Ratings**

Ingredients

2 tbsp. honey
1 pint vanilla ice cream
1 tbsp. packed brown sugar
4 barely ripe peaches, halved and pitted

Directions

1. Prepare your smoker according to the manufacturer's instructions, ensuring it reaches a temperature of around 225°F (107°C).
2. In a small bowl, combine the honey and brown sugar. Stir until well blended.
3. Place the peach halves, cut side up, on the smoker rack. Brush the honey mixture generously over the top of each peach half.
4. Close the smoker and let the peaches smoke for approximately 30-40 minutes, or until they are tender and have absorbed a smoky flavor.
5. Remove the smoked peaches from the smoker and let them cool slightly.
6. Serve the smoked peaches warm or at room temperature, topped with a scoop of vanilla ice cream.

Tips: Choose peaches that are slightly firm and not overly ripe for best results.

Queso Chorizo Meal

 **Preparation time** 10-15 MINUTES |  **Cooking time** 60 MINUTES |  **Servings** 4 |  Ratings

Ingredients

16 ounces Velveeta cheese, cubed
4 ounces cream cheese, cubed
10 ounces Rotel (diced tomatoes and green chilies)
1 lb. cooked Chorizo, chopped

Directions

1. In a medium-sized saucepan, combine the cubed Velveeta cheese, cream cheese, and Rotel over low heat.
2. Stir the mixture continuously until the cheeses have melted and the ingredients are well combined, creating a smooth and creamy texture.
3. Add the chopped cooked Chorizo to the cheese mixture and stir well to incorporate.
4. Continue heating the queso chorizo dip over low heat, stirring occasionally, until it is heated through and the flavors have melded together. Be careful not to let it boil.
5. Once heated, transfer the queso chorizo dip to a serving bowl or keep it warm in a slow cooker or fondue pot.
6. Serve the dip hot with tortilla chips, sliced baguette, or your favorite dippers.

Tips: To make the dip in advance, combine all the ingredients (except the Chorizo) and store in an airtight container in the refrigerator. When ready to serve, reheat the dip in a saucepan over low heat, add the cooked Chorizo, and stir until heated through.

Cool Brie Cheese Appetizer

 **Preparation time** 10-15 MINUTES |  **Cooking time** 60 MINUTES |  **Servings** 4 |  **Ratings**

Ingredients

8-ounce blocks of brie cheese

Directions

1. Remove the brie cheese from its packaging and place it on a serving platter.
2. Allow the brie cheese to come to room temperature for about 30 minutes to soften and enhance its flavors.
3. Optionally, you can score the top rind of the brie cheese with a knife in a crisscross pattern, but this step is not necessary.
4. Serve the brie cheese as is or with accompaniments such as crackers, sliced baguette, fresh fruit, or nuts.

Tips: For a warm and melty brie cheese, preheat the oven to 350°F (175°C). Place the brie cheese on a baking sheet and bake for about 10-15 minutes, or until the cheese is soft and gooey. Add a touch of sweetness by drizzling honey or spreading fruit preserves on top of the brie cheese before serving.

Mesmerizing Banana Foster Dessert

 **Preparation time** 10-15 MINUTES |  **Cooking time** 15-20 MINUTES |  **Servings** 4 | ★★★★★ **Ratings**

Ingredients

10 overripe bananas, peeled and halved lengthwise

Rum and raisin sauce for serving

Directions

1. Preheat a grill or stovetop griddle to medium heat.
2. Place the banana halves, cut side down, on the grill or griddle. Cook for about 2-3 minutes, or until grill marks appear and the bananas are slightly softened.
3. Carefully flip the banana halves using tongs and cook for another 2-3 minutes on the other side.
4. Remove the grilled bananas from the heat and transfer them to serving plates or bowls.
5. Drizzle the rum and raisin sauce generously over the grilled bananas.
6. Serve the mesmerizing banana foster immediately while the bananas are warm and the sauce is deliciously gooey.

Tips: You can make your own rum and raisin sauce by combining rum, raisins, sugar, and a pinch of cinnamon in a small saucepan. Simmer the mixture until the raisins are plump and the sauce has thickened.

Hearty Peaches

 **Preparation time** 10-15 MINUTES |  **Cooking time** 30 MINUTES | 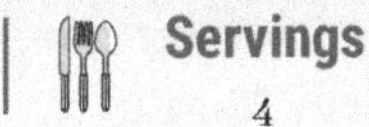 **Servings** 4 | ★★★★★ **Ratings**

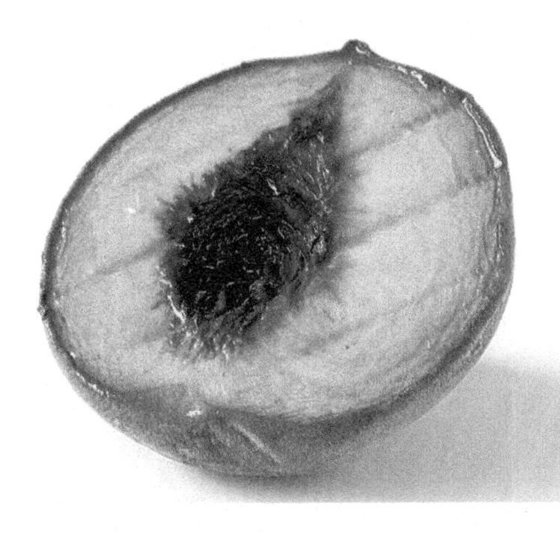

Ingredients

6 fresh peaches

Directions

1. Preheat the grill to medium heat.
2. Wash the peaches thoroughly and pat them dry with a paper towel.
3. Cut the peaches in half and remove the pits.
4. Place the peach halves, cut side down, on the grill grates. Close the lid and grill for about 3-4 minutes, or until the peaches have grill marks and are slightly softened.
5. Carefully flip the peach halves using tongs and grill for an additional 2-3 minutes on the other side.
6. Remove the grilled peaches from the heat and transfer them to a serving platter or individual dessert plates.
7. Serve the hearty peaches as is for a simple and rustic dessert, or pair them with a dollop of whipped cream or a scoop of vanilla ice cream.

Tips: If desired, you can brush the peach halves with a little melted butter or sprinkle them with a touch of cinnamon or brown sugar before grilling for added flavor.

Coconut Bacon

 **Preparation time** 10 MINUTES |  **Cooking time** 30 MINUTES |  **Servings** 2 | 

Ingredients

3 ½ cups flaked coconut
1 tbsp pure maple syrup
1 tbsp water
2 tbsp liquid smoke
1 tbsp soy sauce
1 tsp smoked paprika (optional)

Directions

1. Preheat your oven to 325°F (163°C) and line a baking sheet with parchment paper.
2. In a mixing bowl, combine the maple syrup, water, liquid smoke, soy sauce, and smoked paprika (if using). Whisk well to combine.
3. Add the flaked coconut to the bowl and toss until all the coconut flakes are evenly coated with the liquid mixture.
4. Spread the coated coconut flakes in a single layer on the prepared baking sheet.
5. Bake in the preheated oven for about 15-20 minutes, or until the coconut flakes are golden brown and crispy. Stir the coconut flakes halfway through the baking process to ensure even browning.
6. Remove from the oven and let the coconut bacon cool completely on the baking sheet. As it cools, it will become even crispier.
7. Once cooled, the coconut bacon is ready to be enjoyed. Use it as a topping for salads, soups, sandwiches, or any dish where you want a smoky and savory flavor.

Tips: If you don't have liquid smoke, you can try substituting it with smoked paprika for a milder smoky flavor.

Smoked Corn on the Cob

 **Preparation time** 5 MINUTES |  **Cooking time** 60 MINUTES |  **Servings** 4 | ★★★★ **Ratings**

Ingredients

4 corn ears, husk removed
4 tbsp olive oil
Pepper and salt to taste

Directions

1. Prepare your smoker according to the manufacturer's instructions and preheat it to 225°F (107°C).
2. Brush each corn ear with olive oil, ensuring they are evenly coated.
3. Season the corn ears with salt and pepper to taste, making sure to cover all sides.
4. Place the seasoned corn ears directly on the smoker grates or use a grilling basket for easier handling.
5. Close the smoker lid and let the corn smoke for approximately 1 to 1 ½ hours, or until the kernels are tender and lightly charred. Rotate the corn occasionally for even smoking.
6. Remove the smoked corn from the smoker and let them cool slightly before serving.
7. Serve the smoked corn on the cob as is or with additional butter, salt, and pepper, if desired.

Tips: Soaking the corn ears in water for about 30 minutes before smoking can help keep them moist during the smoking process.

Easy Grilled Corn

 **Preparation time** 5 MINUTES |  **Cooking time** 40 MINUTES |  **Servings** 6 |  **Ratings**

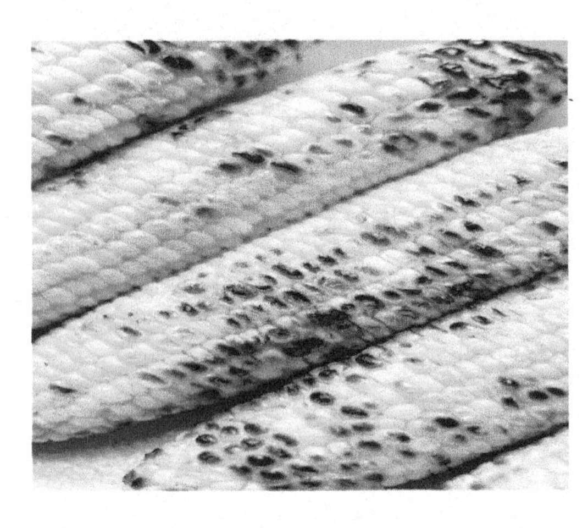

Ingredients

6 fresh corn ears, still in the husk
Pepper, salt, and butter

Directions

1. Preheat your grill to medium-high heat.
2. Peel back the outer husks of each corn ear, but leave them attached at the base. Remove the silk strands and discard.
3. Lightly brush each corn ear with melted butter, ensuring they are evenly coated. Season with salt and pepper to taste.
4. Pull the husks back up to cover the corn, forming a natural protective layer.
5. Place the corn ears on the preheated grill and cook for about 10-15 minutes, turning occasionally. The husks will slightly char and the corn kernels will become tender.
6. Once the corn is cooked, carefully remove the husks using oven mitts or tongs.
7. Serve the grilled corn on a platter and season with additional salt and pepper if desired. Optionally, serve with extra melted butter on the side.

Tips: If you prefer a sweeter taste, you can sprinkle a little sugar or drizzle honey over the buttered corn before grilling.

Seasoned Potatoes on Smoker

 **Preparation time** 10 MINUTES |  **Cooking time** 45 MINUTES |  **Servings** 6 | ★★★★★ **Ratings**

Ingredients

1-½ lb. creamer potatoes
2 tbsp olive oil
1 tbsp garlic powder
¼ tbsp oregano
½ tbsp thyme, dried
½ tbsp parsley, dried

Directions

1. Preheat your smoker to a temperature of 225°F (107°C).
2. Rinse the creamer potatoes under cold water to remove any dirt. Pat them dry with a paper towel.
3. In a bowl, combine the olive oil, garlic powder, oregano, thyme, and parsley. Stir well to create a seasoned oil mixture.
4. Place the creamer potatoes in a large mixing bowl. Pour the seasoned oil mixture over the potatoes and toss them gently to coat evenly.
5. Transfer the seasoned potatoes to a smoker-safe dish or aluminum foil pan. Arrange them in a single layer for even cooking.
6. Place the dish or pan of potatoes in the preheated smoker. Close the smoker lid and let them cook for approximately 1 to 1.5 hours, or until the potatoes are tender. Stir or toss the potatoes occasionally during the cooking process to ensure they cook evenly.
7. Once the potatoes are cooked, remove them from the smoker and let them cool for a few minutes.
8. Serve the seasoned potatoes as a delicious side dish alongside your favorite grilled or smoked meats.

Tips: if you prefer crispy potatoes, you can increase the temperature of the smoker to 375°F (190°C) for the last 10-15 minutes of cooking.

Caprese Tomato Salad

 **Preparation time** 5 MINUTES |  **Cooking time** 60 MINUTES |  **Servings** 4 | 

Ingredients

3 cups halved multicolored cherry tomatoes
1/8 tsp. kosher salt
½ cup fresh basil leaves
1 tbsp. extra-virgin olive oil
1 tbsp. balsamic vinegar
½ tsp. black pepper
¼ tsp. kosher salt
1 ounce diced fresh mozzarella cheese (about 1/3 cup)

Directions

1. In a large mixing bowl, combine the halved cherry tomatoes and sprinkle them with 1/8 teaspoon of kosher salt. Toss gently to coat the tomatoes evenly with the salt. Let them sit for about 10 minutes to release some of their juices.
2. Meanwhile, stack the basil leaves together and roll them tightly into a cylinder. Slice the rolled basil leaves crosswise into thin strips, creating ribbons of basil.
3. After the tomatoes have released their juices, add the basil ribbons, extra-virgin olive oil, balsamic vinegar, black pepper, and ¼ teaspoon of kosher salt to the bowl. Toss the ingredients gently to combine.
4. Add the diced fresh mozzarella cheese to the bowl and gently toss again to distribute it evenly throughout the salad.
5. Let the Caprese tomato salad sit at room temperature for about 10 minutes to allow the flavors to meld together.
6. Serve the salad as a refreshing appetizer or side dish. You can garnish it with additional basil leaves, a drizzle of balsamic glaze, or a sprinkle of freshly ground black pepper, if desired.

Tips: Use a variety of multicolored cherry tomatoes to add visual appeal to the salad. You can choose red, yellow, and orange cherry tomatoes for a vibrant and colorful presentation. Fresh, high-quality ingredients make a difference in this salad. Use the best-quality extra-virgin olive oil, balsamic vinegar, and mozzarella cheese you can find for the best flavor.

Watermelon-Cucumber Salad

 **Preparation time** 12 MINUTES |  **Cooking time** / |  **Servings** 4 | ★★★★★ **Ratings**

Ingredients

1 tbsp. olive oil
2 tsp. fresh lemon juice
¼ tsp. salt
2 cups cubed seedless watermelon
1 cup thinly sliced English cucumber
¼ cup thinly vertically sliced red onion
1 tbsp. thinly sliced fresh basil

Directions

1. In a small bowl, whisk together the olive oil, fresh lemon juice, and salt until well combined. This will be the dressing for the salad.
2. In a large mixing bowl, combine the cubed watermelon, sliced cucumber, sliced red onion, and fresh basil.
3. Drizzle the dressing over the watermelon-cucumber mixture and toss gently to coat all the ingredients with the dressing. Be careful not to crush the watermelon cubes.
4. Let the salad sit at room temperature for about 10 minutes to allow the flavors to meld together.
5. Serve the watermelon-cucumber salad as a refreshing and light appetizer or side dish. It pairs well with grilled meats or can be enjoyed on its own.

Tips: English cucumbers work well in this salad because they have a crisp texture and mild flavor. If you can't find English cucumbers, you can use regular cucumbers, but peel them and remove the seeds before slicing.

Fresh Creamed Corn

 **Preparation time** 5 MINUTES |  **Cooking time** 30 MINUTES |  **Servings** 4 |  **Ratings**

Ingredients

2 tsp. unsalted butter
2 cups fresh corn kernels
2 tbsp. minced shallots
¾ cup 1% low-fat milk
2 tsp. all-purpose flour
¼ tsp. salt

Directions

1. In a large skillet, melt the unsalted butter over medium heat.
2. Add the fresh corn kernels and minced shallots to the skillet. Cook for about 5 minutes, stirring occasionally, until the corn is tender.
3. In a small bowl, whisk together the low-fat milk, all-purpose flour, and salt until the flour is dissolved and no lumps remain.
4. Pour the milk mixture into the skillet with the corn. Stir well to combine.
5. Reduce the heat to medium-low and continue cooking for about 5 minutes, or until the mixture thickens and becomes creamy. Stir occasionally to prevent sticking.
6. Taste and adjust the seasoning if needed, adding more salt if desired.
7. Remove the skillet from the heat and let the creamed corn rest for a few minutes before serving.

Tips: Shallots add a mild onion flavor to the dish. If you don't have shallots, you can substitute them with finely minced onions or omit them altogether.

Spinach Salad with Avocado & Orange

 **Preparation time** 5 MINUTES |  **Cooking time** 20 MINUTES |  **Servings** 4 |  Ratings

Ingredients

1 ½ tbsp. fresh lime juice
4 tsp. extra-virgin olive oil
1 tbsp. chopped fresh cilantro
1/8 tsp. kosher salt
½ cup diced peeled ripe avocado
½ cup fresh orange segments
1 (5-ounce) package baby spinach
1/8 tsp. freshly ground black pepper

Directions

1. In a small bowl, whisk together the fresh lime juice, extra-virgin olive oil, chopped cilantro, and kosher salt to make the dressing.
2. Place the baby spinach in a large salad bowl.
3. Add the diced avocado and fresh orange segments to the salad bowl.
4. Drizzle the dressing over the salad ingredients.
5. Gently toss the salad to coat the spinach, avocado, and orange with the dressing. Be careful not to mash the avocado.
6. Sprinkle freshly ground black pepper over the salad.
7. Serve the spinach salad immediately as a refreshing appetizer or side dish.

Tips: When cutting the avocado, gently score the flesh into cubes and then use a spoon to scoop it out, making it easier to dice.

Raspberry & Blue Cheese Salad

 **Preparation time** 5 MINUTES |  **Cooking time** 20 MINUTES |  **Servings** 4 |  **Ratings**

Ingredients

1 ½ tbsp. olive oil
1 ½ tsp. red wine vinegar
¼ tsp. Dijon mustard
1/8 tsp. salt
1/8 tsp. pepper
5 cups mixed baby greens
½ cup raspberries
¼ cup chopped toasted pecans
1 ounce blue cheese

Directions

1. In a small bowl, whisk together the olive oil, red wine vinegar, Dijon mustard, salt, and pepper to make the dressing.
2. Place the mixed baby greens in a large salad bowl.
3. Add the raspberries and chopped toasted pecans to the salad bowl.
4. Crumble the blue cheese over the salad ingredients.
5. Drizzle the dressing over the salad.
6. Gently toss the salad to coat the greens, raspberries, pecans, and blue cheese with the dressing.
7. Serve the raspberry and blue cheese salad immediately as a refreshing appetizer or side dish.

Tips: To toast the pecans, spread them in a single layer on a baking sheet and bake in a preheated oven at 350°F (175°C) for about 5-7 minutes, or until fragrant and lightly browned. Keep an eye on them to prevent burning.

Grilled Green Onions, Orzo & Sweet Peas

 **Preparation time** 5 MINUTES |  **Cooking time** 15 MINUTES |  **Servings** 4 | ★★★★★ **Ratings**

Ingredients

¾ cup whole-wheat orzo
1 cup frozen peas
1 bunch green onions, trimmed
1 tsp. olive oil
½ tsp. grated lemon rind
1 tbsp. lemon juice
1 tsp. olive oil
¼ tsp. salt
1 ounce shaved Montego cheese

Directions

1. Cook the whole-wheat orzo according to the package instructions. Drain and set aside.
2. In a separate pot, cook the frozen peas in boiling water for 2-3 minutes until tender. Drain and set aside.
3. Preheat a grill or grill pan over medium heat.
4. Toss the trimmed green onions with 1 teaspoon of olive oil. Place the green onions on the grill and cook for 3-4 minutes, turning occasionally, until charred and tender. Remove from the grill and set aside.
5. In a small bowl, whisk together the grated lemon rind, lemon juice, 1 teaspoon of olive oil, and salt to make the dressing.
6. In a large bowl, combine the cooked orzo, peas, and grilled green onions. Pour the dressing over the mixture and toss gently to coat everything evenly.
7. Sprinkle the shaved Montego cheese over the salad.
8. Serve the grilled green onions, orzo, and sweet peas salad as a side dish or a light lunch. It can be enjoyed warm or at room temperature.

Tips: Adjust the amount of lemon juice and grated lemon rind according to your taste preference.

Cinnamon Almonds

 **Preparation time** 10 MINUTES |  **Cooking time** 1 H 30 MINUTES |  **Servings** 4-6 | ★★★ **Ratings**

Ingredients

1 egg white
1 lb. almonds
½ cup brown sugar
½ cup granulated sugar
1/8 tsp. salt
1 tbsp. ground cinnamon

Directions

1. Preheat the oven to 300°F (150°C). Line a baking sheet with parchment paper.
2. In a large mixing bowl, whisk the egg white until frothy and slightly thickened.
3. Add the almonds to the bowl and stir until they are evenly coated with the egg white.
4. In a separate bowl, combine the brown sugar, granulated sugar, salt, and ground cinnamon. Mix well.
5. Add the cinnamon sugar mixture to the bowl with the almonds. Toss and stir until the almonds are thoroughly coated with the mixture.
6. Spread the coated almonds in a single layer on the prepared baking sheet.
7. Bake in the preheated oven for about 30-35 minutes, or until the almonds are golden brown and crispy. Stir the almonds every 10 minutes to ensure even baking.
8. Remove the baking sheet from the oven and let the almonds cool completely on the sheet. They will continue to harden as they cool.
9. Once cooled, transfer the cinnamon almonds to an airtight container or serve immediately as a delicious snack.

Tips: For extra flavor, you can add a pinch of nutmeg or other spices of your choice to the cinnamon sugar mixture.

Roasted Cashews

 **Preparation time** 15 MINUTES |  **Cooking time** 12 MINUTES |  **Servings** 4 |  Ratings

Ingredients

¼ cup rosemary, chopped
2 ½ tbsp butter, melted
2 cups cashews, raw
½ tsp cayenne pepper
1 tsp salt

Directions

1. Preheat the oven to 350°F (175°C). Line a baking sheet with parchment paper.
2. In a mixing bowl, combine the chopped rosemary, melted butter, cayenne pepper, and salt. Stir until well combined.
3. Add the raw cashews to the bowl and toss them in the rosemary mixture, ensuring they are evenly coated.
4. Spread the coated cashews in a single layer on the prepared baking sheet.
5. Roast the cashews in the preheated oven for about 12-15 minutes, or until they are golden brown and fragrant. Stir the cashews halfway through the baking time to ensure even roasting.
6. Remove the baking sheet from the oven and let the cashews cool completely on the sheet. They will continue to harden as they cool.
7. Once cooled, transfer the roasted cashews to an airtight container or enjoy them immediately as a flavorful snack.

Tips: Make sure to keep an eye on the cashews while roasting to prevent them from burning. They can go from golden brown to overdone quickly.

Smoked Jerky

 **Preparation time** 20 MINUTES |  **Cooking time** 6 HOURS |  **Servings** 6-8 |  **Ratings**

Ingredients

1 flank steak (3 lb.)
½ cup brown sugar
1 cup bourbon
¼ cup jerky rub
2 tbsp Worcestershire sauce
1 can chipotle
½ cup cider vinegar

Directions

1. Prepare the marinade by combining the brown sugar, bourbon, jerky rub, Worcestershire sauce, chipotle (including the adobo sauce), and cider vinegar in a mixing bowl. Stir well to combine all the ingredients.
2. Place the flank steak in a large resealable plastic bag or a shallow dish. Pour the marinade over the steak, making sure it is fully coated. Seal the bag or cover the dish and marinate in the refrigerator for at least 4 hours, or preferably overnight, to allow the flavors to develop.
3. Preheat your smoker to a temperature of 180°F (82°C) using hardwood chips or chunks for smoke flavor. If your smoker doesn't have a temperature control, maintain a low heat by adjusting the airflow and using a thermometer to monitor the temperature.
4. Remove the marinated flank steak from the refrigerator and pat it dry with paper towels. Discard the marinade.
5. Place the flank steak on the smoker grates and close the lid. Smoke the steak for approximately 4-6 hours, or until it reaches your desired level of doneness and chewiness. Check the internal temperature with a meat thermometer to ensure it reaches a minimum of 160°F (71°C) for food safety.
6. Once the jerky is smoked to your liking, remove it from the smoker and let it cool completely. The jerky will continue to firm up as it cools.
7. Slice the smoked flank steak against the grain into thin strips, about 1/8 to ¼ inch thick. This will help ensure a tender and chewy texture.
8. Store the smoked jerky in an airtight container or resealable bags. It can be kept at room temperature for up to 2 weeks or refrigerated for longer shelf life.

Tips: For added flavor, you can experiment with different variations of the marinade. Consider adding soy sauce, garlic powder, onion powder, or your favorite spices and seasonings.

Cranberry-Almond Broccoli Salad

 **Preparation time** 10 MINUTES |  **Cooking time** 60 MINUTES |  **Servings** 8 | ★★★★ **Ratings**

Ingredients

¼ cup finely chopped red onion
1/3 cup canola mayonnaise
3 tbsp. 2% reduced-fat Greek yogurt
1 tbsp. cider vinegar
1 tbsp. honey
¼ tsp. salt
¼ tsp. freshly ground black pepper
4 cups coarsely chopped broccoli florets
1/3 cup slivered almonds, toasted
1/3 cup reduced-sugar dried cranberries
4 center-cut bacon slices, cooked and crumbled

Directions

1. In a small bowl, combine the finely chopped red onion, canola mayonnaise, Greek yogurt, cider vinegar, honey, salt, and black pepper. Whisk together until well combined and the dressing is smooth.
2. In a large mixing bowl, add the chopped broccoli florets, toasted slivered almonds, dried cranberries, and crumbled bacon.
3. Pour the prepared dressing over the broccoli mixture. Toss well to coat all the ingredients evenly with the dressing.
4. Cover the bowl with plastic wrap and refrigerate for at least 1 hour to allow the flavors to meld and the broccoli to slightly soften.
5. Before serving, give the salad a gentle toss to redistribute the dressing. Taste and adjust the seasoning if needed.
6. Serve the Cranberry-Almond Broccoli Salad chilled. It can be enjoyed as a side dish or a light lunch option.

Tips: For added crunch, you can include other ingredients like sunflower seeds or chopped celery.

Bacon BBQ Bites

 **Preparation time** 10 MINUTES |  **Cooking time** 25 MINUTES |  **Servings** 2-4 | 

Ingredients

1 tbsp. ground fennel
½ cup brown sugar
1 lb. slab bacon, cut into cubes (1 inch)
1 tsp. black pepper
Salt to taste

Directions

1. Preheat your grill to medium-high heat.
2. In a small bowl, combine the ground fennel, brown sugar, black pepper, and a pinch of salt. Mix well to create the BBQ seasoning.
3. Take the bacon cubes and generously coat them with the BBQ seasoning mixture. Make sure each piece is well coated on all sides.
4. Thread the seasoned bacon cubes onto skewers, leaving a small space between each piece to allow for even cooking.
5. Place the bacon skewers on the preheated grill and cook for about 10-12 minutes, or until the bacon is crispy and slightly charred, turning occasionally to ensure even cooking.
6. Once cooked, remove the bacon BBQ bites from the grill and let them cool for a few minutes before serving.
7. Serve the Bacon BBQ Bites as a delicious appetizer or snack. They can be enjoyed on their own or paired with your favorite dipping sauce.

Tips: You can use wooden or metal skewers for this recipe. If using wooden skewers, make sure to soak them in water for about 30 minutes before threading the bacon to prevent them from burning on the grill.

Fromage Macaroni & Cheese

 **Preparation time** 30 MINUTES |  **Cooking time** 60 MINUTES |  **Servings** 8 | ★★★★ **Ratings**

Ingredients

¼ cup all-purpose flour
½ stick butter
Butter, for greasing
1 lb. cooked elbow macaroni
1 cup grated Parmesan cheese
8 ounces cream cheese
2 cups shredded Monterey Jack cheese
3 tsp. garlic powder
2 tsp. salt
1 tsp. pepper
2 cups shredded Cheddar cheese, divided
3 cups milk

Directions

1. Preheat your oven to 375°F (190°C). Grease a baking dish with butter.
2. In a large saucepan, melt the butter over medium heat. Add the flour and whisk continuously for about 1-2 minutes until the mixture becomes smooth and thick.
3. Gradually pour in the milk while whisking constantly. Continue to cook and whisk until the mixture thickens and comes to a simmer.
4. Reduce the heat to low and add the cream cheese, Parmesan cheese, Monterey Jack cheese, garlic powder, salt, and pepper. Stir until the cheeses are melted and the mixture is smooth and creamy.
5. Remove the saucepan from the heat and add half of the shredded Cheddar cheese. Stir until the cheese is melted and well incorporated into the sauce.
6. In a large mixing bowl, combine the cooked elbow macaroni and the cheese sauce. Mix well until all the macaroni is coated with the sauce.
7. Transfer the macaroni and cheese mixture to the greased baking dish. Sprinkle the remaining shredded Cheddar cheese over the top.
8. Bake in the preheated oven for about 25-30 minutes, or until the cheese is bubbly and golden brown on top.
9. Remove from the oven and let it cool for a few minutes before serving. The Fromage Macaroni and Cheese can be served as a main dish or as a side to accompany your favorite meal.

Tips: Experiment with different types of cheese to customize the flavor of your macaroni and cheese. Gouda, Gruyere, or Fontina are great options to mix with the traditional Cheddar and Monterey Jack cheeses.

Shrimp Cocktail

 **Preparation time** 10 MINUTES |  **Cooking time** 10 MINUTES |  **Servings** 2-4 |  **Ratings**

Ingredients

2 lbs. shrimp, tails on, deveined
Salt and black pepper
1 tsp. Old Bay seasoning
2 tbsp. oil (such as olive oil or vegetable oil)
½ cup ketchup
1 tbsp. lemon juice
2 tbsp. prepared horseradish
1 tbsp. lemon juice
Chopped parsley, for garnish
Hot sauce (optional)

Directions

1. Start by preparing the shrimp. Rinse the shrimp under cold water and pat them dry with a paper towel. Season the shrimp with salt, black pepper, and Old Bay seasoning.
2. Heat the oil in a large skillet or grill pan over medium-high heat. Once the oil is hot, add the seasoned shrimp and cook for 2-3 minutes on each side until they turn pink and opaque. Be careful not to overcook the shrimp, as they can become rubbery. Remove the cooked shrimp from the heat and let them cool.
3. While the shrimp are cooling, prepare the cocktail sauce. In a small bowl, combine the ketchup, lemon juice, prepared horseradish, and additional tablespoon of lemon juice. Mix well until all the ingredients are fully incorporated. Taste and adjust the seasoning if needed.
4. Once the shrimp have cooled, arrange them on a serving platter or individual cocktail glasses. If using individual glasses, place a small bowl with the cocktail sauce in the center.
5. Drizzle the prepared cocktail sauce over the shrimp or serve it on the side. Garnish with chopped parsley for a fresh touch.
6. If desired, offer hot sauce alongside the shrimp cocktail for those who enjoy an extra kick of spiciness.

Tips: Choose large, firm shrimp for the best texture and presentation in your shrimp cocktail. Don't forget to remove the tails before eating the shrimp. You can leave them on for a more elegant presentation or remove them beforehand for easier consumption.

Easy Eggs

 **Preparation time** 10 MINUTES |  **Cooking time** 30 MINUTES |  **Servings** 12 | ★★★★★ **Ratings**

Ingredients

12 hard-boiled eggs, peeled and rinsed

Directions

1. Start by preparing the hard-boiled eggs. Place the eggs in a saucepan and add enough water to cover them completely. Place the saucepan over medium heat and bring the water to a boil.
2. Once the water is boiling, reduce the heat to low and let the eggs simmer for about 10-12 minutes.
3. After the cooking time, remove the saucepan from the heat and carefully drain the hot water. Transfer the eggs to a bowl filled with cold water or run them under cold running water to cool them down quickly.
4. Once the eggs have cooled, gently tap them on a hard surface to crack the shell. Roll the eggs between your hands to loosen the shell, and then peel off the shell starting from the wider end of the egg.
5. Rinse the peeled eggs under cool water to remove any residual shell pieces.
6. The easy eggs are now ready to be served as desired. You can enjoy them as a snack, use them in salads, or prepare deviled eggs or egg salad sandwiches.

Tips: To prevent the eggs from cracking during cooking, you can add a teaspoon of salt or a splash of vinegar to the water before boiling.

Grilled Watermelon juice

 **Preparation time** 10 MINUTES |  **Cooking time** 15 MINUTES |  **Servings** 4 |  Ratings

Ingredients

2 limes

2 tbsp. oil

½ watermelon, sliced into wedges

¼ tsp. pepper flakes

2 tbsp. salt

Directions

1. Preheat your grill to medium-high heat.
2. Squeeze the juice of the limes into a small bowl and set aside.
3. In a separate bowl, combine the oil, pepper flakes, and salt. Mix well to create a marinade.
4. Brush the watermelon wedges with the marinade on all sides, ensuring they are well coated.
5. Place the watermelon wedges directly on the preheated grill and cook for about 2-3 minutes per side. The watermelon should have grill marks and be slightly softened.
6. Remove the grilled watermelon from the grill and let it cool for a few minutes.
7. Cut the grilled watermelon into smaller chunks and transfer them to a blender or food processor.
8. Add the lime juice to the blender and blend until smooth. If needed, you can add a splash of water to achieve the desired consistency.
9. Once blended, strain the watermelon juice through a fine-mesh sieve to remove any pulp or seeds.
10. Serve the grilled watermelon juice chilled or over ice. You can garnish it with a lime slice or mint leaves for added freshness.

Tips: Adjust the amount of salt and pepper flakes according to your taste preferences. You can add more or less depending on how spicy and salty you want the juice to be.

Smoked Mushrooms

 **Preparation time** 5 MINUTES |  **Cooking time** 45 MINUTES |  **Servings** 4-6 |  **Ratings**

Ingredients

4 cups whole baby Portobello mushrooms, cleaned
1 tsp. onion powder
1 tbsp. canola oil
1 tsp. granulated garlic
1 tsp. pepper
1 tsp. salt

Directions

1. Preheat your smoker to a temperature of 225°F (107°C).
2. In a large bowl, combine the mushrooms, onion powder, canola oil, granulated garlic, pepper, and salt. Toss the mushrooms until they are evenly coated with the seasonings.
3. Place the seasoned mushrooms directly on the smoker rack or in a smoker-safe pan or basket.
4. Smoke the mushrooms at 225°F (107°C) for about 1 to 1.5 hours, or until they have reached your desired tenderness. Stir or toss the mushrooms occasionally during the smoking process to ensure even cooking.
5. Once the mushrooms are smoked to perfection, remove them from the smoker and let them cool for a few minutes before serving.
6. Serve the smoked mushrooms as a side dish, add them to salads, sandwiches, or use them as a topping for pizzas and burgers.

Tips: You can use any variety of mushrooms for this recipe, but baby Portobello mushrooms are recommended for their meaty texture and flavor.

SANDWICHES AND SIDES

Delicious Grilled Chicken Sandwich

 **Preparation time** 15 MINUTES |  **Cooking time** 50 MINUTES |  **Servings** 4 | ★★★★ **Ratings**

Ingredients

¼ cup mayonnaise
1 tbsp. Dijon mustard
1 tbsp. honey
4 boneless, skinless chicken breasts
½ tsp. steak seasoning
4 slices American Swiss cheese
4 hamburger buns
2 bacon strips
Lettuce leaves and tomato slices

Directions

1. Preheat the barbecue to medium heat.
2. In a small bowl, mix together mayonnaise, Dijon mustard, and honey. Stir well to create a sauce.
3. Season the chicken breasts with steak seasoning on both sides.
4. Grill the chicken breasts for about 6-8 minutes per side, or until they reach an internal temperature of 165°F (75°C).
5. During the last few minutes of cooking, place a slice of Swiss cheese on each chicken breast to melt.
6. While the chicken grills, cook the bacon in a skillet until crispy. Remove from the pan and place on paper towels to dry.
7. Toast the hamburger buns on the barbecue for a few minutes until slightly golden.
8. Spread the mayonnaise sauce on the bottom half of each bun. Add a grilled chicken breast, crispy bacon, lettuce leaves, and tomato slices.
9. Top with the other half of the bun and serve it hot.

Tips: You can marinate the chicken breasts in your favorite marinade for added flavor before grilling.

Baked Pulled Pork Stuffed Potatoes

 **Preparation time** 10 MINUTES |  **Cooking time** 50 MINUTES |  **Servings** 6 | ★★★★ **Ratings**

Ingredients

4 russet potatoes
Canola oil, as needed
Salt, to taste
2 tbsp. butter, melted
3 cups pulled pork
1 cup Cheddar cheese, shredded
1 cup Mozzarella cheese, shredded
4 tbsp. Barbecue Sweet & Heat BBQ Sauce
Toppings: Sour cream, chopped bacon, chopped green onion

Directions

1. Preheat the oven to 400°F (200°C).
2. Scrub the potatoes clean and pat them dry. Pierce the potatoes several times with a fork.
3. Rub the potatoes with a thin layer of canola oil and sprinkle with salt.
4. Place the potatoes directly on the oven rack and bake for about 50-60 minutes, or until the potatoes are tender and cooked through.
5. Remove the potatoes from the oven and let them cool slightly.
6. Cut each potato in half lengthwise and scoop out the flesh, leaving a thin shell.
7. In a bowl, mash the potato flesh with melted butter. Season with salt to taste.
8. Mix in the pulled pork and half of the shredded Cheddar and Mozzarella cheeses.
9. Spoon the mixture back into the potato shells, dividing it evenly.
10. Drizzle each stuffed potato with Barbecue Sweet & Heat BBQ Sauce.
11. Sprinkle the remaining shredded Cheddar and Mozzarella cheeses on top of each stuffed potato.
12. Place the stuffed potatoes on a baking sheet and return them to the oven. Bake for an additional 10-15 minutes, or until the cheese is melted and bubbly.
13. Remove from the oven and let the potatoes cool slightly.
14. Serve the baked pulled pork stuffed potatoes with a dollop of sour cream, chopped bacon, and chopped green onion on top.

Tips: Customize the toppings with your favorite ingredients such as diced tomatoes, jalapenos, or cilantro.

Baked Pumpkin Seeds

 **Preparation time** 15 MINUTES |  **Cooking time** 45 MINUTES |  **Servings** 10 | ★★★★★ **Ratings**

Ingredients

10 cups pumpkin seeds
4 tsp. melted butter
Java steak dry rub

Directions

1. Preheat the oven to 300°F (150°C).
2. Remove the pumpkin seeds from the pumpkin and rinse them under cold water to remove any pumpkin pulp.
3. Spread the pumpkin seeds out on a baking sheet lined with parchment paper or a silicone baking mat. Let them air dry for about 1 hour, or you can pat them dry with a clean kitchen towel.
4. In a bowl, toss the dried pumpkin seeds with melted butter until they are well-coated.
5. Sprinkle the Java steak dry rub over the pumpkin seeds, ensuring they are evenly seasoned. You can adjust the amount of dry rub according to your taste preference.
6. Spread the seasoned pumpkin seeds in a single layer on the baking sheet.
7. Bake in the preheated oven for about 45-60 minutes, or until the pumpkin seeds are golden brown and crispy. Stir or shake the baking sheet occasionally during baking to ensure even toasting.
8. Remove the baking sheet from the oven and let the pumpkin seeds cool completely before serving.
9. Once cooled, store the baked pumpkin seeds in an airtight container.

Tips: Experiment with flavors by adding a pinch of cayenne pepper for a spicy kick or a sprinkle of cinnamon and sugar for a sweet and savory combination.

Cilantro & Lime Corn

 **Preparation time** 15 MINUTES |  **Cooking time** 15 MINUTES |  **Servings** 4 | ★★★★★ **Ratings**

Ingredients

4 corn cobs
1 tbsp. lime juice
2 tbsp. melted butter
Smoked paprika
1 cup cilantro, chopped

Directions

1. Preheat your grill to medium-high heat.
2. Peel back the husks of the corn cobs, leaving them attached at the base. Remove the silk strands and then fold the husks back over the corn.
3. Place the corn on the grill and cook for about 10-15 minutes, turning occasionally, until the corn is tender and lightly charred.
4. While the corn is grilling, prepare the cilantro and lime mixture. In a small bowl, combine the lime juice and melted butter.
5. Once the corn is cooked, carefully peel back the husks and brush each cob with the cilantro and lime mixture.
6. Sprinkle the corn with smoked paprika to add a smoky and slightly spicy flavor.
7. Return the corn to the grill and cook for another 2-3 minutes, until the butter mixture is melted and the corn is nicely coated.
8. Remove the corn from the grill and sprinkle with chopped cilantro.
9. Serve the cilantro and lime corn hot as a side dish or as part of a barbecue spread.

Tips: For a dairy-free option, substitute the melted butter with olive oil or vegan butter.

Roasted Trail Mix

 **Preparation time** 10 MINUTES |  **Cooking time** 15 MINUTES |  **Servings** 6 | ★★★★★ **Ratings**

Ingredients

1 cup pretzels
1 cup crackers
1 cup mixed nuts and seeds
3 tbsp. butter
1 tsp. smoked paprika

Directions

1. Preheat your oven to 350°F (175°C).
2. In a large mixing bowl, combine the pretzels, crackers, and mixed nuts and seeds.
3. Melt the butter in a small saucepan over low heat.
4. Stir in the smoked paprika until well combined.
5. Pour the melted butter mixture over the pretzel, cracker, and nut mixture. Stir well to coat all the ingredients evenly.
6. Spread the mixture in a single layer on a baking sheet.
7. Place the baking sheet in the preheated oven and roast for about 10-15 minutes, or until the trail mix is golden brown and crispy.
8. Remove from the oven and let it cool completely.
9. Once cooled, transfer the roasted trail mix to an airtight container or individual snack bags for storage.

Tips: Feel free to customize the trail mix by adding other ingredients such as dried fruits, chocolate chips, or coconut flakes.

Grilled Watermelon

 **Preparation time** 5 MINUTES |  **Cooking time** 6 MINUTES |  **Servings** 8 |  **Ratings**

Ingredients

1 watermelon, sliced into thick rounds or wedges
Feta cheese, crumbled
Fresh mint leaves, chopped

Directions

1. Preheat your grill to medium-high heat.
2. Place the watermelon slices directly on the grill grates and cook for about 2-3 minutes per side, or until grill marks form and the watermelon is slightly softened.
3. Remove the grilled watermelon from the grill and let it cool for a few minutes.
4. Transfer the grilled watermelon slices to a serving platter or individual plates.
5. Sprinkle crumbled feta cheese generously over the grilled watermelon.
6. Garnish with freshly chopped mint leaves.
7. Serve immediately and enjoy!

Tips: Make sure your grill grates are clean and well-oiled to prevent sticking.

Grilled Peaches

 **Preparation time** 5 MINUTES |  **Cooking time** 10 MINUTES |  **Servings** 6 | ★★★★★ **Ratings**

Ingredients

½ tbsp. ground cinnamon
3 tbsp. brown sugar
3 peaches, sliced in half and pitted
1 tbsp. melted butter

Directions

1. Preheat your grill to medium heat.
2. In a small bowl, mix together the ground cinnamon and brown sugar.
3. Brush the cut sides of the peaches with melted butter.
4. Sprinkle the cinnamon-sugar mixture evenly over the cut sides of the peaches.
5. Place the peaches, cut side down, directly on the grill grates.
6. Grill for about 4-5 minutes, or until the peaches have grill marks and are slightly softened.
7. Carefully flip the peaches with tongs and grill for an additional 2-3 minutes.
8. Remove the grilled peaches from the grill and serve warm.

Tips: Serve the grilled peaches as they are, or pair them with a scoop of vanilla ice cream or a dollop of whipped cream for a delightful dessert.

Grilled Strawberries

 **Preparation time** 5 MINUTES |  **Cooking time** 5 MINUTES |  **Servings** 4 |  **Ratings**

Ingredients

1 tbsp. lemon juice
4 tbsp. honey
16 strawberries

Directions

1. Preheat your grill to medium heat.
2. In a small bowl, whisk together the lemon juice and honey until well combined.
3. Thread the strawberries onto skewers, about 4 strawberries per skewer.
4. Brush the strawberries with the lemon-honey mixture, coating them evenly.
5. Place the strawberry skewers directly on the grill grates.
6. Grill for about 2-3 minutes per side, or until the strawberries are slightly softened and grill marks appear.
7. Carefully remove the strawberry skewers from the grill and transfer them to a serving plate.
8. Serve the grilled strawberries as they are or pair them with a scoop of vanilla ice cream, yogurt, or whipped cream.

Tips: Experiment with different flavor variations by adding a sprinkle of cinnamon, a drizzle of balsamic glaze, or a sprinkle of chopped mint leaves before grilling.

Smoked Crepes

 **Preparation time** 10 MINUTES |  **Cooking time** 2 HOURS |  **Servings** 6 | ★★★★ **Ratings**

Ingredients

2-lb. apples, sliced into wedges
Apple butter seasoning
½ cup apple juice
2 tsp. lemon juice
5 tbsp. butter
¾ tsp. cinnamon, ground
2 tbsp. brown sugar
¾ tsp. cornstarch
6 crepes

Directions

1. Preheat your smoker to a low temperature, around 225°F (107°C).
2. In a bowl, combine the sliced apples, apple butter seasoning, apple juice, and lemon juice. Toss until the apples are coated evenly.
3. Transfer the apple mixture to a smoker-safe pan or aluminum foil tray.
4. Place the pan of apples in the smoker and close the lid. Let the apples smoke for about 1 hour, or until they are tender and infused with smoky flavor.
5. While the apples are smoking, prepare the cinnamon-brown sugar sauce. In a saucepan over medium heat, melt the butter. Stir in the ground cinnamon, brown sugar, and cornstarch. Cook until the mixture thickens slightly, stirring occasionally. Remove from heat and set aside.
6. Once the apples are smoked and tender, remove them from the smoker and transfer to a serving dish.
7. Warm the crepes according to package instructions or your preferred method.
8. To serve, place a spoonful of the smoked apples onto a warmed crepe and roll it up. Repeat with the remaining crepes and smoked apples.
9. Drizzle the cinnamon-brown sugar sauce over the smoked crepes.
10. Serve immediately and enjoy the smoky, sweet flavors of the smoked apple-filled crepes.

Tips: If you don't have apple butter seasoning, you can substitute with a blend of cinnamon, nutmeg, and allspice.

Apple Crumble

 **Preparation time** 30 MINUTES |  **Cooking time** 1 H 30 MINUTES |  **Servings** 8 |  **Ratings**

Ingredients

2 cups + 2 tbsp. all-purpose flour, divided
½ cup shortening
Pinch of salt
¼ cup cold water
8 cups apples, sliced into cubes
3 tsp. lemon juice
½ tsp. ground nutmeg
1 tsp. apple butter seasoning
1/8 tsp. ground cloves
1 tsp. cinnamon
¼ cup butter

Directions

1. Preheat your oven to 375°F (190°C).
2. In a mixing bowl, combine 2 cups of flour, shortening, and salt. Use a pastry cutter or your fingers to cut the shortening into the flour until it resembles coarse crumbs.
3. Gradually add cold water to the flour mixture, tossing with a fork, until the dough comes together. Form the dough into a ball.
4. On a lightly floured surface, roll out the dough to fit the size of your baking dish. Place the rolled-out dough into the bottom of the baking dish, pressing it against the sides.
5. In a large bowl, combine the sliced apples, lemon juice, nutmeg, apple butter seasoning, ground cloves, and cinnamon. Toss until the apples are coated evenly.
6. Pour the apple mixture onto the prepared crust in the baking dish, spreading it out evenly.
7. In a separate bowl, mix together the remaining 2 tablespoons of flour and the butter until crumbly. Sprinkle this crumb mixture over the apples.
8. Place the apple crumble in the preheated oven and bake for 40-45 minutes, or until the apples are tender and the crumble topping is golden brown.
9. Remove from the oven and let it cool slightly before serving.
10. Serve warm with a scoop of vanilla ice cream or a dollop of whipped cream, if desired.

Tips: Feel free to add nuts such as chopped walnuts or pecans to the crumble topping for extra crunch.

Grilled Pork Burgers

 **Preparation time** 15 MINUTES |  **Cooking time** 1 HOUR |  **Servings** 4-6 |  **Ratings**

Ingredients

1 beaten egg
¾ cup soft bread crumbs
¾ cup grated Parmesan cheese
1 tbsp. dried parsley
1 tsp. dried basil
½ tsp. salt, to taste
½ tsp. garlic powder
¼ tsp. pepper, to taste
2 lbs. ground pork
6 hamburger buns
Toppings: Lettuce leaves, sliced tomato, sliced sweet onion
Lettuce leaves
Sliced tomato
Sliced sweet onion.

Directions

1. In a large bowl, combine the beaten egg, bread crumbs, grated Parmesan cheese, dried parsley, dried basil, salt, garlic powder, and pepper.
2. Add the ground pork to the bowl and mix well until all the ingredients are evenly incorporated.
3. Divide the pork mixture into 6 equal portions and shape each portion into a patty, about ½-inch thick.
4. Preheat your grill to medium-high heat.
5. Place the pork patties on the preheated grill and cook for about 4-5 minutes per side, or until the internal temperature reaches 160°F (71°C) on a meat thermometer.
6. While the patties are grilling, lightly toast the hamburger buns on the grill.
7. Once the patties are cooked through, remove them from the grill and let them rest for a few minutes.
8. Assemble the burgers by placing a cooked pork patty on each toasted bun.
9. Top with lettuce leaves, sliced tomato, and sliced sweet onion, or any other desired toppings.
10. Serve the grilled pork burgers immediately and enjoy!

Tips: Feel free to customize the toppings based on your preferences. Add cheese, avocado, or bacon for extra flavor.

BLT Sandwich

 **Preparation time** 15 MINUTES |  **Cooking time** 35 MINUTES |  **Servings** 4-6 | ★★★★★ **Ratings**

Ingredients

8 slices of bacon
½ romaine heart
Sliced tomato
4 slices of sandwich bread
Tablespoons of mayonnaise
Salted butter
Sea salt, to taste
Pepper, to taste

Directions

1. Cook the bacon in a skillet over medium heat until crispy. Remove the bacon from the skillet and drain on paper towels.
2. Wash and dry the romaine heart, then slice it into thin strips.
3. Slice the tomato into thick slices.
4. Lightly toast the slices of bread.
5. Spread a thin layer of mayonnaise on one side of each toasted bread slice.
6. Place the romaine strips on two of the bread slices, followed by the sliced tomato.
7. Season the tomato slices with a pinch of sea salt and pepper.
8. Lay the cooked bacon slices on top of the tomato.
9. Place the remaining two bread slices, mayonnaise side down, on top of the bacon to complete the sandwiches.
10. Spread a thin layer of butter on the outer sides of each sandwich.
11. Heat a skillet over medium heat and place the sandwiches in the skillet.
12. Cook for about 2-3 minutes on each side, or until the bread is golden brown and crispy.
13. Remove the sandwiches from the skillet and let them cool for a few minutes before slicing in half.
14. Serve the delicious BLT sandwiches while still warm and enjoy!

Tips: Serve the sandwiches with a side of potato chips, coleslaw, or a fresh green salad.

Sweet Pull-Apart Rolls

 **Preparation time** 5 MINUTES |  **Cooking time** 10-12 MINUTES |  **Servings** 8 | ★★★★★ **Ratings**

Ingredients

1/3 cup vegetable oil
¼ cup warm water
¼ cup sugar
2 tbsp. active dry yeast
1 egg
3 ½ cups all-purpose flour, divided
½ tsp. salt
Cooking spray, as needed

Directions

1. In a large mixing bowl, combine the vegetable oil, warm water, and sugar. Stir until the sugar is dissolved.
2. Sprinkle the yeast over the mixture and let it sit for about 5 minutes, or until it becomes frothy.
3. Add the egg to the bowl and mix well.
4. Gradually add 3 cups of the all-purpose flour and the salt to the mixture. Stir until the dough starts to come together.
5. Turn the dough out onto a lightly floured surface and knead it for about 5-7 minutes, or until it becomes smooth and elastic. Add more flour as needed if the dough is too sticky.
6. Place the dough in a greased bowl and cover it with a clean kitchen towel. Let it rise in a warm place for about 1 hour, or until it doubles in size.
7. Preheat the oven to 375°F (190°C) and lightly grease a baking dish.
8. Punch down the dough to release the air, then divide it into small portions and shape them into balls.
9. Arrange the dough balls in the greased baking dish, leaving a little space between each one.
10. Cover the baking dish with the kitchen towel and let the dough rise for another 30 minutes.
11. Bake the rolls in the preheated oven for 20-25 minutes, or until they turn golden brown and sound hollow when tapped.
12. Remove the rolls from the oven and let them cool slightly before serving.

Tips: For added flavor, you can incorporate spices like cinnamon or nutmeg into the dough.

Pretzels

 **Preparation time** 30 MINUTES |  **Cooking time** 1 H 30 MINUTES |  **Servings** 6 |  **Ratings**

Ingredients

1 packet (2 ¼ teaspoons) active instant dry yeast
1 tbsp. sugar
1 ½ cups warm water
2 oz melted butter
4 ½ cups all-purpose flour
Cooking spray
½ cup baking soda
10 cups boiling water
Egg yolks, beaten
Sea salt

Directions

1. In a large mixing bowl, combine the yeast, sugar, and warm water. Let it sit for about 5 minutes until the mixture becomes foamy.
2. Add the melted butter to the yeast mixture and stir to combine.
3. Gradually add the all-purpose flour to the mixture, stirring well after each addition, until a soft dough forms.
4. Turn the dough out onto a floured surface and knead it for about 5 minutes until it becomes smooth and elastic.
5. Place the dough in a greased bowl and cover it with a clean kitchen towel. Let it rise in a warm place for about 1 hour, or until it doubles in size.
6. Preheat the oven to 450°F (230°C) and line a baking sheet with parchment paper. Lightly grease the parchment paper with cooking spray.
7. In a large pot, bring 10 cups of water to a boil. Once the water is boiling, carefully add the baking soda (be cautious as it may cause the water to foam).
8. Divide the dough into small portions and shape them into pretzel shapes or any desired shape.
9. Carefully place the shaped pretzels, one or two at a time, into the boiling water with baking soda. Boil them for about 30 seconds on each side, then remove them using a slotted spoon and place them on the prepared baking sheet.
10. Brush the pretzels with beaten egg yolks and sprinkle them with sea salt.
11. Bake the pretzels in the preheated oven for about 12-15 minutes, or until they turn golden brown.
12. Remove the pretzels from the oven and let them cool slightly before serving.

Tips: These homemade pretzels are best enjoyed on the day they are made, but you can store any left-overs in an airtight container at room temperature for up to 2 days.

Fruits on Bread

 **Preparation time** 30 MINUTES |  **Cooking time** 1 H 30 MINUTES |  **Servings** 8 | ★★★★ **Ratings**

Ingredients

½ cup milk
1 tsp. sugar
¼ cup warm water
2 ½ tsp. active dry yeast (instant)
2 ½ cups all-purpose flour
2 tbsp. melted butter
1 egg
½ tsp. vanilla extract
½ tsp. salt
Vegetable oil
1 tbsp. ground cinnamon
Chocolate spread
Sliced fruits (such as strawberries, bananas, or berries)

Directions

1. In a small saucepan, heat the milk until warm but not boiling. Remove from heat and stir in the sugar until dissolved.
2. In a small bowl, combine the warm water and yeast. Let it sit for about 5 minutes until it becomes frothy.
3. In a large mixing bowl, combine the flour, melted butter, egg, vanilla extract, and salt. Pour in the milk mixture and yeast mixture. Stir until a soft dough forms.
4. Turn the dough out onto a floured surface and knead it for about 5 minutes until it becomes smooth and elastic. Shape the dough into a ball.
5. Lightly oil a clean bowl and place the dough in it, turning it to coat with oil. Cover the bowl with a clean kitchen towel and let the dough rise in a warm place for about 1 hour, or until it doubles in size.
6. Preheat the oven to 375°F (190°C) and line a baking sheet with parchment paper.
7. Punch down the risen dough and transfer it to a floured surface. Roll out the dough into a rectangle about ½-inch thick.
8. Spread the chocolate spread evenly over the dough, leaving a small border around the edges.
9. Sprinkle the ground cinnamon over the chocolate spread.
10. Arrange the sliced fruits over the chocolate spread, pressing them slightly into the dough.
11. Starting from one of the longer edges, roll up the dough tightly into a log shape. Pinch the seams to seal.
12. Using a sharp knife, slice the rolled dough into individual pieces, about 1 inch thick.
13. Place the sliced dough onto the prepared baking sheet, leaving some space between each piece.
14. Bake in the preheated oven for about 15-18 minutes, or until the bread is golden brown and cooked through.
15. Remove from the oven and let it cool slightly before serving.

Tips: Feel free to experiment with different spreads or fillings, such as Nutella, peanut butter, or jam.

Ground Turkey Burgers

 **Preparation time** 15 MINUTES |  **Cooking time** 50 MINUTES |  **Servings** 6 | ★★★★ **Ratings**

Ingredients

1 beaten egg
2/3 cup breadcrumbs
½ cup chopped celery
¼ cup chopped onion
1 tbsp. minced parsley
1 tsp. Worcestershire sauce
1 tsp. dried oregano
½ tsp. salt (or to taste)
¼ tsp. pepper
1-¼ lbs. lean ground turkey
6 hamburger buns
Optional toppings: sliced tomato, sliced onion, lettuce leaves

Directions

1. In a large mixing bowl, combine the beaten egg, breadcrumbs, chopped celery, chopped onion, minced parsley, Worcestershire sauce, dried oregano, salt, and pepper.
2. Add the ground turkey to the bowl and mix all the ingredients together until well combined. Be careful not to overmix, as this can result in tough burgers.
3. Divide the turkey mixture into 6 equal portions and shape each portion into a patty. Ensure the patties are of uniform thickness for even cooking.
4. Preheat your grill or stovetop griddle over medium heat. If using a grill, lightly oil the grates to prevent sticking.
5. Place the turkey patties on the preheated grill or griddle. Cook for about 5-6 minutes per side, or until the internal temperature reaches 165°F (74°C) and the patties are cooked through.
6. While the patties are cooking, you can toast the hamburger buns on the grill or in a toaster if desired.
7. Once the patties are cooked, remove them from the heat and let them rest for a few minutes.
8. Assemble the burgers by placing each turkey patty on a toasted bun. Add your preferred toppings, such as sliced tomato, sliced onion, and lettuce leaves.
9. Serve the ground turkey burgers immediately and enjoy!

Tips: Feel free to add cheese slices or other toppings like avocado or bacon for added flavor.

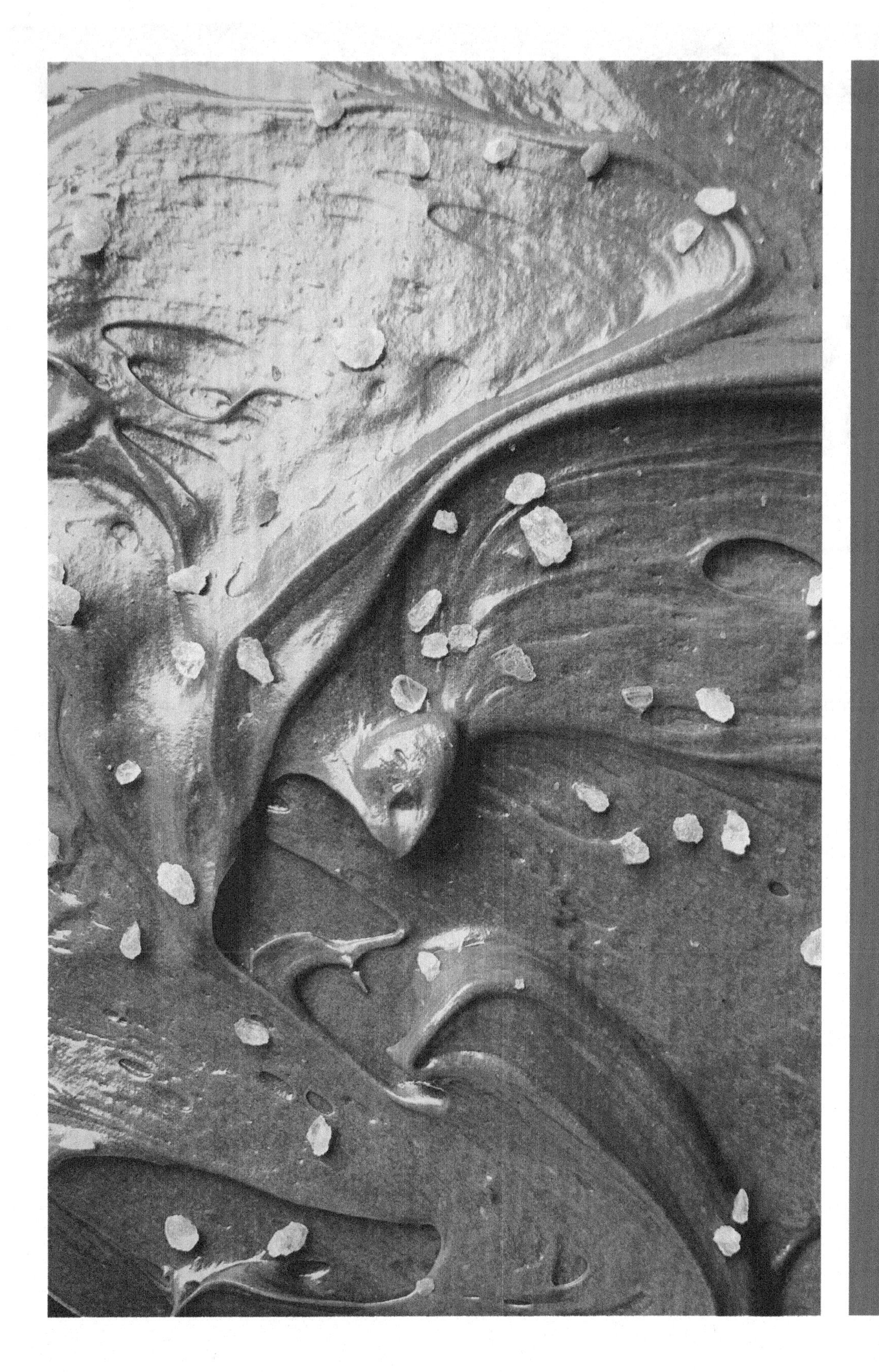

DESSERT

Grilled Pineapple with Chocolate Sauce

 **Preparation time** 10 MINUTES |  **Cooking time** 25 MINUTES |  **Servings** 8 |  **Ratings**

Ingredients

1 pineapple
8 oz bittersweet chocolate chips
½ cup spiced rum
½ cup whipping cream
2 tbsp light brown sugar

Directions

1. Preheat your grill to medium-high heat.
2. Cut the pineapple into slices or wedges, removing the skin and core.
3. In a small saucepan, combine the chocolate chips, spiced rum, whipping cream, and light brown sugar. Place the saucepan over low heat and stir continuously until the chocolate chips have melted and the sauce is smooth. Remove from heat.
4. Brush the pineapple slices with a little olive oil or melted butter to prevent sticking.
5. Place the pineapple slices directly on the grill grates and cook for about 4-5 minutes per side, or until grill marks appear and the pineapple is heated through.
6. Remove the grilled pineapple from the grill and place on a serving platter.
7. Drizzle the warm chocolate sauce over the grilled pineapple slices.
8. Serve immediately and enjoy!

Tips: Serve the grilled pineapple with a scoop of vanilla ice cream or whipped cream for an extra delicious treat.

Caramel Bananas

 **Preparation time** 15 MINUTES |  **Cooking time** 15 MINUTES |  **Servings** 4 | ★★★★★ **Ratings**

Ingredients

1/3 cup chopped pecans
½ cup sweetened condensed milk
4 slightly green bananas
½ cup brown sugar
2 tbsp. corn syrup
½ cup butter

Directions

1. Preheat your grill to medium heat.
2. In a small saucepan, melt the butter over medium heat. Add the brown sugar and corn syrup, stirring until the sugar has dissolved and the mixture is smooth.
3. Stir in the chopped pecans and cook for an additional 1-2 minutes, until the pecans are coated in the caramel sauce. Remove from heat.
4. Peel the bananas and slice them in half lengthwise.
5. Place the banana halves on a sheet of aluminum foil. Drizzle the sweetened condensed milk over the bananas, followed by the caramel pecan sauce.
6. Wrap the bananas securely in the foil, creating a packet.
7. Place the foil packet on the grill and cook for about 10-15 minutes, or until the bananas are tender and caramelized.
8. Carefully remove the foil packet from the grill and let it cool slightly before opening.
9. Serve the caramel bananas warm, either on their own or with a scoop of vanilla ice cream.

Tips: You can also add a sprinkle of cinnamon or a splash of vanilla extract to enhance the flavor of the caramel sauce.

Grilled Layered Cake

 **Preparation time** 10 MINUTES |  **Cooking time** 14 MINUTES |  **Servings** 6 | ★★★★★ **Ratings**

Ingredients

2 pound cakes
3 cups whipped cream
¼ cup melted butter
1 cup blueberries
1 cup raspberries
1 cup sliced strawberries

Directions

1. Preheat your grill to medium heat.
2. Slice the pound cakes horizontally into two equal layers, creating a total of four layers.
3. Brush each cake layer with melted butter on both sides.
4. Place the cake layers on the grill and cook for about 1-2 minutes per side, until they are lightly toasted and have grill marks. Remove from the grill and let them cool slightly.
5. Take one grilled cake layer and spread a generous amount of whipped cream on top.
6. Add a layer of blueberries, raspberries, and sliced strawberries on top of the whipped cream.
7. Place another grilled cake layer on top of the fruit layer and repeat the process of spreading whipped cream and adding fruit.
8. Repeat this process with the remaining cake layers, whipped cream, and fruit, creating a layered cake.
9. Once the cake is assembled, you can garnish the top with additional fruit if desired.
10. Chill the cake in the refrigerator for at least 30 minutes before serving to allow the flavors to meld together.

Tips: Feel free to add a drizzle of chocolate sauce or sprinkle of powdered sugar for added sweetness and decoration.

Nectarine & Nutella Sundae

 **Preparation time** 10 MINUTES |  **Cooking time** 25 MINUTES |  **Servings** 4 | ★★★★★ **Ratings**

Ingredients

2 nectarines, halved and pitted
2 tsp. honey
4 tbsp. Nutella
4 scoops vanilla ice cream
¼ cup pecans, chopped
Whipped cream, for topping
4 cherries, for topping

Directions

1. Preheat your grill to medium heat.
2. Brush the cut side of the nectarines with honey.
3. Place the nectarines on the grill, cut side down, and cook for about 2-3 minutes, until they are slightly caramelized and have grill marks. Flip the nectarines and cook for an additional 2-3 minutes. Remove from the grill.
4. Spread 1 tablespoon of Nutella on each nectarine half, ensuring the cut side is fully covered.
5. Place a scoop of vanilla ice cream on top of each nectarine half.
6. Sprinkle the chopped pecans over the ice cream and drizzle with additional honey if desired.
7. Top each sundae with a dollop of whipped cream and a cherry.
8. Serve immediately and enjoy!

Tips: Feel free to add extra toppings such as chocolate sauce, caramel sauce, or shredded coconut for added flavor and texture.

Smoked Pumpkin Pie

 **Preparation time** 10 MINUTES |  **Cooking time** 50 MINUTES |  **Servings** 8 | ★★★★★ **Ratings**

Ingredients

1tbsp cinnamon
1-½ tbsp pumpkin pie spice
15oz can pumpkin
14oz can sweetened condensed milk.
2beaten eggs
1unbaked pie shell
Topping: whipped cream

Directions

1. Preheat your smoker to 325°F (163°C) using indirect heat.
2. In a mixing bowl, combine the cinnamon, pumpkin pie spice, pumpkin, sweetened condensed milk, and beaten eggs. Stir until well combined.
3. Pour the pumpkin mixture into the unbaked pie shell, spreading it evenly.
4. Place the pie on the smoker grate and close the lid. Smoke the pie for about 1 to 1 ½ hours, or until the center is set and a toothpick inserted into the center comes out clean.
5. Remove the pie from the smoker and let it cool completely on a wire rack.
6. Once cooled, refrigerate the pie for at least 2 hours or overnight to allow it to fully set.
7. Before serving, top the smoked pumpkin pie with whipped cream.
8. Slice and serve the delicious smoked pumpkin pie as a delightful dessert.

Tips: For added texture and flavor, consider sprinkling some crushed graham crackers or chopped nuts on top of the whipped cream.

Smoked Nut Mix

 **Preparation time** 15 MINUTES |  **Cooking time** 20 MINUTES |  **Servings** 12 | ★★★★★ **Ratings**

Ingredients

3 cups mixed nuts (pecans, peanuts, almonds, etc.)
½ tbsp. brown sugar
1 tbsp. dried thyme
¼ tbsp. mustard powder
1 tbsp. extra-virgin olive oil

Directions

1. Preheat your smoker to 225°F (107°C) using indirect heat.
2. In a mixing bowl, combine the mixed nuts, brown sugar, dried thyme, and mustard powder. Toss the nuts until they are evenly coated with the seasonings.
3. Drizzle the extra-virgin olive oil over the nuts and toss again to ensure all the nuts are coated with the oil.
4. Spread the seasoned nuts in a single layer on a smoker-safe tray or pan.
5. Place the tray of nuts on the smoker grate and close the lid. Smoke the nuts for about 1 to 2 hours, or until they have absorbed the smoky flavor and become golden brown. Stir the nuts occasionally during the smoking process to ensure even smoking.
6. Once the nuts are smoked to your desired level, remove them from the smoker and let them cool completely.
7. Transfer the smoked nut mix to an airtight container for storage.

Tips: Experiment with different types of nuts or a combination of your favorites to create a unique flavor profile.

Grilled Peaches & Cream

 **Preparation time** 15 MINUTES |  **Cooking time** 8 MINUTES |  **Servings** 8 | ★★★★★ **Ratings**

Ingredients

4 peaches, halved and pitted
1 tbsp. vegetable oil
2 tbsp. clover honey
1 cup cream cheese, softened
Honey and nuts for garnish (optional)

Directions

1. Preheat your grill to medium-high heat.
2. Brush the cut side of each peach half with vegetable oil to prevent sticking.
3. Place the peaches on the grill, cut side down. Grill for about 3-4 minutes, or until the peaches have grill marks and are slightly softened.
4. Flip the peaches over and brush the tops with honey. Grill for an additional 2-3 minutes, or until the peaches are tender.
5. While the peaches are grilling, prepare the cream cheese by combining it with honey and nuts (if desired) in a small bowl. Mix well until the ingredients are evenly incorporated.
6. Remove the grilled peaches from the grill and let them cool slightly.
7. Serve the grilled peaches with a dollop of the honey and nut cream cheese mixture on top.
8. Optionally, drizzle some additional honey and sprinkle some nuts on top for garnish.

Tips: For an extra special touch, you can serve the grilled peaches and cream with a scoop of vanilla ice cream or a sprinkle of granola.

Pellet Grill Apple Crisp

 **Preparation time** 20 MINUTES |  **Cooking time** 60 MINUTES |  **Servings** 15 | ★★★★ **Ratings**

Ingredients

Apples:
10 large apples, peeled, cored, and sliced
½ cup all-purpose flour
1 cup dark brown sugar
½ tbsp. ground cinnamon
½ cup sliced butter
Crisp Topping:
3 cups old-fashioned oatmeal
1 ½ cups softened salted butter
1 ½ tbsp. ground cinnamon
2 cups brown sugar

Directions

1. Preheat your pellet grill to 350°F (175°C).
2. In a large bowl, combine the sliced apples, flour, dark brown sugar, and ground cinnamon. Toss until the apples are coated evenly.
3. Pour the apple mixture into a greased 9x13-inch baking dish. Arrange the sliced butter over the top of the apples.
4. In another bowl, mix together the oatmeal, softened butter, ground cinnamon, and brown sugar until well combined. The mixture should be crumbly.
5. Sprinkle the oatmeal mixture evenly over the apples, covering them completely.
6. Place the baking dish on the preheated pellet grill and bake for about 40-45 minutes, or until the apples are tender and the crisp topping is golden brown and crispy.
7. Remove from the grill and let it cool for a few minutes before serving.

Tips: Serve the pellet grill apple crisp warm with a scoop of vanilla ice cream or a dollop of whipped cream for a delicious dessert.

Spicy Barbecue Pecans

 **Preparation time** 15 MINUTES |  **Cooking time** 1 HOUR |  **Servings** 2 |  **Ratings**

Ingredients

16 ounces raw pecan halves
3 tbsp. melted butter
2 ½ tsp. garlic powder
1 tsp. onion powder
1 tsp. black pepper
2 tsp. salt
1 tsp. dried thyme

Directions

1. Preheat your grill to medium heat.
2. In a large bowl, combine the melted butter, garlic powder, onion powder, black pepper, salt, and dried thyme. Stir until well mixed.
3. Add the pecan halves to the bowl and toss them in the butter and spice mixture until they are coated evenly.
4. Grease a grill basket or aluminum foil with butter to prevent the pecans from sticking.
5. Place the coated pecans in the grill basket or on the greased foil in a single layer.
6. Grill the pecans over medium heat, stirring occasionally, for about 10-15 minutes or until they are lightly browned and fragrant. Be careful not to burn them.
7. Remove the pecans from the grill and let them cool completely before serving.

Tips: You can adjust the amount of spices according to your taste preferences. If you prefer a milder flavor, reduce the amount of garlic powder and black pepper.

Barbecue Blackberry Pie

 **Preparation time** 10 MINUTES |  **Cooking time** 40 MINUTES |  **Servings** 8 |  **Ratings**

Ingredients

Butter, for greasing
½ cup all-purpose flour
½ cup milk
2 pints blackberries
2 cups sugar, divided
1 box refrigerated pie crusts
1 stick melted butter
1 stick butter
Vanilla ice cream (for serving)

Directions

1. Preheat your barbecue grill to medium heat.
2. Grease a pie dish with butter to prevent sticking.
3. In a mixing bowl, combine the all-purpose flour, milk, and 1 cup of sugar. Stir until well combined and smooth.
4. Gently fold in the blackberries until they are evenly coated with the flour mixture.
5. Roll out one pie crust and place it into the greased pie dish. Trim any excess crust hanging over the edges.
6. Pour the blackberry mixture into the pie crust.
7. Roll out the second pie crust and place it on top of the blackberry filling. Seal the edges by pressing the top and bottom crusts together. Create vents in the top crust to allow steam to escape.
8. Place the pie dish on the grill and close the lid. Cook for about 45 minutes to 1 hour, or until the crust is golden brown and the filling is bubbly.
9. While the pie is still hot, brush the melted butter over the top crust. Sprinkle the remaining 1 cup of sugar evenly over the buttered crust.
10. Let the pie cool for a few minutes before serving. Serve warm with a scoop of vanilla ice cream on top.

Tips: You can use homemade or store-bought pie crusts for this recipe.

S'mores Dip

 **Preparation time** / |  **Cooking time** 15 MINUTES |  **Servings** 6-8 | 

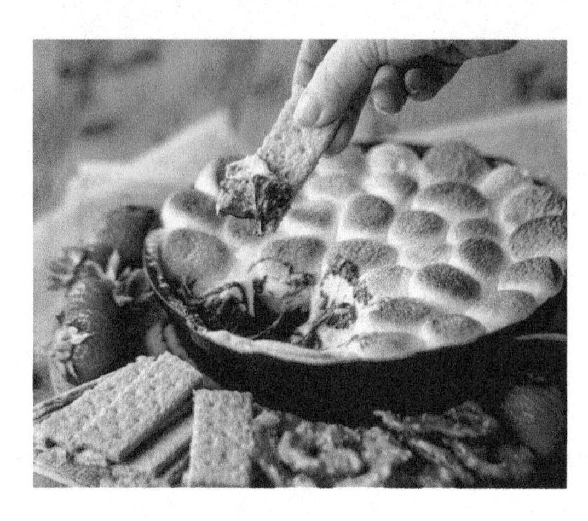

Ingredients

12 ounces semisweet chocolate chips
¼ cup milk
2 tbsp. melted salted butter
16 ounces marshmallows
Apple wedges (for dipping)
Graham crackers (for dipping)

Directions

1. Preheat your barbecue grill to medium heat.
2. In a heatproof skillet or oven-safe dish, combine the semisweet chocolate chips, milk, and melted butter.
3. Place the skillet or dish on the grill and close the lid. Heat until the chocolate chips are melted and the mixture is smooth, stirring occasionally to ensure even melting.
4. Once the chocolate mixture is melted and smooth, remove the skillet or dish from the grill.
5. Carefully arrange the marshmallows on top of the melted chocolate in a single layer, covering the entire surface.
6. Return the skillet or dish to the grill and close the lid. Cook for a few minutes until the marshmallows are golden brown and toasted. Keep a close eye on them to prevent burning.
7. Once the marshmallows are toasted to your desired level, remove the skillet or dish from the grill.
8. Serve the s'mores dip immediately with apple wedges and graham crackers for dipping.

Tips: You can also serve the dip with other dippable items like pretzels or strawberries.

Bacon Chocolate Chip Cookies

 **Preparation time** 10 MINUTES |  **Cooking time** 30 MINUTES |  **Servings** 24 | ★★★★ **Ratings**

Ingredients

8 slices of cooked and crumbled bacon
2 ½ tsp. apple cider vinegar
1 tsp. vanilla extract
2 cups semisweet chocolate chips
2 eggs, at room temperature
1 ½ tsp. baking soda
1 cup granulated sugar
½ tsp. salt
2 ¾ cups all-purpose flour
1 cup light brown sugar
1 ½ sticks (12 tbsp.) softened butter

Directions

1. Preheat your barbecue grill to medium heat.
2. In a large mixing bowl, cream together the softened butter, granulated sugar, and light brown sugar until light and fluffy.
3. Add the eggs, one at a time, beating well after each addition. Stir in the apple cider vinegar and vanilla extract.
4. In a separate bowl, whisk together the all-purpose flour, baking soda, and salt.
5. Gradually add the dry ingredients to the butter mixture, mixing until just combined.
6. Stir in the chocolate chips and crumbled bacon, ensuring they are evenly distributed throughout the dough.
7. Drop rounded tablespoonfuls of dough onto a greased or lined baking sheet.
8. Place the baking sheet on the grill and close the lid. Bake for about 10-12 minutes, or until the cookies are golden brown around the edges.
9. Remove the baking sheet from the grill and let the cookies cool for a few minutes on the sheet before transferring them to a wire rack to cool completely.

Tips: Make sure the bacon is cooked until crispy and then crumble it into small pieces.

Cinnamon Sugar Pumpkin Seeds

 **Preparation time** 12 MINUTES |  **Cooking time** 30 MINUTES |  **Servings** 8-12 | ★★★★★ **Ratings**

Ingredients

Seeds from a pumpkin
2 tbsp. sugar
1 tsp. cinnamon
2 tbsp. melted butter

Directions

1. Preheat your barbecue grill to medium heat.
2. Remove the seeds from a pumpkin and separate them from any pumpkin pulp or fibers. Rinse the seeds in a colander under cold water to remove any remaining pulp.
3. Spread the pumpkin seeds on a clean kitchen towel or paper towels and pat them dry thoroughly.
4. In a small bowl, combine the sugar and cinnamon, and mix well.
5. Place the dried pumpkin seeds in a medium-sized bowl. Pour the melted butter over the seeds and toss to coat them evenly.
6. Sprinkle the cinnamon sugar mixture over the butter-coated pumpkin seeds. Stir well to ensure that the seeds are evenly coated with the cinnamon sugar mixture.
7. Transfer the coated pumpkin seeds to a grill basket or a piece of aluminum foil that has been greased with cooking spray or butter.
8. Place the grill basket or foil with the pumpkin seeds on the preheated grill. Close the lid and grill for about 10-15 minutes, or until the seeds are toasted and golden brown, stirring occasionally to prevent burning.
9. Remove the pumpkin seeds from the grill and let them cool completely before serving.

Tips: Make sure to remove any excess moisture from the pumpkin seeds before coating them with butter to ensure crispiness.

Apple Cobbler

 **Preparation time** 20 MINUTES |  **Cooking time** 1 H 30 MINUTES |  **Servings** 8 |  **Ratings**

Ingredients

8 Granny Smith apples, peeled, cored, and sliced
1 cup sugar
2 eggs
2 tsp. baking powder
2 cups plain flour
1 ½ cups sugar

Directions

1. Preheat your barbecue grill to medium heat.
2. In a large bowl, combine the sliced apples and 1 cup of sugar. Mix well to coat the apples with sugar.
3. In a separate bowl, beat the eggs. Add the baking powder and plain flour to the beaten eggs and mix until a dough-like consistency is formed.
4. Roll out the dough on a floured surface to fit the size of your baking dish.
5. Grease a baking dish and transfer the sliced apples into it. Spread them evenly.
6. Sprinkle the remaining 1 ½ cups of sugar over the apples.
7. Place the rolled-out dough on top of the apples, covering them completely.
8. Transfer the baking dish to the preheated grill. Close the lid and grill for about 30-40 minutes, or until the apple filling is bubbly and the crust is golden brown.
9. Remove the apple cobbler from the grill and let it cool for a few minutes before serving.

Tips: Serve the apple cobbler warm with a scoop of vanilla ice cream or a dollop of whipped cream for a delicious treat.

Chocolate-Hazelnut & Strawberry Grilled Pizza

 **Preparation time** 10 MINUTES |  **Cooking time** 6 MINUTES |  **Servings** 4 | 

Ingredients

2 tbsp. all-purpose flour, plus more as needed
½ store-bought pizza dough (about 8 ounces)
1 tbsp. canola oil
1 cup sliced fresh strawberries
1 tbsp. sugar
½ cup chocolate-hazelnut spread

Directions

1. Preheat your barbecue grill to medium heat.
2. Sprinkle the flour onto a clean surface. Roll out the pizza dough on the floured surface to your desired thickness, shaping it into a round or rectangular shape.
3. Brush the rolled-out dough with canola oil to prevent sticking.
4. Place the dough directly onto the preheated grill. Close the lid and grill for about 2-3 minutes, or until the bottom is lightly charred and the dough is cooked through. Flip the dough and grill for an additional 2-3 minutes on the other side.
5. In a small bowl, combine the sliced strawberries and sugar. Toss gently to coat the strawberries with sugar and let them macerate for a few minutes.
6. Remove the grilled pizza dough from the grill and transfer it to a serving plate or cutting board.
7. Spread the chocolate-hazelnut spread evenly over the grilled dough, leaving a small border around the edges.
8. Arrange the macerated strawberries on top of the chocolate-hazelnut spread.
9. Cut the dessert pizza into slices and serve warm.

Tips: If the dough sticks to the grill, lightly sprinkle more flour on both sides of the dough before grilling. Feel free to add other toppings such as sliced bananas, shredded coconut, or chopped nuts to customize your dessert pizza.

Ice Cream Bread

 **Preparation time** 10 MINUTES |  **Cooking time** 1 HOUR |  **Servings** 12-16 |  **Ratings**

Ingredients

1 ½ quarts full-fat butter pecan ice cream, softened
1 tsp. salt
2 cups semisweet chocolate chips
1 cup sugar
1 stick melted butter
Butter, for greasing
4 cups self-rising flour

Directions

1. Preheat your barbecue grill to medium heat.
2. In a large mixing bowl, combine the softened butter pecan ice cream, salt, chocolate chips, sugar, and melted butter. Mix well until all ingredients are evenly incorporated.
3. Gradually add the self-rising flour to the ice cream mixture, stirring gently until a thick dough forms. Be careful not to overmix.
4. Grease a loaf pan or baking dish with butter to prevent sticking. Transfer the dough into the greased pan and spread it out evenly.
5. Place the pan on the preheated grill, close the lid, and bake for about 45-55 minutes, or until the bread is golden brown and a toothpick inserted into the center comes out clean.
6. Remove the pan from the grill and let the bread cool for a few minutes. Then, carefully remove the bread from the pan and transfer it to a wire rack to cool completely.
7. Once the bread has cooled, slice it into thick slices and serve.

Tips: Experiment with different flavors of ice cream to create variations of this bread. Try using chocolate, vanilla, or strawberry ice cream for different taste experiences.

Banana Boats

 **Preparation time** 30 MINUTES |  **Cooking time** 10 MINUTES |  **Servings** 4 |  **Ratings**

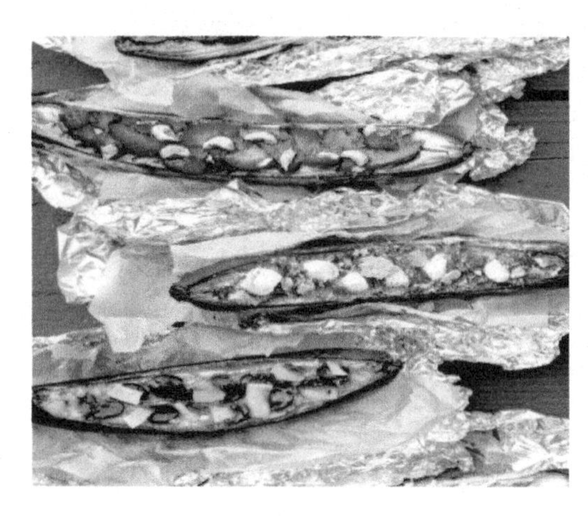

Ingredients

4 green bananas
Chocolate chips
Miniature marshmallows
Peanut butter chips
Crushed cookies

Directions

1. Preheat your barbecue grill to medium heat.
2. Make a lengthwise cut along the top of each banana, creating a slit for the toppings.
3. Stuff each banana with a combination of chocolate chips, miniature marshmallows, peanut butter chips, and crushed cookies. You can customize the fillings based on your preference.
4. Wrap each banana tightly in aluminum foil, ensuring that the fillings are sealed inside.
5. Place the foil-wrapped bananas on the preheated grill, close the lid, and cook for about 10-15 minutes, or until the bananas are soft and the fillings are melted.
6. Carefully remove the banana boats from the grill and let them cool for a few minutes.
7. Open the foil and enjoy the warm and gooey banana boats straight from the grill. Be cautious as they may be hot.

Tips: Serve the banana boats as they are or top them with a scoop of vanilla ice cream or a drizzle of chocolate sauce for an extra indulgent treat.

Grilled Pineapple Sundaes

 **Preparation time** 30 MINUTES |  **Cooking time** 5 MINUTES |  **Servings** 4 | ★★★★ **Ratings**

Ingredients

4 fresh pineapple spears
Vanilla ice cream
Jarred caramel sauce
Toasted coconut

Directions

1. Preheat your barbecue grill to medium heat.
2. Place the pineapple spears directly on the grill grates and cook for about 5 minutes on each side, or until grill marks appear and the pineapple is tender.
3. Remove the grilled pineapple spears from the grill and let them cool slightly.
4. While the pineapples are cooling, prepare your sundae bowls or dishes. Scoop a generous serving of vanilla ice cream into each bowl.
5. Place one grilled pineapple spear on top of each scoop of ice cream.
6. Drizzle jarred caramel sauce over the grilled pineapple and ice cream.
7. Sprinkle toasted coconut on top as a delicious garnish.
8. Serve the grilled pineapple sundaes immediately while the pineapple is still warm and the ice cream is creamy.

Tips: You can enhance the flavor of the grilled pineapple by brushing it with a mixture of honey and cinnamon before grilling.

Chocolate Chip Cookies

 **Preparation time** 20 MINUTES |  **Cooking time** 45 MINUTES |  **Servings** 12 | ★★★★ **Ratings**

Ingredients

1 cup salted butter, softened
1 cup sugar
1 cup light brown sugar
2 tsp vanilla extract
2 large eggs
3 cups all-purpose flour
1 tsp baking soda
½ tsp baking powder
1 tsp natural sea salt
2 cups semi-sweet chocolate chips or chunks

Directions

1. Preheat your oven to 350°F (175°C) and line baking sheets with parchment paper.
2. In a large mixing bowl, cream together the softened butter, sugar, and light brown sugar until light and fluffy.
3. Add the vanilla extract and eggs to the butter mixture and beat well until fully incorporated.
4. In a separate bowl, whisk together the all-purpose flour, baking soda, baking powder, and sea salt.
5. Gradually add the dry ingredients to the wet ingredients, mixing until just combined. Be careful not to overmix the dough.
6. Fold in the semi-sweet chocolate chips or chunks until evenly distributed throughout the dough.
7. Drop rounded tablespoonfuls of dough onto the prepared baking sheets, spacing them about 2 inches apart.
8. Bake in the preheated oven for 10-12 minutes, or until the edges are golden brown.
9. Remove from the oven and let the cookies cool on the baking sheets for a few minutes before transferring them to a wire rack to cool completely.

Tips: For an extra chewy texture, refrigerate the dough for at least 1 hour before baking.

Delicious Smoked Apple Pie

 **Preparation time** 10-15 MINUTES |  **Cooking time** 20-30 MINUTES |  **Servings** 4 | ★★★★ **Ratings**

Ingredients

5 apples (such as Granny Smith or Honeycrisp), peeled, cored, and thinly sliced

¼ cup sugar

1 tbsp. cornstarch

Flour (as needed for dusting)

1 refrigerated pie crust

¼ cup peach preserves

Directions

1. Preheat your smoker to 350°F (175°C) and prepare it for indirect grilling.
2. In a mixing bowl, combine the sliced apples, sugar, and cornstarch. Toss well to coat the apples evenly.
3. Lightly dust your work surface with flour and roll out the refrigerated pie crust to fit a 9-inch pie dish.
4. Place the rolled-out crust into the pie dish, making sure it covers the bottom and sides.
5. Spread the peach preserves evenly over the bottom of the pie crust.
6. Arrange the apple slices over the peach preserves, creating a mound in the center.
7. Carefully fold the edges of the pie crust over the apples, creating a rustic, crimped look.
8. Place the pie in the preheated smoker and let it smoke for about 45-60 minutes, or until the apples are tender and the crust is golden brown.
9. Remove the smoked apple pie from the smoker and let it cool slightly before serving.

Tips: Serve the smoked apple pie warm with a scoop of vanilla ice cream or a dollop of whipped cream for a delightful dessert experience.

Peanut Butter Cookies

 **Preparation time** 5 MINUTES |  **Cooking time** 25 MINUTES |  **Servings** 24 |  **Ratings**

Ingredients

1 egg
1 cup sugar
1 cup peanut butter

Directions

1. Preheat your grill or smoker to 350°F (175°C) and prepare it for indirect grilling.
2. In a mixing bowl, combine the egg, sugar, and peanut butter. Mix well until the ingredients are fully incorporated.
3. Shape the cookie dough into small balls, about 1 inch in diameter, and place them on a greased baking sheet or a sheet of aluminum foil.
4. Place the baking sheet or foil with the cookie dough balls onto the grill grates or in a smoker-safe baking dish.
5. Bake the cookies in the grill or smoker for about 10-12 minutes, or until they are lightly golden and set.
6. Remove the cookies from the grill or smoker and let them cool on a wire rack before serving.

Tips: You can add extra flavor to your peanut butter cookies by incorporating ingredients like chocolate chips, chopped nuts, or dried fruits into the dough.

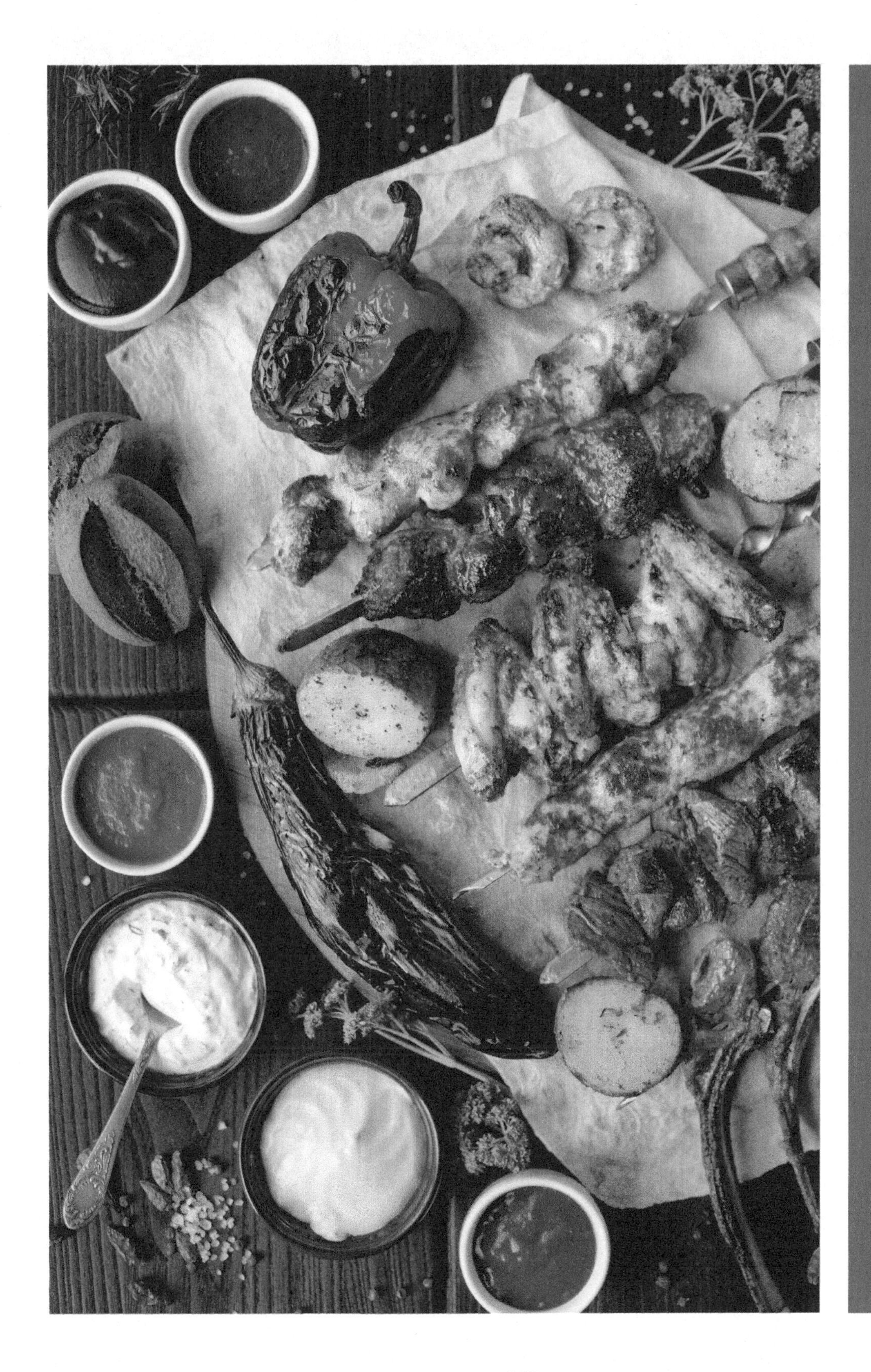

SPECIALS

Citrus Herb Salt

 **Preparation time** 15 MINUTES |  **Cooking time** 2 HOURS |  **Servings** 4 |  **Ratings**

Ingredients

1 cup high-quality coarse kosher salt
2 tsp. dried rosemary
2 tsp. dried thyme
2 tsp. granulated garlic
Zest of 2 limes
Zest of 1 lemon

Directions

1. In a bowl, combine the kosher salt, dried rosemary, dried thyme, granulated garlic, lime zest, and lemon zest.
2. Stir well to ensure that all the ingredients are evenly mixed.
3. Transfer the mixture to an airtight container or jar for storage.
4. Use as a flavorful seasoning for your grilled dishes by sprinkling it over meats, vegetables, or even salads.
5. Store the citrus herb salt in a cool, dry place for up to several months.

Tips: Feel free to experiment with different herbs or citrus zests to customize the flavor of the salt.

Corned Beef Pastrami

 **Preparation time** 5 DAYS |  **Cooking time** 3 HOURS |  **Servings** 6 | ★ **Ratings**

Ingredients

1.5 lb corned beef brisket
Coarse ground pepper (about 1.5 cups)
2 tbsp. granulated garlic
2 tbsp. onion flakes
2 tbsp. ancho chili powder
Ancho espresso rub (store-bought or homemade)

Directions

1. Preheat your smoker or grill to a low and steady temperature of around 225°F (107°C).
2. Rinse the corned beef brisket under cold water to remove any excess brine. Pat it dry with paper towels.
3. In a bowl, combine the coarse ground pepper, granulated garlic, onion flakes, and ancho chili powder. Mix well to create a spice rub.
4. Generously coat the entire surface of the corned beef brisket with the spice rub, pressing it into the meat.
5. Place the seasoned brisket on the smoker or grill and cook it low and slow for several hours until the internal temperature reaches around 195°F (90°C). This will ensure the meat is tender and fully cooked.
6. Once cooked, remove the corned beef brisket from the smoker or grill and let it rest for about 15 minutes.
7. Slice the pastrami thinly against the grain and serve it as desired. It can be enjoyed on its own, in sandwiches, or as part of various dishes.
8. Optionally, you can further enhance the flavor by applying an ancho espresso rub before serving.

Tips: For an even more pronounced flavor, you can marinate the corned beef brisket in a brine mixture of your choice for a few days before smoking or grilling.

Halloumi Cheese & Vegetables

 **Preparation time** 20 MINUTES |  **Cooking time** 2 HOURS |  **Servings** 8 | ★★ **Ratings**

Ingredients

2 tbsp. olive oil
1 tbsp. dried roasted garlic
1 tbsp. Herbs de Provence
1 jar marinara sauce
Salt and pepper to taste
2 green zucchinis
2 yellow zucchinis
2 red onions
2 sweet potatoes
4 Roma tomatoes
6 large-cap (stuffing) mushrooms
2 packages Halloumi cheese

Directions

1. Preheat your grill to medium-high heat.
2. In a small bowl, combine the olive oil, dried roasted garlic, and Herbs de Provence to create a marinade.
3. Slice the green zucchinis, yellow zucchinis, red onions, sweet potatoes, Roma tomatoes, and mushrooms into thick slices.
4. Brush the vegetable slices with the marinade on both sides, ensuring they are well coated.
5. Slice the Halloumi cheese into thick slices.
6. Place the vegetables and Halloumi cheese slices directly on the grill grates and cook for about 4-5 minutes per side, or until grill marks appear and the vegetables are tender.
7. Remove the grilled vegetables and cheese from the grill and season with salt and pepper to taste.
8. Serve the grilled vegetables and Halloumi cheese with a side of marinara sauce for dipping.

Tips: Make sure to brush the vegetables and cheese with the marinade evenly to enhance the flavors.

Grilla Savory BBQ Ranch Dip

 **Preparation time** 20 MINUTES |  **Cooking time** 30 MINUTES |  **Servings** 6 | 

Ingredients

2 cups sour cream
3 tbsp. Grilla BBQ sauce
1 tbsp. Grilla AP Rub
1 packet Hidden Valley Ranch dressing mix

Direction

1. In a mixing bowl, combine the sour cream, Grilla BBQ sauce, Grilla AP Rub, and Hidden Valley Ranch dressing mix.
2. Stir well until all the ingredients are thoroughly combined.
3. Cover the bowl and refrigerate for at least 1 hour to allow the flavors to meld together.
4. Before serving, give the dip a quick stir to ensure all the ingredients are evenly distributed.
5. Serve the Grilla Savory BBQ Ranch Dip with your favorite chips, crackers, or vegetable sticks.

Tips: Feel free to garnish the dip with some chopped fresh herbs, such as parsley or chives, for added freshness and visual appeal.

Grilla Grilled Bologna

 **Preparation time** 10 MINUTES |  **Cooking time** 4 HOURS |  **Servings** 4 | ★ **Ratings**

Ingredients

1 lb. stick of bologna
1 cup Grilla AP Rub
1 bottle Grilla BBQ Sauce

Directions

1. Preheat your grill to medium-high heat.
2. Slice the stick of bologna into thick slices, about ½ inch thick.
3. Coat each slice of bologna with Grilla AP Rub, ensuring all sides are evenly covered.
4. Place the bologna slices directly on the preheated grill grates.
5. Grill the bologna for about 3-4 minutes per side, or until it is nicely browned and heated through.
6. During the last minute of grilling, brush each slice of bologna with Grilla BBQ Sauce to glaze and add extra flavor.
7. Remove the grilled bologna from the grill and serve hot.

Tips: This recipe works well with other deli meats too, so feel free to try it with ham, turkey, or roast beef.

Grilled London Broil Flank Steak

 **Preparation time** 5 MINUTES |  **Cooking time** 15 MINUTES |  **Servings** 6 | ★★★★ **Ratings**

Ingredients

3 tbsp. crumbled blue cheese
2 tbsp. butter
1 tsp. chives, finely chopped
¼ cup Grilla AP Rub
2 to 3-lbs. beef flank steak
2 tbsp. olive oil

Directions

1. Preheat your grill to high heat.
2. In a small bowl, mix together the crumbled blue cheese, butter, and chives until well combined. Set aside.
3. Rub the flank steak with Grilla AP Rub, ensuring all sides are evenly coated.
4. Drizzle the steak with olive oil and gently massage it into the meat.
5. Place the seasoned flank steak on the preheated grill and cook for about 4-5 minutes per side for medium-rare, or adjust the cooking time to your desired level of doneness.
6. During the last minute of grilling, spread the blue cheese butter mixture on top of the steak and allow it to melt slightly.
7. Remove the steak from the grill and let it rest for a few minutes before slicing.
8. Slice the grilled flank steak against the grain into thin strips.
9. Serve the grilled London broil flank steak with your favorite sides and enjoy!

Tips: London broil flank steak is best cooked to medium-rare or medium to ensure tenderness. Avoid overcooking as it may result in a tougher texture.

Delicious Donuts on a Grill

 **Preparation time** 5 MINUTES |  **Cooking time** 10 MINUTES |  **Servings** 6 | ★★★★★ **Ratings**

Ingredients

1 ½ cups powdered sugar
1/3 cup whole milk
½ tsp. vanilla extract
16 ounces prepared biscuit dough
Oil spray, for greasing
1 cup chocolate sprinkles

Directions

1. Preheat your grill to medium heat.
2. In a bowl, whisk together the powdered sugar, milk, and vanilla extract until well combined. Set aside.
3. Roll out the prepared biscuit dough on a lightly floured surface to about ½-inch thickness.
4. Use a round cookie cutter or a glass to cut out donut shapes from the dough. You can also use a smaller cutter to remove the center, creating a traditional donut shape.
5. Lightly grease the grill grates with oil spray to prevent sticking.
6. Place the donuts directly on the grill grates and cook for about 2-3 minutes per side, or until they are golden brown and cooked through. Make sure to keep an eye on them to avoid burning.
7. Remove the grilled donuts from the grill and let them cool slightly.
8. Dip each donut into the prepared powdered sugar glaze, ensuring they are fully coated.
9. Sprinkle chocolate sprinkles over the glazed donuts while the glaze is still wet.
10. Allow the glaze to set for a few minutes before serving.

Tips: Serve the grilled donuts warm for the best taste and texture.

Smoked Nut Mix

 **Preparation time** 15 MINUTES |  **Cooking time** 20 MINUTES |  **Servings** 12 | ★★★★★ **Ratings**

Ingredients

3 cups mixed nuts (such as pecans, peanuts, almonds, etc.)
½ tbsp. brown sugar
1 tbsp. dried thyme
¼ tsp. mustard powder
1 tbsp. extra-virgin olive oil

Directions

1. Preheat your smoker to a low temperature, around 225°F (110°C).
2. In a mixing bowl, combine the mixed nuts, brown sugar, dried thyme, and mustard powder. Toss to coat the nuts evenly with the seasonings.
3. Drizzle the olive oil over the nut mixture and toss again to ensure all the nuts are coated with the oil.
4. Spread the seasoned nuts evenly in a single layer on a baking sheet or aluminum foil.
5. Place the baking sheet with the nuts in the smoker and close the lid.
6. Smoke the nuts for about 1 to 1 ½ hours, or until they are golden brown and have absorbed the smoky flavor.
7. Remove the smoked nuts from the smoker and let them cool completely before serving.
8. Once cooled, store the smoked nut mix in an airtight container to maintain freshness.

Tips: If you prefer a spicier flavor, you can add a pinch of cayenne pepper or chili powder to the seasoning mixture.

Grilled Peaches & Cream

 **Preparation time** 15 MINUTES |  **Cooking time** 8 MINUTES |  **Servings** 8 | ★★★★★ **Ratings**

Ingredients

4 peaches, halved and pitted
1 tbsp. vegetable oil
2 tbsp. clover honey
1 cup cream cheese, softened (preferably with honey and nuts)

Directions

1. Preheat your grill to medium-high heat.
2. In a small bowl, whisk together the vegetable oil and honey until well combined.
3. Brush the cut sides of the peaches with the oil and honey mixture, ensuring they are evenly coated.
4. Place the peaches cut side down on the grill grates and cook for about 3-4 minutes, or until they have grill marks and are slightly softened.
5. Carefully flip the peaches using tongs and continue grilling for another 2-3 minutes.
6. Remove the grilled peaches from the grill and let them cool slightly.
7. Serve the grilled peaches with a dollop of softened cream cheese on top.
8. Drizzle any remaining honey mixture over the peaches and cream cheese.
9. Optional: Garnish with a sprinkle of chopped nuts or a drizzle of additional honey for extra flavor and presentation.
10. Enjoy the grilled peaches and cream as a delightful and refreshing summer dessert.

Tips: Serve the grilled peaches and cream with a scoop of vanilla ice cream or a sprinkle of granola for added texture and sweetness.

Spicy Barbecue Pecans

 **Preparation time** 15 MINUTES |  **Cooking time** 1 HOUR |  **Servings** 2 | ★★★★ **Ratings**

Ingredients

2 ½ tsp. garlic powder
16 ounces raw pecan halves
1 tsp. onion powder
1 tsp. pepper
2 tsp. salt
1 tsp. dried thyme
Butter, for greasing
3 tbsp. melted butter

Directions

1. Preheat your grill or smoker to medium heat.
2. In a small bowl, combine the garlic powder, onion powder, pepper, salt, and dried thyme to create the spicy barbecue seasoning.
3. Place the pecan halves in a large mixing bowl and drizzle the melted butter over them. Toss to coat the pecans evenly with the butter.
4. Sprinkle the spicy barbecue seasoning over the pecans and toss again to ensure they are well coated with the seasoning.
5. Grease a grill basket or a sheet of aluminum foil with butter to prevent sticking.
6. Spread the seasoned pecans in a single layer on the greased grill basket or foil.
7. Place the grill basket or foil with the pecans on the preheated grill or smoker and close the lid.
8. Smoke the pecans for about 20-25 minutes, or until they become fragrant and slightly toasted, stirring occasionally to prevent burning.
9. Remove the smoked pecans from the grill and let them cool completely.
10. Once cooled, transfer the spicy barbecue pecans to an airtight container or serving dish.
11. Serve as a snack or use them as a flavorful addition to salads, cheese boards, or other dishes.

Tips: These spicy barbecue pecans also make a great homemade gift. Package them in a decorative jar or tin for a delightful snack to share with friends and family.

Feta Cheese Stuffed Meatballs

 **Preparation time** 12 MINUTES |  **Cooking time** 35 MINUTES |  **Servings** 6 |  Ratings

Ingredients

Pepper
Salt
¾ cup Feta cheese, crumbled
½ tsp. thyme
2 tsp. chopped oregano
Zest of 1 lemon
1 lb. ground pork
1 lb. ground beef
1 tbsp. olive oil

Directions

1. Preheat your grill or oven to medium-high heat.
2. In a mixing bowl, combine the ground pork, ground beef, thyme, oregano, lemon zest, salt, and pepper. Mix well until all the ingredients are evenly incorporated.
3. Take a small portion of the meat mixture (about the size of a golf ball) and flatten it in your palm.
4. Place a spoonful of crumbled Feta cheese in the center of the flattened meat and carefully fold the edges of the meat around the cheese, sealing it completely. Roll the meatball gently between your palms to shape it into a round ball. Repeat with the remaining meat mixture and Feta cheese.
5. Drizzle the olive oil over the stuffed meatballs and gently toss them to coat with the oil.
6. Place the meatballs on the grill grates or on a baking sheet if using the oven.
7. Grill or bake the meatballs for about 15-20 minutes, or until they are cooked through and reach an internal temperature of 160°F (71°C).
8. Remove the meatballs from the grill or oven and let them rest for a few minutes before serving.
9. Serve the Feta cheese stuffed meatballs as a delicious appetizer or as a main course with your favorite sides.

Tips: Make sure to seal the meatballs tightly around the Feta cheese to prevent it from leaking out during cooking.

Butternut Squash

 **Preparation time** 30 MINUTES |  **Cooking time** 2 HOURS |  **Servings** 4-6 | ★★★ **Ratings**

Ingredients

Brown sugar
Maple syrup
6 tbsp. butter
Butternut squash, peeled, seeded, and cut into cubes or slices

Directions

1. Preheat your grill or oven to medium heat.
2. In a small saucepan, melt the butter over low heat. Add brown sugar and maple syrup to the melted butter and stir until the sugar is dissolved. Set aside.
3. Place the butternut squash cubes or slices on a grilling tray or a baking sheet.
4. Brush the melted butter mixture over the butternut squash, coating all sides.
5. If grilling, place the grilling tray on the grill grates. If baking, place the baking sheet in the oven.
6. Grill or bake the butternut squash for about 20-25 minutes, or until it is tender and lightly caramelized, flipping or turning the pieces occasionally for even cooking.
7. Remove the butternut squash from the grill or oven and let it cool for a few minutes before serving.
8. Serve the grilled or roasted butternut squash as a side dish or as part of a salad or other main course.

Tips: For added flavor, sprinkle some cinnamon or nutmeg over the butternut squash before grilling or baking.

Beef Burgers

 **Preparation time** 5 MINUTES |  **Cooking time** 4 MINUTES |  **Servings** 4 |  **Ratings**

Ingredients

1 ¼ lbs. lean ground beef
1 small onion, minced
¼ cup teriyaki sauce
3 tbsp. Italian-flavored bread crumbs
2 tbsp. grated Parmesan cheese
1 tsp. salt
1 tsp. freshly ground black pepper
3 tbsp. sweet pickle relish
4 Kaiser rolls, toasted

Directions

1. In a mixing bowl, combine the ground beef, minced onion, teriyaki sauce, bread crumbs, Parmesan cheese, salt, pepper, and sweet pickle relish. Mix well until all the ingredients are evenly incorporated.
2. Divide the mixture into 4 equal portions and shape them into burger patties, about ½-inch thick.
3. Preheat your grill to medium-high heat.
4. Place the burger patties on the grill grates and cook for about 4-5 minutes per side, or until they reach your desired level of doneness.
5. During the last few minutes of cooking, you can add a slice of cheese on top of each patty if desired, and allow it to melt.
6. Remove the burger patties from the grill and let them rest for a couple of minutes.
7. Assemble the burgers by placing each patty on a toasted Kaiser roll.
8. Add your favorite toppings such as lettuce, tomato, onion, and condiments like ketchup or mayo.
9. Serve the beef burgers immediately and enjoy!

Tips: Toasting the Kaiser rolls adds a nice crunch and helps hold the burger together.

Spiced Lamb Burger

 **Preparation time** 5 MINUTES |  **Cooking time** 5 MINUTES |  **Servings** 4 | 

Ingredients

1 ¼ lbs. lean ground lamb
1 tbsp. ground cumin
¼ tsp. ground cinnamon
½ tsp. salt
½ tsp. freshly ground black pepper
Whole-wheat pitas
½ medium cucumber, peeled and sliced
½ cup Simple Garlic Yogurt Sauce

Directions

1. In a mixing bowl, combine the ground lamb, ground cumin, ground cinnamon, salt, and black pepper. Mix well to evenly distribute the spices.
2. Divide the mixture into 4 equal portions and shape them into burger patties, about ½-inch thick.
3. Preheat your grill to medium-high heat.
4. Place the lamb patties on the grill grates and cook for about 4-5 minutes per side, or until they reach your desired level of doneness.
5. During the last few minutes of cooking, you can lightly toast the whole-wheat pitas on the grill.
6. Remove the lamb patties from the grill and let them rest for a couple of minutes.
7. Assemble the burgers by placing each patty inside a whole-wheat pita. Top with sliced cucumber and drizzle with the Simple Garlic Yogurt Sauce.
8. Serve the spiced lamb burgers immediately and enjoy!

Tips: If you prefer a stronger spice flavor, you can increase the amount of ground cumin and ground cinnamon.

Garlicky Pork Burgers

 **Preparation time** 5 MINUTES |  **Cooking time** 10 MINUTES |  **Servings** 4 | ★★★★★ **Ratings**

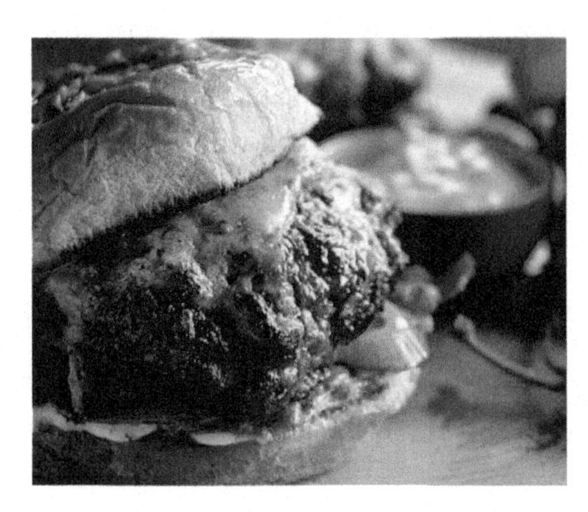

Ingredients

1 lb. ground pork
1 tsp. salt
1 tsp. black pepper
4 cloves garlic, chopped
4 hard rolls, split, or 8-10 slider buns

Directions

1. In a mixing bowl, combine the ground pork, salt, black pepper, and chopped garlic. Mix well until the ingredients are evenly incorporated.
2. Divide the mixture into 4 equal portions for regular-sized burgers or adjust the size for slider buns.
3. Preheat your grill to medium-high heat.
4. Place the pork patties on the grill grates and cook for about 4-5 minutes per side, or until the internal temperature reaches 160°F (71°C).
5. While the patties are cooking, you can lightly toast the hard rolls or slider buns on the grill.
6. Remove the pork patties from the grill and let them rest for a couple of minutes.
7. Assemble the burgers by placing each patty inside a hard roll or slider bun.
8. Add your preferred toppings and condiments, such as lettuce, tomato, onion, pickles, or your favorite sauce.
9. Serve the garlicky pork burgers immediately and enjoy!

Tips: For added juiciness, you can brush the patties with a little olive oil before grilling.

Pineapple Cake

 **Preparation time** 20 MINUTES |  **Cooking time** 1 HOUR |  **Servings** 8 |  **Ratings**

Ingredients

1 cup sugar
1 tbsp. baking powder
1 cup buttermilk
2 eggs
½ tsp. salt
1 jar maraschino cherries
1 stick butter, divided
¾ cup brown sugar
1 can pineapple slices
1 ½ cups flour

Directions

1. Preheat your grill to medium heat or preheat your oven to 350°F (175°C).
2. In a mixing bowl, combine the sugar, baking powder, buttermilk, eggs, salt, and flour. Mix well until the batter is smooth.
3. In a 9-inch round cake pan or a disposable aluminum cake pan, melt 4 tablespoons of butter over the heat or in the oven.
4. Sprinkle the brown sugar evenly over the melted butter.
5. Arrange the pineapple slices on top of the brown sugar. Place a maraschino cherry in the center of each pineapple slice.
6. Pour the cake batter over the pineapple slices, spreading it evenly.
7. If using a grill, place the cake pan on the grill grates. Close the lid and grill for about 30-35 minutes, or until a toothpick inserted into the center of the cake comes out clean. If using an oven, place the cake pan in the preheated oven and bake for about 30-35 minutes, or until a toothpick inserted into the center of the cake comes out clean.
8. Remove the cake from the grill or oven and let it cool in the pan for a few minutes.
9. Invert the cake onto a serving plate, allowing the pineapple slices to be on top.
10. Serve the pineapple cake warm or at room temperature. It can be enjoyed on its own or served with whipped cream or vanilla ice cream.

Tips: Make sure to grease the cake pan well before adding the butter and brown sugar to prevent sticking.

Pulled Hickory-Smoked Pork Butts

 **Preparation time** 30-45 MINUTES |  **Cooking time** 6 HOURS |  **Servings** 20 | ★ **Ratings**

Ingredients

2 (10-pound) boneless pork butts, vacuum-sealed or fresh

1 cup roasted garlic–seasoned extra-virgin olive oil

¾ cup Pork Dry Rub, Jan's Original Dry Rub, or your preferred pork rub

Directions

1. Preheat your smoker to a temperature of 225°F (107°C) using hickory wood for smoke flavor.
2. Prepare the pork butts by trimming off excess fat and silver skin. Pat them dry with paper towels.
3. Rub the pork butts with the roasted garlic–seasoned extra-virgin olive oil, making sure to coat all sides.
4. Generously season the pork butts with the pork dry rub, massaging it into the meat to ensure even coverage.
5. Place the seasoned pork butts on the smoker grates, fat side up.
6. Close the smoker lid and cook the pork butts at 225°F (107°C) for approximately 1 hour per pound, or until the internal temperature reaches 195-205°F (90-96°C). This slow and low cooking process will result in tender and flavorful pulled pork.
7. Monitor the smoker temperature throughout the cooking process, adjusting the airflow and adding more hickory wood chunks as needed to maintain a steady smoke.
8. Once the pork butts reach the desired internal temperature, remove them from the smoker and let them rest for about 30 minutes.
9. Using two forks or meat claws, shred the smoked pork butts into pulled pork.
10. Serve the pulled hickory-smoked pork butts on buns or alongside your favorite barbecue sides. Drizzle with additional barbecue sauce if desired.

Tips: For optimal flavor, marinate the pork butts overnight in the roasted garlic–seasoned olive oil and dry rub before smoking.

Pork Sirloin Tip Roast Three Ways

 **Preparation time** 20 MINUTES |  **Cooking time** 1½ TO 3 HOURS |  **Servings** 4-6 | ★★★★★ **Ratings**

Ingredients

Apple-injected Roasted Pork Sirloin Tip Roast:

1 (1½ to 2 lbs.) pork sirloin tip roast

¾ cup 100% apple juice

2 tbsp. roasted garlic–seasoned extra-virgin olive oil

5 tbsp. Pork Dry Rub or your preferred barbecue rub, such as Plowboys BBQ Bovine Bold

Directions

1. Preheat your smoker to a temperature of 225°F (107°C) using a combination of apple and hickory wood for smoke flavor.
2. Prepare the pork sirloin tip roast by patting it dry with paper towels.
3. Using a meat injector, inject the pork roast with the apple juice, distributing it evenly throughout the meat.
4. Rub the entire surface of the roast with the roasted garlic–seasoned extra-virgin olive oil.
5. Sprinkle the Pork Dry Rub or your preferred barbecue rub generously over the entire surface of the roast, ensuring even coverage.
6. Place the seasoned pork sirloin tip roast on the smoker grates.
7. Close the smoker lid and cook the roast at 225°F (107°C) for approximately 1.5 to 2 hours, or until the internal temperature reaches 145°F (63°C).
8. Remove the roast from the smoker and let it rest for about 10 minutes before slicing.
9. Slice the roasted pork sirloin tip roast and serve it as a main dish or use it in sandwiches or wraps.

Tips: Use a meat thermometer to ensure the pork reaches the recommended internal temperature of 145°F (63°C) for safe consumption.

Aromatic Smoked Duck Breast

Preparation time
15 MIN + MARINATE

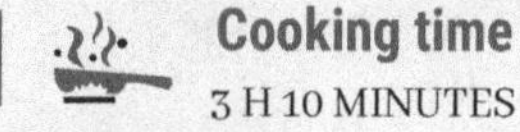
Cooking time
3 H 10 MINUTES

Servings
5

Ratings

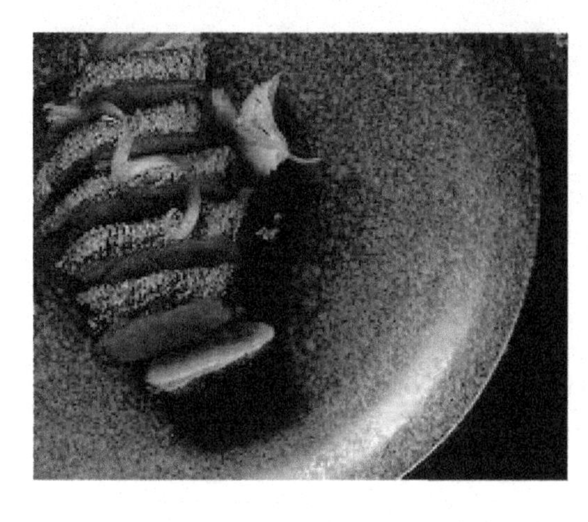

Ingredients

3 lbs. duck breast
For Marinade:
3 cups apple juice
1 tbsp. salt
1 and ½ tbsp. sugar
2 tbsp. soy sauce
¾ tsp. paprika
¾ tsp. garlic powder
1 tsp. dried basil
¾ tsp. pepper

Directions

1. In a bowl, combine the apple juice, salt, sugar, soy sauce, paprika, garlic powder, dried basil, and pepper to create the marinade.
2. Place the duck breast in a resealable plastic bag or a container with a lid.
3. Pour the marinade over the duck breast, making sure it is fully coated. Seal the bag or cover the container and refrigerate for at least 2 hours or overnight for better flavor penetration.
4. Preheat your smoker to a temperature of 225°F (107°C), using your choice of wood chips for smoke flavor.
5. Remove the duck breast from the marinade and discard the marinade.
6. Place the duck breast on the smoker grates, skin side up.
7. Close the smoker lid and smoke the duck breast at 225°F (107°C) for approximately 2 to 3 hours, or until the internal temperature reaches 165°F (74°C) for safe consumption.
8. Once cooked, remove the duck breast from the smoker and let it rest for about 10 minutes before slicing.
9. Slice the smoked duck breast and serve it as a main dish or use it in salads, sandwiches, or other recipes.

Tips: Use skin-on duck breast for a richer flavor and crispier skin.

Smoked Quails

 **Preparation time** 15 MIN + MARINATE |  **Cooking time** 1 H 10 MINUTES |  **Servings** 4 | 

Ingredients

5 lbs. quails
For Marinade:
2 cups orange juice
1 cup soy sauce
2 tbsp. minced garlic
½ cup brown sugar
¼ cup olive oil
1 tbsp. pepper
1 cup chopped onion

Directions

1. In a bowl, combine the orange juice, soy sauce, minced garlic, brown sugar, olive oil, pepper, and chopped onion to create the marinade.
2. Place the quails in a resealable plastic bag or a container with a lid.
3. Pour the marinade over the quails, making sure they are fully coated. Seal the bag or cover the container and refrigerate for at least 2 hours or overnight for better flavor penetration.
4. Prepare your smoker and preheat it to a temperature of 225°F (107°C), using your choice of wood chips for smoke flavor.
5. Remove the quails from the marinade and discard the marinade.
6. Place the quails on the smoker grates.
7. Close the smoker lid and smoke the quails at 225°F (107°C) for approximately 2 to 3 hours, or until the internal temperature reaches 165°F (74°C) for safe consumption.
8. Once smoked, remove the quails from the smoker and let them rest for a few minutes before serving.
9. Serve the smoked quails as a main dish, accompanied by your favorite side dishes or sauces.

Tips: Keep an eye on the internal temperature of the quails to ensure they are fully cooked and safe to eat.

Cajun Crab Stuffed Shrimp & Jicama Corn Salad

 **Preparation time** 20 MINUTES |  **Cooking time** 5 MINUTES |  **Servings** 4 | ★★★★★ **Ratings**

Ingredients

For Cajun Crab Stuffed Shrimp:

12 stuffed shrimp

16 oz. lump crab meat

1 medium-size red onion, finely diced

½ tbsp. minced garlic

Cajun seasoning, to taste

1 lime, juiced

Zest of 1 lime

2 jalapeno peppers (optional), finely diced

16 g Ritz Crackers, crushed

2 slices bacon, cooked and crumbled

For Jicama Corn Salad:

1 medium-size jicama, peeled and diced

1 cup corn kernels, cooked

¼ cup red onion, finely diced

¼ cup fresh cilantro, chopped

Juice of 1 lime

Salt and pepper, to taste

Directions

1. Preheat your grill or oven to medium-high heat.
2. In a mixing bowl, combine the lump crab meat, diced red onion, minced garlic, Cajun seasoning, lime juice, lime zest, diced jalapeno peppers (if using), and crushed Ritz Crackers. Mix well until all the ingredients are evenly incorporated.
3. Take each stuffed shrimp and carefully remove the stuffing, creating a cavity for the crab mixture.
4. Stuff each shrimp with the Cajun crab mixture, pressing it firmly into the cavity. Arrange the stuffed shrimp on a greased grill pan or baking sheet.
5. Place the stuffed shrimp on the preheated grill or in the oven and cook for about 10-12 minutes, or until the shrimp is cooked through and the stuffing is golden brown.
6. While the shrimp is cooking, prepare the jicama corn salad. In a separate mixing bowl, combine the diced jicama, cooked corn kernels, finely diced red onion, chopped cilantro, lime juice, salt, and pepper. Toss well to combine.
7. Once the stuffed shrimp are cooked, remove them from the grill or oven and let them cool for a few minutes.
8. Serve the Cajun crab stuffed shrimp on a platter, garnished with the crumbled bacon.
9. Serve the jicama corn salad alongside the stuffed shrimp as a refreshing and flavorful side dish.

Tips: Be gentle when removing the stuffing from the shrimp to create a cavity for the crab mixture. Take care not to tear the shrimp. Press the crab mixture firmly into the shrimp cavities to ensure the stuffing stays intact during cooking.

Made in the USA
Coppell, TX
10 December 2024